Designing Teaching Improvement Programs

Designing Teaching Improvement Programs

Jack Lindquist, Editor
William Bergquist
Claude Mathis
Chester Case
Thomas Clark
Lance Buhl

A Sourcebook based on pilot projects supported by the W. K. Kellogg Foundation of Battle Creek, Michigan.

Library of Congress Card Number 79-51475

Foreword

This sourcebook represents one approach employed by the W.K. Kellogg Foundation to increase the impact of a series of successfully completed projects. The Foundation has long felt that the potential social impact of pilot projects, such as the ones described in this book, can seldom be realized unless the lessons learned are shared with other institutions and organizations with similar concerns. Hence, the Kellogg Foundation regularly supports a variety of dissemination and utilization activities, including workshops, conferences, social consultations, audio visual presentations, and even the publication of "action brochures" or books.

This book has been designed specifically to share the lessons learned about the development of teaching improvement programs. Its authors are talented innovators. They have been directly involved with several of the more than 25 Foundation-assisted projects concerned with collegiate staff development as well as with a number of similar projects not related to the Kellogg series. Their experiences are shared in this publication.

Intended as a resource tool, *Designing Teaching Improvement Programs* should be a stimulating and informative publication for those concerned with improving the educational process of colleges and universities. Although the book is intended to provide insight into the operation of the various programs, it is not intended to be a "how to" publication. Those wishing to implement similar programs or adapt specific aspects of any of the programs are counseled to use the publication in conjunction with private consultations with appropriate people.

The Kellogg Foundation will judge the value of its support of this publication by the extent to which it increases the impact of its original investments in a variety of approaches to collegiate staff development. The final measure of its success, however, will be the degree to which the teaching-learning process is improved to better serve students across the nation.

Robert E. Kinsinger
Vice President
W. K. Kellogg Foundation

DESIGNING TEACHING IMPROVEMENT PROGRAMS

Table of Contents

Foreword v

Preface xi

Chapter One — Approaches to Collegiate Teaching Improvement
by Jack Lindquist

Introduction 3
Subject Mastery 6
Instructional Resources 7
Instructional Development 8
Research and Dissemination 9
Student Ratings of Instruction 11
Personal and Professional Development 11
Organization Development 13
Administrative Development for Teaching Improvement 15
Preparation for New Academic Programs 16
Local Socialization 17
Conceptual Frameworks for Teaching Improvement Programs 18

Chapter Two — Teaching and Learning
by Jack Lindquist

Introduction 25
The Nature of the Student 25
The Nature of the Professor as Teacher 29
Learning Objectives 34
Teaching-Learning Process 36
The Teaching-Learning Context 38
Summary Teaching-Learning Guidelines 42

Chapter Three — The Liberal Arts College
by William Bergquist

Introduction 47
Purposes 48

Structure 55
Staffing 58
Activities 68
Financing 75
Evaluation 78
A Hypothetical Example 79

Chapter Four — The University Center
by Claude Mathis

Introduction 93
Purposes 100
Structure 102
Staffing 106
Activities 110
Financing 119
Evaluation 121
Personal Reflections 122

Chapter Five — Staff Development for the Community College
by Chester Case

Introduction 131
Structure 142
Staffing 144
Activities 150
Financing 154
Evaluation 157
Personal Reflections 160

Chapter Six — The Nontraditional Setting
by Thomas Clark

Introduction 165
Purposes 182
Structure 184
Staffing 188
Activities 190
Financing 203
Evaluation 204
Personal Reflections 205

Chapter Seven — Professional Development in the Interinstitutional Setting
by Lance Buhl

Introduction 209
Purpose 210
Structure 221
Staffing 223
Activities 228
Financing 235
Evaluation 240
Personal Reflections 245

Chapter Eight — Summary Recommendations
by Jack Lindquist

Introduction 253
The Purpose of Teaching Improvement 253
Structure 256
Staffing 257
Program Activities 258
Finances 260
Evaluation 261
Strategies for Program Implementation 263
Resistances to Teaching Improvement Programs 264
Strategies for Change 267
Tips of the Trade 270
The Emerging Challenge 274

Appendix A — Selected Teaching Improvement Programs
          The Liberal Arts College 279

Appendix B — Selected Teaching Improvement Programs
          The University Center 301

Appendix C — Selected Teaching Improvement Programs
          The Community College 311

Appendix D — Selected Teaching Improvement Programs
          Interinstitutional Setting 331

Bibliography 359

Project List 368

Preface

I was meandering along a back road called "academic reform" when I happened upon a flurry of activity called "faculty development." The year was 1973. I wondered what all the commotion was about. What did all these workshops and seminars and consultations have to do with making American colleges and universities better places for students to learn? I quickly learned to like and respect the faculty development leaders I met. The five contributors to this volume have become special friends and respected colleagues. I soon developed similar appreciation for the faculty members and administrators who, at no small risk, were trying to improve their teaching and leadership. And slowly it dawned on me that one of the most powerful strategies for significant academic improvement is not elaborate planning or nimble politics, important though they may be, but slow and steady encouragement and aid to the individual professionals in whose hands the quality of higher learning ultimately lies. I became a believer in "faculty development." The last few years, I have spent much of my time helping such programs get underway.

But what is "faculty development" or "teaching improvement?" How is it done? How can it be made to make a meaningful difference in the lives of professors and students? About some innovations, we are blessed with extensive and impressive research which tells us what we want to know about that thing's effectiveness and about the best way to do it. Not so in the case of programs to improve college teaching. Most "faculty development" or "instructional development" programs are less than a decade old in 1978. Excellent rationales, useful conceptual frameworks, helpful surveys of the field and many program descriptions are available to the developer of a program to improve college teaching. Many of these writings are cited within this book. But such resources do not share what has been *learned* from experience in the 1960's and 1970's regarding how to go about the improvement of college teaching in any particular kind of college setting.

This book does not answer that need with systematic research. Such inquiry is yet to be made (and is much needed). What is available, however, is personal learning gained by teaching improvement leaders. Several practitioners have come to prominence in higher education because of their insights about what a teaching improvement program should be. The five contributors to this volume are among those frequently sought for their advice on the matter. In each case, the contributor has depth of experience as director of one teaching improvement program, plus breadth of experience as a consultant to many other programs and as a student of pertinent literature. None claims the objectivity of the neutral researcher. All wish they had more rigorous evidence than is to be had. But I argued to them that the insights of widely experienced practitioners like themselves could be of immense help to colleagues.

Contributors were asked, "If you were just beginning, or renewing, a college teaching improvement program, what would you do? What *purposes* would you pursue? How would you *structure* and *staff* such a program? What kinds of *functions* and *activities* would you include? How would you tackle the hard questions of *finance* and *evaluation*?" Chapters Three through Seven are their answers. Each has focused on a different collegiate setting: the liberal arts college, the university, the community colleges, the nontraditional program and the interinstitutional arrangement. Personal learnings useful to colleagues elsewhere turn out to be much more difficult to write about than show-and-tell descriptions or academic scholarship and research. This book was a year and several meetings in the making.

The result seems well worth the effort. Various chapters have been used in workshop presentations and institutional consultation. Audiences consistently have been appreciative. We believe, however, that it is the book as a whole which offers the most helpful guidance for developers of teaching improvement programs. The first two chapters provide general background useful as foundation for all later program models. Chapters Three through Seven have more in common than in conflict; the reader primarily interested in programs for community colleges can gain much from reading chapters on the university and the consortium. It is the redundancy of conclusions across settings which lends insight to any one chapter. The best indication of common discoveries regarding how to go about college teaching improvement is found in Chapter Eight, which synthesizes the prior seven chapters into general guidelines for initiating such a program in any postsecondary setting. Finally, Chapter Eight's "Initiation and Implementation" guidelines are culled from aiding program development in literally hundreds of colleges and universities. An added feature is an appendix containing brief descriptions of several model programs.

The chapters have their differences as well. William Bergquist presents a new way to consider faculty development services depending on the degree of change a professor may need to undergo — from minor tinkering in a course to changing one's whole career. He also pictures a low-cost way to get teaching improvement off the ground. Claude Mathis reviews various kinds of teaching improvement strategies useful in small colleges as well as in universities. Chester Case urges us to think of teaching improvement in the context of a comprehensive staff development curriculum. Thomas Clark discusses individual student differences which should guide teaching improvement efforts everywhere. And Lance Buhl suggests a "Conditions for Teaching" model appropriate wherever the goal is not just assistance to a few professors but substantial improvement in teaching across the institution.

For whom is this book meant? Most directly, we have in mind faculty development committees, academic administrators and/or teaching improvement coordinators who seek to launch new programs or renew existing ones. Secondarily, the book should be a useful picture of the state of the art for any student of higher education or teaching. It is designed to supplement rather than duplicate such work as Gaff's *Toward Faculty Renewal*, Bergquist and Phillips' two volumes of *A Handbook for Faculty Development*, Centra's *Faculty Development Practices in U.S. Colleges and Universities* and the many articles and single institution reports now available.

Several persons besides the contributors deserve special thanks for making this book a reality. Robert Kinsinger of the W.K. Kellogg Foundation encouraged the project from its inception, and the Foundation itself funded not only this volume but many of the model programs upon which it is based. James Richmond of Kellogg contributed valuable editorial assistance and review, as did Steven Phillips of the University of Puget Sound, JB Lon Hefferlin of Jossey-Bass Publishers, and Robert Wilson of the University of California-Berkeley. Directors of dozens of faculty development programs gave of their time and knowledge. Laura Wilson, Thelma Scott and Jennifer Grimes helped gather and edit program information, and Jennifer Grimes painstakingly edited every word you will read. Sandra Colombo assembled the bibliography and Cari Gittleson prepared the manuscript more times than she cares to remember.

What began as several isolated assignments became collaboration. We learned in the process that our experiences had taught us that we could have saved ourselves considerable trouble if we had known enough to write such a book five years ago. We hope you find it helpful in your own efforts to make college teaching more effective for college learners.

Jack Lindquist

1

Approaches to Collegiate Teaching Improvement

by Jack Lindquist

Jack Lindquist has worked for the last fifteen years to help make colleges and universities more effective for students. He has been a student dean, a medical researcher, an English instructor, a debate coach, a residence hall staff trainer and director and a director of international programs along the way. On the way, he accumulated a B.A. and M.A. in English literature and a Ph.D. in Higher Education, all from the University of Michigan. Recently, he directed Strategies for Change and Knowledge Utilization, *an action-research project focused on the improvement of undergraduate education. He has authored a book called* Strategies for Change: Academic Innovation as Adaptive Development *from that experience, and his section on "Implementation" in* Developing the Curriculum: A Handbook for Faculty and Administration *is also based in part on the Strategies project. Also recently, he served as policy analyst for Empire State College. Currently, he is director of the Kellogg Use of Innovations Project and a faculty member in the University of Michigan's Center for the Study of Higher Education. He is aiding the Foundation as it learns how best to share the learnings of model programs meant to improve health, education, and agriculture.*

Chapter One is meant to put current college teaching improvement programs in a historical perspective. What has been done in the name of "teaching improvement" or "faculty development" in the last twenty years? Lindquist identifies ten rather different emphases, each of which is dominant in some program or other. He maintains, however, that these emphases are not so much alternatives to select among but integral parts of a teaching improvement program which does make a real difference for faculty and students.

Introduction

The roots of college teaching lie in undergraduate school, where the next generation's professors experience college teachers, and in graduate school, where they are steeped in some discipline and socialized into the professorial role. For many, those roots run deep. The tree which springs from that base is a replica of what the professor experienced as a student, the experience of a particular subject taught a particular way. For most professors, the species of teaching tree is similar: a lecture/discussion focused on an academic subject, based on a set of readings, and evaluated by essay and multiple choice examinations. There are other trees in postsecondary education, such saplings as mediated instruction and experiential learning, but they are overshadowed by the forest of traditional teaching.

The common variety of college teaching is not necessarily bad. A clear and exciting lecture accompanying equally stimulating and informative readings, supplemented by illuminating discussions and synthesizing examinations, all delivered to students who want to learn that subject and find that teaching method helpful, can be a superb learning experience. We all can remember at least one such college course. Problems arise only when this model, or other approaches, is not done particularly well or is done with students whose learning objectives and style, whose background and present situation, do not fit this method of teaching. Then, a professor needs to find more effective ways to enable learning among diverse students.

Enter "teaching improvement services." They come in all varieties, from sabbatical leaves to interpersonal skills workshops. What they have in common is an institutional investment in the continuing development of professors as teachers. They say to the professor, "Your ability as a teacher is important enough that this institution will provide you the resources you need in order to increase your effectiveness."

But what resources work? The answer to that question has changed in the last twenty years. Table One depicts ten different approaches to teaching improvement, each used somewhere in higher education. They are listed in roughly the sequence of their development in the last two decades. I will argue in this chapter that these approaches are not alternatives but parts of a necessary whole. Parts have been added as their need became clear, but these new parts augment, rather than replace, the old. To return to the tree metaphor, the roots of subject mastery and the trunk of instructional development need the limbs and branches and leaves of

Table 1

Strategies for Improving College Teaching

Strategy	Activities	Teaching Improvement Objectives
1. Subject Mastery	Sabbaticals, leaves, conference attendance, workload time for scholarship and research, small grants, promotion and tenure review of scholarly mastery.	To raise faculty members' understanding of the subjects they teach.
2. Instructional Resources	Provisions of technological or prepackaged teaching aids and assistance in using them.	To increase the quality, range, variety and flexibility of teaching resources used by professors and students.
3. Instructional Development	Technical assistance to professors and departments in the diagnosis of teaching improvement needs and the design, method, and evaluation of teaching solutions.	To improve the design and method of teaching.
4. Research and Dissemination of Teaching and Learning	Academic research and publication or oral presentaion of findings and implications concerning how diverse students learn and how teaching can aid that process.	To increase professional knowledge of teaching-learning theory, research, and practice and to encourage use of promising teaching approaches.
5. Student Ratings of Instruction	Administration and feedback (public or private) of student evaluations of a course and teacher.	To motivate professors to rectify course and teaching problems perceived by students. Also to evaluate faculty performance and permit student selection of teachers rated highly by peers.

6. Personal and Professional Development	Workshops and consultations to help meet the developmental interests and concerns of faculty members and administrators.	To help professionals reduce personal obstacles to teaching effectiveness and strengthen opportunities for personal and professional advancements related to teaching.
7. Organization Development	Institutional diagnosis, feedback, action-planning, team-building, training, and formative evaluation regarding such matters as institutional goal clarity and accomplishment, effectiveness of interpersonal and group processes, role definition and support.	To create an organizational setting conducive to and supportive of teaching improvement.
8. Administrative Development	Workshops and consultation concerning management information and techniques, academic leadership, conflict management, the nature of students, personnel practices, curriculum and organization and the management of change.	To increase administrative ability to stimulate, facilitate, and supervise teaching improvement.
9. Preparation for New Programs	All the activities (1) through (8), but focused on enabling participants in new academic programs to master their new professional roles.	To effectively implement new academic programs.
10 Local Socialization	Self study and feedback on local mission, students, program, resources, problems; student-faculty retreats and workshops; faculty orientation seminars and manuals; participation in local governance; teaching awards.	To raise faculty understanding and interest in local goals, students, and professional roles.

local socialization, instructional resources, student ratings, personal and professional development, organization development, research on learning and teaching, administrative development and training for non-traditional programs in order to create a whole and healthy learning experience for the wide variety of learners who attend our colleges and universities.

Subject Mastery

College teachers teach subjects. They are professors of biology, nursing, English, engineering. Their undergraduate and graduate education was meant in good part to develop mastery of their subject. But knowledge keeps developing, and professors need to keep up. So colleges and universities support conference attendance, sabbaticals, visiting scholars and colloquia programs, research grants, workload time to read and conduct studies, salary and promotion policies which reward continuous achievement in one's specialty.

These are not new teaching improvement services. They are old and pervasive. Although the amount of money and time given to such services varies with a local institution's financial situation, most colleges and universities have policies and procedures intended to help a professor maintain subject mastery.

In recent years, some new twists have been added to these services. Some professors find that they need to master a new subject, often because theirs is not drawing students or because of a new, interdisciplinary curriculum. Faculty development programs such as those at Illinois State University (132) and the Kansas City Regional Council for Higher Education (117) seek to support such transitions. Stanford's Center for Teaching and Learning offers seminars and institutes on teaching interdisciplinary subjects. (118) A number of institutions have small grant programs for professors who need time and money to develop a new specialty, and sabbaticals can serve that purpose nicely. The time seems right for some enterprising university to offer in-service postdoctoral or doctoral programs to professors who wish to master a new area while continuing to teach their current area part-time.

Many college leaders have said that a problem with these traditional development services that is their payoffs in terms of teaching improvement are elusive. Professors take the sabbatical, attend the conference, win the small grant, but little visible change in teaching effectiveness (or research productivity, for that matter) occurs. In part, the lack of visible payoff on these investments may be a function of the subtlety of effects. It may be hard to see a new twist on theory or a new enthusiasm for one's subject derived from a conference or sabbatical, but it may occur nonetheless. Still, there may be much slippage in a system of supports without much in the way of controls. Some institutions, therefore, award travel or sabbatical or small grant monies and assign workload attention to subject mastery on the basis of a specific "professional growth contract." Professors are asked to declare improvement objectives related to their own developmental needs and to institutional needs, then request institutional support for particular activities designed to accomplish their growth objectives. Often, a dissemination component is included so that professors must share with colleagues what they have learned at a conference or on sabbatical. Gordon College has developed a model of the growth contract which is being adapted in many other postsecondary settings. (49, 126)

The major question being asked of traditional practices to improve professorial subject mastery is not the appropriateness of such investments but the sufficiency of this approach as the only institutional means for improving teaching. In particular, questions have been raised about the *process* side of higher learning. First-rate content delivered in a manner incomprehensible to students is not effective teaching if learning is the purpose. One response to this concern has been to make some sabbatical, small grant, colloquia and travel funds available for faculty members who want to use these resources to improve some aspect of their teaching process rather than, or as well as, content. Several other strategies have been developed in the last decade primarily to improve the teaching-learning process.

Instructional Resources

A teacher, a book and a classroom have been the basic ingredients in the college teaching process. That formula has much to recommend it and is not about to be abandoned by professors. But technology has added new resources. Computers, television, film, tape recorders, overhead projectors and the programs developed for them can augment first-hand contact between professor and student or book and student. They can make material visually and audibly vivid. They can even interact with individual students. A professor's impact can be strengthened by films of the quality of *Ascent of Man*, learning guides of the quality of *Psychology Today*'s introduction to psychology, video-tapes which provide students immediate pictures of themselves in action and computer-assisted instruction which immediately responds to each individual learner in a variety of ways.

Many professors have an understandable uneasiness about educational technology. It was not a familiar part of their education, except for language laboratories. It seems more difficult to use than it turns out to be. Some think it will displace instead of augment the professor's or book's contact with students. It can have a dehumanizing feel. It suggests that professors are in the entertainment rather than the education business. And much technology as well as "software" is still somewhat crude, not sufficiently sophisticated to warrant wide use. Both Evans (39) and House (57) have researched professorial reluctance to leap into the age of technology.

Still, many universities and community colleges have made heavy investment in instructional resources. As the technology improves and as professors get more comfortable with it, the basic teacher-student relationship can be richly supported. Perhaps key to this use of technology is institutional support for professors to train themselves in the use of instructional resources, to develop better "software" and to learn how to integrate technology into teaching in such ways that they are freed to concentrate on the most difficult and complex aspects of helping students to learn. To aid this kind of teaching improvement, instructional resource staff and faculty development staff need to work closely together. A good model of this collaboration is Northwestern University's Center for the Teaching Professions, which includes the instructional resources office within it. Claude Mathis elaborates on that model in Chapter Four.

Instructional Development

A second institutional support for the process side of teaching improvement is commonly called "instructional development." It usually consists of an office staffed by persons expert in helping individual professors or departments diagnose teaching improvement needs, design new approaches, develop the skill to do the new method and evaluate its effectiveness. First established in medical schools during the late 1950's, this model emerged on university campuses such as Michigan State and Syracuse less than a decade later. Alexander and Yelón's *Instructional Development Agencies in Higher Education* (1) presents a useful overview of such programs, while more detailed pictures are available in monographs describing the Michigan State (30) and Syracuse (33) programs. The New

Hampshire College and University Council has applied the Syracuse approach with success to various kinds of colleges (127), although this strategy is most frequently found in large universities and community colleges.

One such service, the University of Massachusetts "Clinic to Improve University Teaching" (now merged into the Center for Instructional Resources and Improvement), has formulated a six-step teaching improvement process, complete with instruments and procedures. This process has proved popular in a wide variety of settings and is described in detail in the second volume of the Bergquist-Phillips *A Handbook for Faculty Development.* (7)

Direct consultation to professors who seek to improve their courses has much to recommend it. Centra finds that this assistance is the most highly rated approach to teaching improvement among faculty development leaders. (16) It offers expert, individualized assistance to professors in areas they learned little about in graduate school, namely the design and method of teaching. It is voluntary, so "clients" are motivated to try what they learn. It usually results in a relationship between consultant and client which continues long enough to gain some depth on the teaching problem and solution. It rests on a body of learning theory but is quite flexible in interpretation and use. The professors who use such services usually appreciate them, and their teaching performance in areas they choose to improve usually rises, say they and their students.

Again, the problem with instructional development is not its appropriateness but its sufficiency. It is only one branch of the teaching improvement tree. It must rely on volunteer "clients," never a very large group and often the most effective teachers. It is often limited to improving classroom instruction, not subject mastery or advising or student learning skills or nontraditional teaching or the personal problems which may be blocking professors and students or changing the institutional environment for encouraging and rewarding good teaching. Some instructional development services, such as Syracuse's, are branching out into these areas as they recognize the complexity and systemic nature of teaching improvement. The label "instructional development" is coming to mean much more than technical assistance in improving the classroom instruction of voluntary clients.

Research and Dissemination

Wilbert McKeachie's *Teaching Tips* was one of the first books to introduce teaching-learning research to college professors. (72) It remains, after several revisions, one of the most helpful guides around. With the advent first of centers for the study of higher education such as Michigan's and Berkeley's and then of centers for research on teaching such as Michigan's and Tennessee's, universities began to make formal investments in yet another strategy for improving college teaching: conduct research on learning and teaching, write it up, then disseminate it through publications, conferences and seminars.

This approach has increased rather rapidly the literature pertinent to the improvement of college teaching, as is noted in Chapter Two. There is still much to learn, but the developer of teaching improvement programs can be guided by useful research regarding the nature of college learners and their development, the effectiveness of various teaching strategies for various purposes and the impact of non-classroom experiences upon learning. A good model for publications on such topics is Stanford Erickson's *Memo to the Faculty* series. (37)

Major problems with this approach are the considerable expense involved in conducting such research and preparing publications, as well as the inadequacy of formal publications and presentations as the main means for getting one's message used. The first problem can be eased by joining forces with institutional research offices which can mount studies of students, of the teaching-learning process, of organizational support or resistance to teaching improvement and of educational outcomes. An alternative is to establish a small grants program to encourage professors to conduct their own research into such matters, perhaps with the aid of social science students desiring field experience or work-study. Consortial arrangements can reduce the costs of such research for any one institution and can add the benefits of cross-institutional comparisons. At the very least, local leaders can collect and distribute teaching-learning publications developed elsewhere.

The second problem, research use, can be alleviated by adding interpersonal interaction to formal presentations. Workshops and consultation can permit an audience to discuss research findings with one another and with the experts. Actual observation and trial of the new methods presented in literature adds first-hand contact to written or oral description. Various strategies and tactics for getting teaching-learning information used will be discussed in Chapter Eight. The point worth emphasizing here is that information alone is unlikely to move anyone other than the few persons already open to that message.

Student Ratings of Instruction

One argument voiced in the late 1960's was that the way to improve college teaching was to confront professors with what their students thought of their teaching. Various student rating forms of considerable reliability have been developed and widely used. Among the most popular are the Purdue University "cafeteria" instrument, which permits professors to select items upon which to be rated, (32) the Kansas State University IDEA system, which allows professors to select preferred learning objectives about which students rate course and teacher effectiveness, (59, 113) and the University of Massachusetts TABS instrument, which asks students to rate their professors on thirty-eight specific teaching skills or behaviors. (106, 116)

Does teaching improve as a result of student ratings? John Centra, a student of this question, finds that some professors do take ratings to heart and make attempts to improve if students rate them much lower than they rate themselves.(17) Bette and Glen Erickson have found that when ratings are followed by systematic technical assistance to help interpret the scores and design improvements, professors do improve their ratings in the areas they seek to improve. (36)

Student ratings by themselves, however, are often insufficient aids to improvement. The scores are not credible or meaningful to many faculty members. A score on how "well-organized" is a professor does not say just what students find either organized or not. Even if the professor agrees with a low rating, she may not know how to improve. And students are rather poor judges of whether course content is up to snuff or not.

Two responses to these problems are visible in current teaching improvement efforts. One is to integrate student ratings with instructional development so that professors have expert assistance in moving from ratings to improvements. A skilled colleague or "support group" can fulfill this facilitative role, given some training for the task. The second response is to integrate student ratings with colleague evaluations and research on students as the information base upon which to shape professional growth contracts. In this way, the formal evaluation system is tied to student ratings but in a less threatening, more meaningful sense than simply reporting scores to the tenure and promotion committee.

Personal and Professional Development

During the 1960's, considerable attention was paid to the fact that college students are developing human beings, not merely tuition dollars or I.D. numbers or so many cranial cavities to cram with knowledge. (20, 63, 99) The argument was made that teachers must take the developmental needs, levels and interests of learners into account. Higher education should become more "student-centered."

In the early 1970's, many of the same developmentalists who had urged attention to the person of the student urged institutional attention to the person of the professor. Professors are developing adults who face such strains as a very tight job market, classrooms too full of extremely diverse students, institutions rife with adversarial clashes, and personal transitions which raise serious questions about identity and future directions. Mervin Freedman, (45) "The Group for Human Development in Higher Education," (52) William Bergquist and Steven Phillips, (7) Jerry Gaff, (48) and Harold Hodgkinson (56) are among the writers and speakers who stressed that faculty development should have as a central purpose the human development of professors on their own terms, not merely as teaching and publishing machines.

In-service programs which attend to the personal side of professorial life often include "life planning" or "career transitions" or "couples" workshops. They often feature workshops and seminars in which colleagues share special knowledge or skills with one another not only to spread such news around but also to provide a break in routine and a chance to make presentations or learn new things just for the intrinsic enjoyment such activities can bring. Sometimes "support groups" of colleagues are formed for the personal support and enjoyment they can generate among colleagues experiencing some strain in their lives.

When developmental programs shift attention to teaching, the emphasis often is on the personal side of that enterprise. Attention is paid to the professor's openness toward and respect for students, to the faculty-student relationship in and out of class, to the developmental needs and learning styles students bring to a course, to the enjoyment of teaching and learning. Some developmentalists regard the student as primary "client" and some keep the faculty member uppermost in mind, but both believe you cannot separate the task from the person in education.

Programs which stress personal and developmental issues can tend to slight the more technical side of teaching, whether that be computer-assisted instruction or scholarly advancement. Also, because higher education is a very rational affair, some professors and administrators become uneasy when it is suggested that they might consider the "affective" side of teaching and learning. Still, if personal development and human relationships are central aspects of education, as much research and theory suggests, then this recent attention to the development of professors and students can be one of the most important limbs on our teaching improvement tree.

Organization Development

Many programmatic efforts to improve college teaching fail not because they are ineffective, but because the institution and professional associations do not really support teaching improvement. The system is against it. Faculty members too often get behind instead of ahead by concentrating on improvement of their teaching, for the payoffs are elsewhere. Some institutional leaders penalize faculty risk-takers and experimenters rather than encourage them. Many institutions simply allow no time to develop and refine some new approach. Professional development leaders quickly find that their job is institutional change as well as individual assistance.

Strategies for creating positive institutional conditions for teaching improvement often are called "organization development." (47) They adapt the theories and procedures used by applied behavioral science to improve the organizational "health" of business, industries, churches, social agencies and public schools. They have in common with personal development a concern for the "human side of enterprise," the ways in which faculty members and administrators relate to one another in the process of identifying and reducing obstacles to more effective institutional functioning. The University of Cincinnati was the first teaching improvement center to use "OD" with schools and departments. (11) A project led by Walter Sikes, called "Training Teams for Campus Change," applied organization development tactics to change attempts in several colleges and universities, and Sikes remains an invaluable resource in initiating this kind of approach. (102) After initiation of the project by Arthur Chickering and William Hannah, I directed a somewhat similar national institutional renewal project called "Strategies for Change." (68) Bergquist and Phillips include this OD dimension in their familiar heuristic regarding important components in faculty development, (7) and their handbooks include organization development exercises. Lance Buhl, as you will see in Chapter Seven, places emphasis in his teaching improvement approach on the application of organization development principles to the creation of positive conditions for teaching. And Jerry Gaff's "Project on Institutional Renewal Through the Improvement of Teaching" also stresses the development of institutional supports for teaching improvement. (134)

Programs which include this institutional dimension usually contain common elements. One is training and maintenance of an "action-research team" of faculty members, students and administrators. The team acts as catalyst and facilitator for the assessment of local improvement needs, the discovery and formulation of solutions and the difficult act of gaining acceptance for those solutions. New academic programs or faculty development services may result, but a major goal is to create the kind of institutional climate of openness, trust, and collaboration which can encourage and support teaching innovations. Often, administrative development is included because of the key role authorities can play in creating such a climate.

Personal and organization development are disturbing to many academicians. They admit and confront feelings which other improvement strategies such as instructional development, subject mastery and research on teaching avoid as unrelated to or beneath the purely rational world of academics. "How are you feeling?" becomes as important a question as "How are you doing?" Needs for staff security, for power and status, for esteem in one's own eyes as well as others and for self-fulfillment become major agenda items rather than coffee table gossip. In Pirsig's terms, personal and organizational development seek to attend both to the romantic and classical sides of our nature. (96) These developmental approaches have in common with more "rational-technical" strategies a concern to improve the professional's or organization's "productivity," however that gets defined, but the developmentalists also hold as prime concerns the sense of well-being among those engaged in this production. Are students, professors, administrators feeling included, supported, respected? Are they able to achieve their personal objectives through or around their work? Are they enjoying themselves? The assumptions, supported by studies of organizational development in institutions other than colleges and universities, is that the organization's effectiveness increases as its members increase their sense of worth and satisfaction. (44)

My own view is that organization development has a great deal to offer teaching improvement if it is adapted to fit the norms and styles of the academic world. Its "touchy-feely" and "T-group" labels, used perjoratively, generally are undeserved. Indeed, it is much more hard-headed and data-based than strategies which depend on lengthy committee discussions that ignore underlying human resistances, engage in little systematic inquiry and have no apparent theory to guide them. As is true of the other strategies I have mentioned, OD appears to be an important branch on our teaching improvement tree.

Administrative Development for Teaching Improvement

Administrators are no more prepared to lead and manage than professors are to teach. Natural inclination and some experience watching other administrators seem to be the basic prerequisites besides scholarly achievements. It stands to reason that if college administrators are to become as knowledgeable and skillful as they need to be to improve teaching and learning, in-service development is necessary. Yet there are very few such programs around. The American Council on Education's Office of Leadership Development, (131) the Higher Education Management Institute's Management Development and Training Program, (130) and the Council for the Advancement of Small College's administrative development project (112) are examples of interinstitutional in-service opportunities, but rarer are local, single institution models such as the one at DeAnza Community College in California. (31) There is a rumble under foot, however, marked by a recent administrative development conference under the auspices of the American Association for Higher Education and the Council for the Advancement of Small Colleges and a book on the subject being edited by John Shtogren. (100)

Early projects in this area can be instructive of later ones. One such effort is Virginia Commonwealth University's attempt to help department chairpersons aid faculty development. Its three-year evaluation, based on a round of interviews with about twenty-five chairpersons, suggests the general ingredients in an effective administrative development program. (121) The strongest aspect of the program, said chairpersons, was the opportunity it provided to meet with other chairpersons, compare notes, and lend mutual support. An obvious, but sometimes overlooked, fact is that we are discussing the further development of oftentimes veteran professionals, but professionals who work in isolation from one another even in the same school or department. Get them together, provide a little structure and facilitation, and they will teach each other.

A persistent message from these administrators was that universities are not businesses. The language is different, the organizational structures and relationships are different, the purposes are different, the work is different. Management development techniques borrowed from non-academic settings need adaptation to fit the real world of academic administration if they are to be much use to very many administrators. A related message was that cook-book programs not focused on their pressing problems are less helpful than direct assistance regarding what ails participating administrators. The call was for individualized responses to the particular needs, situation and style of each chairperson, for they are as diverse a lot as their students and faculty.

The Virginia Commonwealth chairpersons also said that it was hard to follow-up on development workshops, no matter how stimulating, because they needed additional help and stimulation or because other job demands overwhelmed their attempts to focus on teaching improvement. Follow-up consultation and continued meetings with a support group of other "developing" administrators were urged. More significant, perhaps, was the implicit message that unless the institution as a whole rethought the chairperson role, little time or interest would be available for teaching improvement. Program leader John Shtogren found that over half the average chairperson's job was bound up in administrative detail, leaving smaller amounts for scholarship, program development and teaching. The average chairperson devoted only seven percent of his time to faculty development and wanted to spend only ten percent. As the job is currently defined and rewarded in practice, faculty development is not exactly a hot item on many chairpersons' itineraries.

It all sounds familiar. We would like to improve learning and teaching, but we get little help, time and payoff for doing it. Five ingredients in effective student, faculty and administrative development are evident: 1) focus development on the solution of problems perceived by those undergoing the experience, 2) encourage and facilitate peer teaching and reinforcement whenever peers have some expertise and support to give, 3) individualize development to fit the objectives, style, background and circumstances of each "client," 4) provide follow-up aid and support after learning events, and 5) strive to create an environment and workload conducive to improvement efforts. As obvious as these suggestions may appear, just consider all the ways we slight them, or find we cannot attain them, in teaching students as well as in professional development.

Preparation for New Academic Programs

A decade ago, most of the energy of college innovators was devoted to getting approval for living-learning programs, interdisciplinary study of contemporary problems, open admissions policies, field experience and independent study, pass-fail grading and peer teaching, audio-tutorial instruction and the Keller Plan, individualized education and competency liberal education. Once we got the faculty and administration to sanction such innovations, we figured we were home free. We professionals certainly could figure out how to make these new approaches to teaching and learning work.

Then we discovered what change researchers were learning at about the same time. (9, 51) A decision to change can be a long, long way from change itself. New teaching roles and attendant skills must be learned. Often, new content must be taught. New working groups and leaders must be developed, and a way must be found to get along with the traditional higher education world. Innovations never work at first try, so formative evaluation and adjustment is needed. Because understanding and commitment to a new program is never what it ought to be either within or beyond the program, continuous education and persuasion regarding our mission and means must occur. New staff must be oriented and new thrusts must be created so that the new program itself gets renewed.

All of these needs point to in-service professional development. And early in the 1970's, such innovative colleges as Mars Hill, Evergreen State, Davis and Elkins, Sterling, New College-Alabama and Santa Cruz turned major attention to helping their staffs learn how to do the new programs they had developed. One such effort was launched at Empire State College and a network of other individualized education institutions, with funding by the Danforth Foundation. Thomas Clark discusses this approach in Chapter Six.

To direct teaching improvement efforts at new academic programs appears to be a particularly potent strategy. Often such programs are created with faculty involvement and are staffed by volunteers, so there is some degree of faculty commitment to the new venture. Because teaching roles are new, professors readily can admit they do not know how to do them without losing face. New program goals can provide clearer benchmarks against which to define teaching-learning effectiveness, and a more manageable focus, than the diffuse mission of an entire university. Changing the structure, content and method of whole programs can make more significant changes in student learning than tinkering with method in a traditional course. Clark and others in similar situations, therefore, have found new program staff eager to participate in faculty development and very appreciative of its benefits. I would not want to try a new academic program without such help.

Local Socialization

College teachers are trained and socialized in graduate research universities to be scholars and researchers, not teachers. That job is effectively done, so well done that when they find themselves in primarily teaching institutions without time or resources for research and without the prestige of their graduate institution, many wish they were someplace else. Parkside is not Madison, Western is not Michigan, Fresno is not Berkeley, Findlay is not Amherst, and Bunker Hill is not Harvard by any stretch of imagination. Jencks and Riesman observe this strong pull of the "top" few institutions in national research reputation. (62) To counter this orientation away from the mission and needs of local colleges and universities, schools traditionally hold brief orientation sessions for new faculty, hand out an incredibly tedious faculty manual and conduct a tea or two. Many primarily teaching institutions have found that these devices are not enough to break the spell of the elite models. More extensive retreats (or "advances," as some call them), self-study projects, workshops on the nature and needs of our students, faculty social hours prior to senate meetings, teaching and service awards and bag lunch seminars on local issues have been introduced as ways to involve faculty in the needs and rewards of teaching in this particular institution.

Los Medanos College goes a step farther. It hires faculty members fresh out of graduate school; then, with money saved by their comparatively low salaries, it reduces their courseload and gives them a year-long, intensive orientation to the Los Medanos mission, student body, curriculum and teaching methods as well as an orientation to themselves as community college teachers. If teaching institutions are to break the grip of graduate/ research universities, such a thorough counter socialization may well be necessary. Chester Case discusses this point more fully in Chapter Five.

Conceptual Frameworks for Teaching Improvement Programs

Two decades ago, professors were supported in their efforts to improve teaching primarily by sabbaticals, small grants, conference travel funds and visiting scholar programs. Since that time, these valuable aids have been augmented by instructional resource centers, instructional development offices, student ratings of instruction, personal and career development services, organization development, research on teaching and learning, extensive orientations to local institutions, administrative development and preparation to teach in nontraditional programs. All these approaches seem to have merit, but how do they relate to one another?

Several attempts have been made to organize various teaching improvement services into some conceptual framework. One of the most frequently used perspectives is that developed by William Bergquist and Steven Phillips and modified somewhat by Jerry Gaff. (7, 48) They propose that services should focus on the personal needs of the professor, the professional responsibilities of that person and the organizational context in which that person tries to improve. This heuristic, (see Chapter Three) emphasizes that any change in teaching has personal, technical and situational aspects. The problem may lie in any of the three dimensions, or in all three, and an effective teaching improvement program had better be able to work on all three fronts.

John Centra, building inductively from a national survey of faculty and instructional development practices, concludes that programs cluster into four general types of activity which he labels "Instructional Assistance Practices," "High Faculty Involvement," "Traditional Practices," and "Emphasis on Assessment." (16) Instructional assistance, the most highly rated approach by Centra's respondents, I grouped on Table One into "instructional resources" and "instructional development." A specialist in teaching process or technology works with faculty clients to help them diagnose teaching problems and to develop solutions. High faculty involvement activities, second ranked in effectiveness, include workshops, seminars, mentor relationships and other means by which colleagues learn with one another's help about their institution, about teaching and advising methods, about new trends in higher education and about themselves and their students as developing adults. The third cluster, traditional practices, includes visiting scholars programs, teaching awards, sabbaticals, workshops and seminars focused on research skills, workload reduction and grants to improve instruction, and travel funds. The common thread is provision of time and money for development rather than stress on technical assistance or colleague interaction concerning teaching-learning information. This cluster is rated below the first two by program leaders. Last in their estimation is the assessment emphasis, including periodic performance reviews, student ratings and colleague or administrative assessments of teaching. Perhaps the threat and subsequent defensiveness which accompanies personnel evaluation, the difficulty in gaining meaningful assessments of an act as private and complex as teaching and the lack of follow-up assistance to professors who receive low assessments make this approach less effective in accomplishing teaching improvement than the others. Table Two displays the four clusters.

Table Two

Factor Analysis of the Approximate Use of Faculty Development Practices*

	Factor Loading
Group 1 (Factor 1): High Faculty Involvement	
Workshops, seminars, or program to acquaint faculty with goals of the institution and types of students enrolled.	.65
"Master teachers" or senior faculty work closely with new or apprentice teachers.	.61
Faculty with expertise consult with other faculty on teaching or course improvement.	.60
Workshops or program to help faculty improve their academic advising and counseling skills.	.57
Personal counseling provided individual faculty members on career goals, and other personal development areas.	.53
Workshops or presentations that explore general issues or trends in education.	.51
Informal assessments by colleagues for teaching or course improvement.	.48
System for faculty to assess their own strengths and areas needing improvement.	.46
Group 2 (Factor 2): Instructional Assistance Practices	
Specialists to assist individual faculty in instructional or course development by consulting on course objectives and course design.	.75
Specialists to help faculty develop teaching skills such as lecturing or leading discussions, or to encourage use of different teaching-learning strategies such as individualized instruction.	.70
Specialists to assist faculty in constructing tests or evaluating student performance.	.69
Assistance to faculty in use of instructional technology as a teaching aid (e.g., programmed learning or computer-assisted instruction).	.65
Specialists on campus to assist faculty in the use of audio-visual aids in instruction, including closed-circuit television.	.56
Workshops or presentations that explore various methods or techniques of instruction.	.42

*John Centra, *Faculty Development Practices in U.S. Colleges and Universities* (1b)

Group 3 (Factor 3): Traditional Practices

Visiting scholars program that brings people to the campus for short or long periods.	.58
Annual awards for excellence in teaching.	.52
Sabbatical leaves with at least half salary.	.43
Workshops or seminars to help faculty improve their research and scholarship skills.	.43
Summer grants for projects to improve instruction or courses.	.43
Temporary teaching load reductions to work on a new course, major course revision, or research area.	.39
Use of grants by faculty members for developing new or different approaches to courses or teaching.	.37
Travel grants to refresh or update knowledge in a particular field.	.33

Group 4 (Factor 4): Emphasis on Assessment

There is a periodic review of the performance of all faculty members, whether tenured or not.	.55
Travel funds available to attend professional conferences.	.47
Systematic ratings of instruction by students used to help faculty improve.	.41
Formal assessments by colleagues for teaching or course improvement (i.e., visitations or use of assessment form).	.40
A policy of unpaid leaves that covers educational or development purposes.	.40
Systematic teaching or course evaluations by an administrator for improvement purposes.	.40

Bergquist, Phillips and Gaff help us identify the major topics of teaching improvement practices: the personal needs of the professor and the student, the tasks of teaching and learning, plus the situation in which the professor teaches and the student tries to learn. Centra, in turn, helps us identify the primary methods of teaching improvement. First and continuously there should be activities which involve staff members in learning together about teaching and learning goals, problems and potential solutions. Then, time and money as well as technical assistance should be provided so that staff members can develop and skillfully implement their own solutions to the problems they see. This "social learning" and "problem-solving" approach to teaching improvement, which I discuss at greater length elsewhere, (69) appears to assume that the central institutional role in teaching improvement is to provide information linkage and problem solving facilitation as faculty members themselves assume major responsibility for improving teaching. Teaching improvement is too dependent upon the willing commitment of the teacher; the professor cannot be forced to improve by formal policy and personnel review. When such review does enter the picture, as it must in personnel decisions,this perspective again suggests that judgments should follow at a fairly non-threatening distance.

If we look at the focus and method of teaching improvement services as that picture emerges from practice and from recent conceptualizations, we can pose several questions that a teaching improvement leader might ask about his program. Do we have time, material resources, skill and activities which enable faculty to learn together about themselves and about their students as developing persons? Do we have the time, money, skill and activities to help faculty resolve the personal concerns they and their students have? Do we have equally effective means for learning together about teaching and learning problems as well as means for improving the content and method of instruction? And are we effective in asserting the organizational conditions which encourage and inhibit effective teaching and learning as well as in aiding the improvement of that situation?

The ten teaching improvement approaches discussed earlier provide most of the parts needed to answer these questions positively. The challenge of the next decade may be to integrate these components into a flexible and powerful whole.

Teaching and Learning

by Jack Lindquist

Introduction

Whatever does it mean to "improve college teaching?" How can we recognize a more or less "developed" faculty member, administrator or student when we see one? These are critical, but troublesome, questions to ask when designing or renewing teaching improvement programs. We need some standard, some definition of effective teaching and fully developed professionals, to guide our work. But dare we ask?

Perhaps, like a clever real estate agent, we should let our "clients," those faculty members who seek to improve, do the defining. That approach makes sense. We are talking about changing their knowledge, attitudes and behaviors; one cannot force such changes on professionals who do not see the changes as their solutions to their problems in pursuit of their improvement goals. The problem with leaving the definition of teaching improvement and professional development entirely up to the faculty, however, is that theirs is a limited perspective. They know their subject and have learned teaching from experience; few are well-versed in teaching-learning theory and research. Few know ways to teach which are different from their own. Few know in any depth the nature and learning experiences of their students.

I assume a good many people will, and should, get into the act of defining "teaching improvement" and "professional development," although the infancy of this movement has meant that teaching improvement leaders, in the absence of clear definitions from others, seem to be the primary shapers of those terms. This said, what guidelines can be offered to the professor, student and development leader as they attempt to define teaching improvement? Five topic areas seem to me to provide the information and convictions necessary to determine what is, and what needs, improvement: 1) the nature of the student, 2) the nature of the teacher, 3) the desired learning outcomes, 4) the teaching/learning process, and 5) the improvement circumstances. This chapter briefly discusses each of the five topics, then directs the reader to more extensive information and assistance. No one definition of teaching improvement or development will be posited, for that complex of five factors should generate a somewhat different general definition for each institution or program as well as a different specific definition for each professor.

The Nature of the Student

A student is a student is a student, traditional teaching formulations apparently assumed. If you can teach one, you can teach them all; or, conversely, only a few students are teachable at the college level. The rest are hopeless causes.

In recent years, the student has been re-introduced as a crucial variable in effective teaching, and ways are being found to enable professors to help an increasing diversity of students. Both respect for the individual and a democratic commitment to bring higher learning to the full range of adult Americans are beginning to attach some reality to the rhetoric. We are a long way from providing equal educational opportunity, and we are only beginning to discover what must lie behind the "open door" in order to accomplish Patricia Cross's nice phrase, "education for each." (27) But we are on our way, thanks in part to teaching improvement programs which help faculty members understand and appreciate their students and which aid them in teaching not only the devout apprentices in their specialty but also dilettantes and the students who wish they were someplace else; not only the eager participant or competitive learners but also the dependent, the collaborative and the independent students; not only the white middle class but also minority and lower socio-economic groups; not only deductive but inductive learners; not only conservatives but radicals; not only students with stable personal lives but ones whose lives are in turmoil or flux; not only students aching to attain truth, beauty and justice but those aching for a job and a little self-respect; not only eighteen year olds but sixty year olds.

There are several ways teaching improvement programs can help faculty members gain a better understanding of the nature of their students and the implications for teaching. One approach is to assist in the interpretation of available information regarding student academic backgrounds and test scores. Such information is lying around most colleges but often sits on the registrar's and institutional researcher's shelves. In working one-on-one with a professor or in facilitating self-study, the teaching improvement facilitator can help professors see the range in background, preparation and ability of their students. The facilitator can play a crucial role in helping professors guard against the possible tendency to fulfill prophecy by treating students with weaker prior records as less able than those with strong records, thereby perpetuating low self-concept and weak performance. (97a) The strong message is to help professors respect and appreciate all their students, for teaching effectiveness may depend on that positive attitude. Some freshmen seminars and self-studies therefore have chosen as a major goal the discovery of hidden talents and motivations in what appear on the surface to be unable and unmotivated students.

Besides examining past student records and test scores or engaging in freshman seminars, faculty can gain greater understanding of students through surveys of student backgrounds and interests. Three good examples are the "Student Information Form" (105) given to hundreds of thousands of freshmen each year, the "College Student Questionnaire," (24) and the "Student Biographical Inventory." (104) Such surveys obtain student profiles on educational and socio-economic background, on learning goals and on various personal traits relevant to learning such as degree of persistence, independence and reading ability. These surveys can be sub-grouped by academic program unit, even by course (with caution because of low numbers) and then can be the focus of discussion in teaching improvement workshops, with students present to put flesh and bones on the numbers.

Supplementing surveys should be other forms of information on students such as in-depth interviews and "portfolios of prior learning," (103) for surveys do not permit the flexibility of inquiry and specificity of evidence often needed to understand one's students. Teaching improvement facilitators can help professors learn how to design and conduct such interviews and portfolios within the context of a course. A teaching improvement team can take on such interviews and portfolios as a project in "Understanding Our Students." Again, students should be involved in the analysis and interpretation of such information, for it comes from them and pertains to them in important ways.

Also increasing in use are surveys of learning styles. We are beginning to discover that students do learn in different ways, and that information can help teachers respond to individual differences. The Grasha-Riechmann "Student Learning Styles Questionnaire," published in the first volume of Bergquist and Phillips' *A Handbook for Faculty Development,* (7) helps identify independent, participant, competitive, avoidant, dependent and collaborative learners. But other similar groupings emerge from responses to the "Myers-Briggs Type Indicator" (86) and the "Student Orientations Survey." (106) Tests of intellectual style help separate students who are field dependent or independent, potentially significant differences for the most effective teaching approach to each type. (81)

Each of these learning styles instruments can be taken by professors as well as students so that teachers can see the fit between their preferred learning style and those of their students. Teaching improvement facilitators then can help professors adjust their teaching so that a wider diversity of learning styles are accommodated. The awareness of such variations in itself is often a powerful incentive for professors to become more sensitive to differences in the way their students learn.

I noted in Chapter One the emergence of a literature regarding the college student. That literature affords yet another way to increase professional understanding of students. Bag lunch seminars, symposiums, article circulation and workshop sessions can be devoted to discussion of such works. For instance, Becker, Geer and Hughes' *Making the Grade*, (6) a study which found that university students are strongly oriented toward grades, can form the basis for student-faculty-administrative discussions of what motivates students to learn *besides* the threat of low grades or the promise of higher ones. Chickering's *Education and Identity*, (20) with its postulation of seven vectors of student development can ground a seminar on the learning needs of young adults, and his *Conceptual Framework for College Development* (18) is equally helpful in laying an intellectual foundation for educating older adults. Cross's *Beyond the Open Door* (28) is a good starting point for examination of the nature of the "new student" who has appeared in our colleges during the last decade or so. Heist's *The Creative College Student* (54) can begin serious consideration of how to aid or stimulate creativity, too often a neglected potential. Perry's *Forms of Intellectual and Ethical Development in the College Years* (94) invites discussion of what levels and stages of development in thinking and valuing are prevalent among one's students.

The point is not that such books hold all the keys to understanding our students. Rather, they provide conceptual frameworks and research evidence which, when merged with local analysis of local students, can move faculty members to a richer, more complex perspective regarding the nature and needs of the students they teach.

Perhaps the most important teaching improvement aid to faculty in understanding their students is help in interviewing the students themselves, whether in the course of academic advising, during classes or in informal contacts. Two kinds of aids can strengthen such inquiries. One is training in questioning, paraphrasing and probing in a systematic but open manner as free as possible of quick assumptions, judgments and attributions by the professor. Most faculty members and administrators are not trained in such skills, and few of us come by them naturally; yet, without thorough and undistorted diagnosis of our students, we are likely to miss connections in our teaching.

The second aid to personal diagnosis is a set of categories for questioning. Tom Clark, in Chapter Seven, delineates several categories of individual differences which have relevance for teaching. I think one should try at least to learn the student's background in the subject and interest in it, her educational, career and personal development objectives, her pace and style of learning, the logistical problems impinging on learning (like three kids, or a full-time job, or a serious personal difficulty, or no money whatsoever) and her self-concept. With such knowledge, a professor can begin to design teaching practices and learning experiences which support rather than thwart learning.

In most of these areas, teaching improvement programs are only beginning to find good ways to help professors understand students more fully. But promising starts are everywhere, and there is little question that serious consideration of the nature of students should be a central aspect of in-service programs to improve college teaching.

The Nature of the Professor as Teacher

Teaching improvement depends in good part on the knowledge, skills, attitudes and values of the person doing the teaching. To state that professors are diverse individuals, like students, is to beg the obvious; some teaching improvement programs, however, neglect the teacher in their concern to attend to the teaching task. It is as if teaching and learning are ferris wheels which professors run and students ride. The students are interchangeable, and the only thing one needs to know about the professor is whether or not he knows how to work the machine. Teaching and learning, however, take place in humans. The faculty member and student are the critical variables, not the wheel, and each one is different. One only needs to compare the conceptually oriented, well-established professor who knows and trusts only one teaching approach, say the Socratic dialogue, and who has no use for students who are not apprentice scholars in his discipline, with the pragmatic assistant professor infatuated with field experience as *the* way to learn, to see that helping both professors learn Personalized System of Instruction at the same time in the same way is liable not to work. It is liable to be disaster.

Several methods are being used to help professors get better acquainted with themselves as college teachers. One is the "development interview," conducted by a colleague or teaching improvement facilitator and focused on such matters as how the professor came to be a college teacher, what have been his particular high points and disappointments in teaching, what educational outcomes in students does he seek, what obstacles to greater effectiveness does he face and what specific changes or improvements in his teaching as well as his broader personal and professional life does he hope to achieve in the next year or so. Such interviews are discussed in Freedman and Sanford's "The Faculty Member Yesterday and Today," (46) and such a set of questions is included in the first volume of Bergquist and Phillips' *Handbook*. (7) A special dividend of this method is that interviewees themselves usually find such questioning a rare and valuable opportunity to reflect upon themselves as college teachers. These interviews also form an excellent prelude to faculty development workshops or consultations, for they warm the participant to the topic while generating good information for designing the workshop. Surveys also have their place in the study of professors as teachers. Two handy instruments, both used in several collegiate settings and both in the second volume of Bergquist-Phillips' *Handbook*, are Gaff's "The Faculty Questionnaire" and Lindquist and Guerrin's "The Professional Development Questionnaire." (7) These examine faculty backgrounds, educational objectives, teaching styles and practices, relations with students and professional development interests. A workshop or retreat which used such data as a basis for discussing the nature and needs of our "Professors as Teachers," with professors and students present to lend first-hand impressions and testimonials, can help identify major professorial variables to be heeded in teaching improvement. Such workshops also could include exercises to help professors clarify their own values and aspirations as they relate to teaching. Again, volume two of the Bergquist-Phillips *Handbook* has such exercises (7), as does *Integrating Professional and Personal Growth* by Wells and Munson. (85)

Perhaps the most significant part of such self-examination is the clarification and rank-ordering of faculty concerns. Every faculty member I ever interviewed said he or she wanted to help diverse students develop as persons, develop intellectually, master a discipline, get ahead in life; but there is only so much teaching time in a professor's life. If "covering the subject" is the number one priority, personal and intellectual development may either lose out or be serendipitous by-products of a forced march through the syllabus. The critical question, often, is "How can I *both* cover the subject and aid the student to develop as a person and thinker?"

Besides interviews and surveys, there is a growing literature on professors as teachers. Anderson and Murray's *The Professors: Work and Life Style Among Academicians* (2) contains essays by notable students of academic life such as Barzun, Veblen, Chomsky, Jencks and Riesman. One or more of these essays could lead off a workshop or seminar discussion of how faculty approach their work and how that approach facilitates or inhibits teaching improvement. Axelrod's *The University Teacher as Artist* (4) nicely differentiates the teacher-craftsman from the teacher-artist, and a discussion might center on which students might benefit from "didactic" or "evocative" teaching. Mann's *The College Classroom* (77) is a systematic research inquiry into types of college teachers and can be used in conjunction with Axelrod's more conceptual approach. Cohen and Brawer's *Confronting Identity: The Community College Instructor* (23) invites consideration of how to reconcile the personal concerns of college teachers and the expectations of their institutions. Eble's *Professors as Teachers* (34) also depicts the problems faced by professors who would be teachers first. It and *Faculty Development in a Time of Retrenchment* (52) are good background reading for discussion regarding the need for faculty services and incentives. A provocative article for discussion of faculty attitudes toward students is Warren's "Student Behavior Underlying Faculty Judgments of Academic Performance," (108) which obtained from three hundred professors in fifteen institutions their descriptions of how a good student and a poor one differ from an average one in one of their classes. Concerning fundamental academic values and biases, there are few better stimuli to discussion than Jencks and Reisman's *The Academic Revolution* (62) and Parsons and Platt's *The American University*. (92)

As for faculty members and administrators as developing adults, Hodgkinson's "Adult Development: Implications for Faculty and Administrators" (56) has spurred many a lively discussion. If the theories of Gould, Levinson, Loevinger (70) and others bear up, teaching improvement services may be able to predict certain development concerns among faculty at certain stages in their development. Young professors and administrators just getting into their careers may be expected to be very interested in learning how to master particular tasks and learning how to "get into" the field. Training and socialization into college teaching make sense during this period, and because young adults tend to be strongly influenced by older "mentors" who act as models and guides, a formal mentoring program using older faculty *chosen by* younger ones would make sense. For professors a few years into teaching, a transition period may occur in which they question initial commitments. Is this the career for me? Is this the spouse for me? How can I change my new life from the dull routine it has become? In-service programs which help staff members in this re-examination of initial directions and which introduce innovations to rekindle the romance of college teaching would appear useful at this time.

For professors in their mid-thirties, the evidence of research on adult development suggests a strong urge both to settle down and to advance one's career. Getting tenure, getting published, building a family, getting known, becoming influential in campus governance and disciplinary associations are strong urges. Unless the institution and its teaching improvement program can manage to define teaching excellence as the route to higher status, influence, esteem and personal fulfillment, it may not attract many professors in this age group or may frustrate those it attracts. An exception may be the faculty development leader. Many in-service programs are run by persons in their mid-thirties who are finding teaching improvement leadership a promising route to career advancement. Also, those faculty members who have taken leadership roles in developing new curricula may be eager for assistance in how to teach those programs most effectively. Mentors no longer have strong influence in this period, so colleague sharing or technical assistance which gives considerable autonomy and status to the professional seem more appropriate approaches.

Next comes the infamous "mid-life transition," that time when it becomes doubtful that I'll become president and when it is clear that my life is probably half over. Death takes on personal meaning. Do I want to go on the same way? The divorce and job shift rates rise. Once again, in-service development which offers personal and career counseling, sabbatical opportunities to reflect and regroup, opportunities to try new roles and new teaching approaches, life-planning which confirms past accomplishments while giving focus and meaning to the future all hold promise for professors in this period.

Once the pain of "middlescence" passes (if it does), the evidence suggests a mellowing period. I won't be president, but life holds plenty of value anyway. Persons in their mid-forties and beyond may take a more relaxed approach to professional and personal life. This relaxation may mean decay into campus deadwood or petrification into hard rock resistors of change, but Erickson finds that it also can mean a strong interest in "generativity," in helping younger people grow and advance. Senior professors with such interests can become skilled mentors of younger faculty and students. Teaching improvement programs can help them carry out that role in a way which improves th effectiveness both of mentor and "mentee." I am impressed at the number of senior faculty members who have played key roles in helping renew or change learning and teaching.

They are secure in status and esteem, have major scholarly achievements under their belts, have settled into their institution for the remainder of their career, know everybody and know how to get things done.

The existing literature constitutes far from a mature understanding of the professor as teacher. There needs to be much more systematic research on both students as learners and professors as teachers. Still, books and articles on the subject offer more information and conceptual insight than most professors have the time or opportunity to compile. They can expand the perspective of local studies and stimulate new thinking regarding what the professor brings to the teaching act. Coupled with surveys and interviews, such studies should provide a solid foundation upon which to build the teaching act itself.

Learning Objectives

"Improvement" or "development" are hard to define unless it is clear what their intent is. What are professor and student trying to accomplish? Too often, one gets only vague answers to that question. Professors will say they want to "cover" the subject or promote "critical thinking," while students comment that they want to "broaden" themselves or get a "good" job. What do such words mean?

Teaching improvement services, especially instructional development specialists, focus part of their time on helping professors (and, more rarely students) clarify their learning objectives. Taxonomies of educational objectives such as Bloom's and Krathwohl's (10, 65) and guides to setting objectives such as Mager's, (75) are frequently used to add precision and clarity to this act. Some advising and "mentoring" programs, such as those Tom Clark discusses in Chapter Seven, also help professors learn how to aid students in clarifying their learning objectives.

'In general, these objectives might be organized in four categories: 1) learning to know and comprehend, 2) learning to think, 3) learning to do, and 4) learning to be. Our educational system tends to stress the first objective and hope that in the course of mastering some body of knowledge, the other objectives will be fulfilled. If you know chemistry or English literature, chances are you will be a master thinker and problem-solver, a fine practitioner of work related to those subjects and an upstanding human being. As knowledge expands, that assumption gets tested to the extreme, for mastering a subject consumes more and more of one's time. Many recent collegiate innovations seek to increase emphasis on thinking, doing and being, in part on the assumption that because mastering a field is a never-ending task, the best preparation is to learn how to think, how to work and how to lead a personal life of enjoyment, responsibility and integrity. It is, perhaps, a chicken-egg debate, with the disciplinary and professional educators on one side and the liberal educators on the other; but it rarely is so clear a dichotomy. A political scientist or physicist may teach subject mastery with little attention to other learning objectives, yet call his courses part of liberal education of the whole person and find eloquent support for that claim. Certainly one service a teaching improvement facilitator can offer is to provide a forum and conceptual tools which can help professors, administrators and students become clearer, and more intentional, regarding just what knowledge, skills and attitudes should be the outcomes of teaching and learning.

Probably because of our stress on knowledge as the essential product of higher learning, much teaching improvement activity is focused on that learning outcome. The focus is didacticism, disseminating knowledge so that it is received and understood. Individual consultations or workshop sessions concern the organization and pace of courses; the clarity with which material is presented; the level of complexity and kind of language or metaphors used so that the message is understood; the use of discussions, demonstrations, simulations, media and field observations to increase comprehension. Mastery learning programs such as the Personalized Systems of Instruction (98) are introduced as ways to increase the level of comprehension among most of one's students. Because professors tend to think of themselves as content specialists, because the culture is transmitted in part by disseminating knowledge and because mastery of content is an important prerequisite to effective functioning in a profession, a central service of teaching improvement programs should be to help professors increase student knowledge and comprehension of academic subjects.

Learning to think, to discover knowledge for oneself and to solve mental problems, is often stated by professors as an objective of their teaching. John Cardinal Newman goes so far as to say that "liberal education, viewed in itself, is simply the cultivation of the intellect, as such, and its object is nothing more or less than intellectual excellence." (87) Many professors still hold with Newman and Robert Maynard Hutchins that the essential objective of higher learning should not be mastery of any particular specialty but "cultivation of the intellect."

The problem is, how do you cultuvate an intellect? Ironically, some students who have little academic knowledge have highly refined thinking abilities, as witnessed by the low income student who has maneuvered her way through twenty or thirty years of ghetto stress and strain but has not heard of Newton or Durkheim. She can solve problems which would stagger most professors. But does she have a cultivated intellect, and if not, how can she develop one? Other students, who have been largely dependent and passive recipients of didactic education in the "best" suburban schools, may be able to fill up an essay on Newton or Durkheim but not be able to think for themselves. Are their intellects cultivated or capable of cultivation?

Teaching improvement services which focus on learning to think generally assist professors in clarifying what they mean by such phrases as "critical thinking" or "creative problem-solving," then introduce them to active learning experiences designed not to lead students to "The Answer" but to assist students in formulating their own answers. It is what Axelrod calls "evocative" rather than "didactic" teaching, instruction for inquiry rather than mastery. (4) In some programs, advisement becomes an important opportunity to teach problem-solving as students are helped to formulate their own learning objectives and plans rather than having them dictated by the catalog or advisor. Simulations and games, open-ended class discussions, student task groups, independent projects, papers calling not simply for knowledge but for analysis and application, and field or work experiences all can be designated and conducted to emphasize thinking. Useful literature for teaching students to think is the work of developmentalists such as Perry, Kohlberg, Piaget and Chickering. (94, 64, 95, 20) McKeachie observed in his presidential address to the American Psychological Association that the major shift in psychology regarding learning and teaching is this turn in attention from straightforward stimulus-response association, the stuff of Skinner and behaviorism, to cognitive development. He notes the shift this way: "Today, we would not, like [William] James, advise teachers to think of their students as little association machines. Rather we see students and people in general as active, curious, social human learners." (71) That shift in thinking has important implications for college teaching, and teaching improvement facilitators would do well to heed the new work in cognitive development.

Major issues for professors who want to teach thinking as well as content are, "What do I do when students don't come up with the right answer?" or "What if the time it takes to get students to think for themselves results in less than full coverage of the subject?" Teaching improvement facilitators will need to provide occasions and devices which help professors, departments or the institution in general determine which learning objective is primary for which students in what subjects at what levels. Students, of course, ought to have a say in the matter too. Put another way, the key question becomes, Who should solve the mental problems if students are to learn how to think: professor or student?

Learning to do, or developing application skills, is a common teaching objective in vocational or basic skills courses but often is left to chance in academic disciplines and professions. In the latter areas, the assumption seems to be that if you know the subject, you can apply it. We all know, however, many professors who are highly knowledgeable about political science or education or medicine but who do not have much skill in applying that knowledge to practical problems. Put them out in government or primary schools or a rural hospital and they flounder. Bring practitioners in for summer seminars with professors and discover that the "real world" and the "ivory tower" are leagues apart.

There is enough need to help professors improve the application skills in students, and enough student motivation to be able to get a job and perform well in it, that teaching improvement services should place some stress on aiding faculty in helping students learn how to apply knowledge. Alfred North Whitehead argues that application is an essential part of knowing, not an activity to be omitted from teaching:

> In the process of learning there should be present, in some sense or other, a subordinate activity of application. In fact, the applications are part of the knowledge. For the very meanings of things known are wrapped up in their relationships beyond themselves. Thus unapplied knowledge is knowledge shorn of its meaning. (109)

Such devices as cooperative work experiences, field placements and internships, laboratory work, simulations, role playing and interpersonal skills training (for jobs in which one must work with others, meaning almost every job one can imagine) are employed to develop application skills. In each case, teaching skills in helping to design applications of knowledge, supervise and assist application, and help students reflect on what worked and why, are somewhat different than the skills used in disseminating knowledge or evoking thinking, although interrelated. They need attention in faculty development.

Often neglected or relegated to student services is "learning to be," the deliberate attempt to assist students in gaining understanding of themselves and others, clarifying purposes, developing a positive self-concept, broadening sensitivities, creating a coherent set of values, becoming a responsible member of their family, community and society. Such matters are not academic, say many professors, nor are they by-products of mastering advanced calculus or Shakespeare. Yet some in-service programs find that these concerns are important to professors regarding their own development and often are pressing matters for young adults or older students "in transition."

Because student services staffs often are most interested in the personal development of students and most able to assist it, teaching improvement programs may direct their personal development services toward those staff members, as well as toward the minority of professors for whom learning to be is a major teaching objective. Also, attention can be paid to making informal, out-of-class contacts between students and faculty or students and peers effective influences on personal growth. Wilson, Gaff and their associates find that the personal relationships between faculty members and students are powerful opportunities to aid student development (110), while Feldman and Newcomb's synthesis of wide-ranging research on students confirms the power of peer relationships. (41) Many teaching improvement programs neglect to aid faculty and students in making informal contacts conducive to personal growth. They miss an important opportunity to aid learning.

Several authors such as Bloom and Chickering offer summary categories of the learning objectives to which teaching improvement services might attend. Learning to know, learning to think, learning to do and learning to be are alternative categories. To put these objectives somewhat differently, I have included below a useful set by Stanford Erickson. In designing or renewing teaching improvement programs, leaders might check to see whether they are providing helpful services to improve accomplishment of each one of these learning objectives:

1. *Verbal learning of factual knowledge*: knowing and understanding information, principles, and concepts.
2. *Acquisition of performance skill*: being able to apply knowledge and understanding to the accomplishment of some task.
3. *Concept formation*: the ability to acquire and manipulate abstract ideas.
4. *Method, process, and problem-solving*: capacity to define and solve problems, to learn how to learn.
5. *Changing attitudes and values*: in liberal education, often a "freeing" from narrow beliefs about what is good and true and beautiful to a broader, more complex, and more open way of holding one's assumptions.

6. *Personal development*: development of personal security, acceptance, self-esteem, self-fulfillment, identity. (38)

We can expect that the most demand for teaching improvement services will be related to the first four objectives on Erickson's list, but I join other writers on professional development and teaching in encouraging serious attention to the last two categories as well. We split up college learning into a smorgasbord which too often has the same dish (verbal learning of factual knowledge) served up in a dozen bland ways to students who are hungry for something else. Teaching improvement services would do well were they to help faculty serve well-balanced and tasty learning meals when and where students are hungry to eat.

Teaching-Learning Process

It is one thing to decide to go to town on a wintry day, to pick the most likely vehicle and the road to get you there. Actually getting there is another matter. The best laid plans of professors and students may go awry in practice. A fourth part of the definition of what needs improving or developing is thus teaching-learning practices themselves, and their outcomes.

A first, and regularly repeated, teaching improvement step is to learn what is happening in teaching and learning. How do local professors go about teaching, and what alternative approaches are used by other professors in other places but for similar students and objectives? How do students go about learning? Surveys such as the "Experience of College Questionnaire" (40) can provide such information as what percentage of teaching time is spent disseminating information and what percentage of student time is spent notetaking and memorizing as opposed to, say, active participation in discussion and analysis or synthesis. A sample of students and professors can be asked to keep diaries of their daily teaching and learning activities for a week or two, and members of a teaching improvement team can interview them to elaborate on the usefulness of various activities so that a vivid picture of teaching and learning can be obtained. Classes, advising sessions and informal contacts can be videotaped or recorded by participant observers. Teams of colleagues can make site visits to other classes or campuses to see how teaching and learning take place elsewhere. And once such pictures are taken, workshops, meetings, and individual consultations can be used to feed back the information and consider its meaning with faculty members and students.

Because professors often have a hard time standing back from their own practices to examine them in a critical light, an important teaching improvement service is to develop an insightful picture of what one is actually doing. The picture may be an illumination of one's own practices or the comparison which results from seeing how someone else teaches math to freshmen or biology to upperclass majors. A lens through which to take these pictures may be teaching-learning theory. Is what we are doing consistent with the best available knowledge regarding how to help students obtain certain learning objectives?

The most meaningful way to focus on teaching-learning practices is the least developed: evidence of learning outcomes. At the level of direct testing on course materials, professors and students have decent information on how many students performed how well. If base-line testing at the beginning of a course is coupled with clear outcome criteria, final tests can indicate immediate progress. Student ratings of instruction also can provide immediate impressions of the effectiveness of teaching. If such data are collected before and after an attempt to improve teaching, one can get a reading on whether teaching and learning actually did improve, although care should be taken because effectiveness is liable to decrease until a new practice is mastered. Also, because much information learned superficially, not used thereafter and not of high interest to students is likely to be forgotten rapidly, immediate testing should be followed up by later examination to see whether potential improvements result in enduring learning.

All these matters of testing improvement by outcomes measures are complicated evaluation and research issues. Most professors will be unfamiliar with ways to determine teaching improvement based on student learning. In truth, most professional evaluators are only beginning to get a handle on the problem. If, however, an evaluation and learning research specialist collaborates with faculty members and students in generating and interpreting evidence of student change related to teaching, faculty and administration can enjoy far better information than they now have regarding teaching effectiveness. A promising model for assessing learning outcomes is the Program Effectiveness and Related Costs (PERC) Project of Empire State College and affiliated institutions. (90)

The Teaching-Learning Context

Professors and students are not off by themselves, given *carte blanche* to do as they please. They teach and learn within the context of institutional goals, norms, budgets, formal structures and peer influences. They are hemmed in by broader boundaries such as the job market, disciplinary associations and government regulations. The definition of teaching improvement must take into account this situation, often a predicament, in which professors try to teach and students do their best to learn.

If, for example, the setting is a conservative one in which risk-taking is discouraged, in which heavy teaching loads and pressures to publish allow little time for improvement, in which there is little trust between and among faculty and administration, in which students and faculty have very little in common, and in which there is almost nothing in the way of expert assistance for the professor who seeks to improve teaching, it will take a magnifying glass to find much teaching improvement. And that situation, unfortunately, is a familiar one in American higher education. It is the reason that teaching improvement leaders such as Lance Buhl (see Chapter Seven) put such stress on creating positive conditions for teaching.

At least these seven conditions can have great impact on efforts to improve college teaching:

1. Formal and informal goals which stress the importance of teaching and learning.
2. Professional incentives and rewards which stress the importance of teaching and learning.
3. Considerable individual freedom to innovate and experiment in teaching and learning.
4. Program structures which encourage and support teaching improvement.
5. Workload time available for teaching improvement.
6. Expertise, materials and advocacy to help professors and students become able to carry out teaching improvements.
7. A good fit between the backgrounds and interests of faculty and backgrounds and interests of students.

If a professional development program took upon itself the task of strengthening these seven conditions for teaching improvement, it would become controversial but probably would be putting its energy in the right directions. In institutions which have low amounts of these seven conditions, the best in-service leaders can hope is to help the few stalwarts who are willing to improve despite the system.

Consider each condition in turn. In many colleges and universities, the stated mission of the institution gives teaching and learning a prominent position, but the statement is too general and ambiguous to be much help. And too often, the real mission has to do more with securing survival and attaining status in the eyes of funders and of prestigious colleagues, whether or not the paths to these goals include the improvement of teaching and learning. Some teaching improvement programs have sought to clarify and raise the importance of teaching goals by holding workshops on setting educational objectives and by conducting institutional, school or departmental goals studies with the use of such instruments as the "Institutional Goals Inventory." (61) If, through such activities, teaching-learning objectives become more explicit and accepted, as is the case in some "competency liberal education" colleges, teaching improvement in the direction of those objectives is facilitated.

Professional incentives and rewards too often give negative sanctions to teaching improvement. What is encouraged and rewarded by collegues may be scholarly productivity and by administrators the processing of as many students as possible; in both cases only minimum expectations and rewards for excellence exist for helping a wide diversity of students advance in knowledge, skills and attitudes. Teaching improvement efforts can encourage shifts in such norms by educating faculty and administrative leaders to the needs of diverse students (say, by workshops, studies, articles, seminars), by establishing among interested faculty norms which value teaching excellence and improvement (say, by teaching grants and awards, limited membership support groups), by altering faculty selection and promotion policies to include teaching excellence as one path to tenure or by cost-effectiveness studies which put the accent on effectiveness. Usually, the task is not to make everyone shift from a norm of productivity (in publications and numbers of students) to one of teaching excellence but to add the latter as one way to get ahead.

Freedom to experiment is not likely in institutions whose leaders maintain that one must be certain of consequences before acting or who do not trust individual professionals to take their own initiatives. Teaching improvement involves experimentation by individuals who cannot be sure of the results beforehand. Organization development is particularly germane to this strengthening of freedom and trust, for its activities focus in part on data gathering, feedback, and follow-up consultation and training designed to study and improve the degree of organizational support for innovation. Few organization development interventions have taken place at the institutional level in colleges and universities, but they are more common in subunits such as schools and departments, the levels at which freedom to experiment can be supported most easily. Often, however, higher authorities also will need to be involved in such interventions so that as leaders they are seen as equally supportive of individual initiatives.

Departmental structures reinforce and facilitate the teaching of disciplinary specialties and a focus more on content than on student. They are designed to advance the discipline and prepare apprentices in it, not for other purposes. If teaching improvement efforts are designed to meet those objectives, departments can be helpful, especially if their leaders value teaching and learning. If, however, the objective of teaching improvement is intellectual or personal development with the focus on the student, other structures or program units become necessary. The contract learning structure described by Tom Clark in Chapter Six is designed to focus teaching on the student rather than a subject.

Such units sound peculiar in their unfamiliarity, but some colleges are redesigning undergraduate liberal education structures around themes, competencies or contracts. Their advantage is that they direct an entire program unit toward nontraditional learning outcomes rather than expecting such outcomes to be the indirect consequence of structures organized mainly to train a student in a particular discipline or profession. Teaching improvement leaders can encourage development of program structures befitting teaching and learning goals and can aid such units in improving their effectiveness through orientation, training and formative evaluation.

Most college teachers have to steal time from other parts of life — scholarship, service, family, church and community, recreation, personal renewal — in order to improve their teaching. Normal faculty workloads simply do not allow time to gain the knowledge and skill needed to improve teaching. Why bother if so much must be sacrificed with so little reward? Various approaches have been used to gain time for improvement: teaching improvement sabbaticals and leaves, special fellowships, small grants, time and money to attend conferences and workshops, calendar rearrangements to create time exclusively for professional development, temporary reassignment from teaching to faculty development, reduced teaching or committee loads. All have the potential to free up a professor for improvement, but unless that time is protected from normal demands and unless assistance and guidance is available to make that time constructive, it may disappear without improvement. A professional growth contract which explicitly states how the time will be used for what purpose, as well as how the institution will provide protection and assistance, has been found to be helpful for such purposes.

The teaching improvement service itself can constitute the sixth condition for improvement: expertise, materials and advocacy. The task is to establish a skilled and committed group of people bound and determined to help faculty members who want to improve their teaching. One continuous job of teaching improvement leaders should be to build and maintain this force.

Finally, strengthening the fit between faculty and student backgrounds and interests is more than a recruitment problem, although it is that. An elitist faculty and a populist student body are not going to work well together, no matter what. But in-service programs which educate faculty to the particular strengths and objectives of their students, which help faculty build from those strengths and objectives toward their own concerns, and which help students learn how to fulfill their own potential by reaching out to faculty can help close the gap. Student-faculty self-studies and retreats, freshman seminars, student-faculty workshops and training on how to relate to one another, "studenting" workshops, class-room exercises and essays which reveal student potential and interests to professors while revealing the faculty member's humanity to students, all can create a better fit between students and faculty.

Creating these seven conditions for improvement in teaching and learning is no small order. I know no institution which can brag of significant advancement in all areas, and few have made much progress in any. But with skill and perserverance, the job is not impossible, especially in institutions supposedly committed to teaching.

Summary Teaching-Learning Guidelines

In his presidential address to the American Psychological Association, Wilbert McKeachie summarized much more knowledgeably than I can the progress which has been made in understanding how students can be helped to learn. In a nutshell, he concludes that "what we have learned is that learning is *more complex* than we had earlier believed." (71) It must account, variably, for student, professor, objectives, process, context. It perhaps is never the same experience twice. Yet McKeachie makes nine points in this hypothetical "Talk to Teachers" which seem to me to be excellent reminders when designing and implementing programs to improve college teaching. I paraphrase those points below.

1. Treat students as learning organisms, humans constantly engaged in seeking, organizing, coding, storing, retrieving, using, and evaluating

information. They are not passive receptacles, even when they look that way.

2. Make use of the social milieu. It can be a powerful aid, or source of resistance, to learning.

3. Identify the critical features of the skill or knowledge or attitude to be learned, for those features will set direction and limits to teaching and learning.

4. Stress the importance not just of acquiring knowledge but of strategies for learning, learning how to learn by oneself.

5. Be alert that learning in a classroom from a professor may have different consequences than learning from peers or from experience.

6. Encourage active learning by getting students to talk, write, do, interact, teach others.

7. Regard the teacher as a potential model of how to learn and how to relate to learners. Seek to create models who are warm, personal encouragers of learners.

8. Emphasize a flexibility of approach to account for interactions among student characteristics, teacher characteristics, goals, subject matter and method.

9. Attend to situational variables, in particular the creation of settings small enough to attend to individuals and to build social support for learning.

McKeachie's formula is a familiar one to us, for it is the one which faculty development leaders are learning to apply to their work with professors. We see again the need to attend to student differences, to differences in the subject and outcomes to be learned, and to differences in the learning context. Perhaps our wisest maxim in teaching improvement is to treat students as we treat professors, and to treat both as developing, problem-solving persons.

3

The
Liberal Arts
College

by William Bergquist

Bill Bergquist is well-known to reformists and innovators in higher education, for they are often implementing projects which Bill thought up. He has played a key role in advancing the "faculty development" movement in this country by initiating and guiding several interinstitutional projects, by initiating the Professional and Organizational Development Network in Higher Education, by conceptualizing faculty development as personal, instructional and organizational development, and by editing with Steven Phillips the two volumes of A Handbook for Faculty Development. *He is also a co-author of* A Comprehensive Approach to Institutional Development *and* Developing the Curriculum: A Handbook for Faculty and Administrators.

Bill attended undergraduate school at Occidental College, spent two years studying religion and psychology at Harvard and completed his M.A. and Ph.D. in psychology at the University of Oregon. He taught psychology at the University of Idaho and has directed the Office of Special Higher Education Programs at the Western Interstate Commission on Higher Education. He now works as an independent consultant to higher education, working with such diverse systems as the California State University and Colleges, Association for Innovation and the American Association for Higher Education, and is chief consultant to the Council for the Advancement of Small Colleges.

This chapter concerns faculty development in small liberal arts colleges. It is based on Bergquist's considerable experience in such institutions and on a survey of small college faculty development practices. Readers from other settings will find of special interest Bergquist's delineation of five succeedingly difficult degrees of change a faculty member may need aid in accomplishing. Also, he describes a low-budget strategy for getting faculty development started on any campus. And because faculty members in liberal colleges often have the same backgrounds and concerns as do faculty anywhere, the findings of Bergquist's survey should be of help to most institutions.

Introduction

It is fashionable in the late 1970's to speak of one's heritage. My own roots in the field of faculty development are to be found in four liberal arts colleges in New York State and in forty-five other small colleges located throughout the United States. During the past three years, I have been involved with many other kinds of colleges and universities in establishing faculty development programs, yet I always look forward to visiting the liberal arts college — not only because I have learned so much in this setting, but more importantly, because this is the most challenging type of institution in which to do faculty development.

On the one hand, the liberal arts college is amenable to change: it is usually small and accessible; it is also oriented toward instruction, so faculty need not be convinced of their role as teachers; and it is usually a setting in which personal values and concerns readily intermingle with one's professional life and institutional commitments. On the other hand, the liberal arts college faculty often have access to very few resources for the improvement of their instruction. Furthermore, many faculty work in one or two-person departments; they have no colleagues with whom to share ideas and enthusiasm in their area of expertise. Perhaps most importantly, the liberal arts college is often the bastion of traditional teaching. Excellence in teaching is pursued but confined to the area of lecturing and teacher-led discussions. Any attempt to introduce alternative methodologies or to encourage faculty to discuss their untested assumptions about teaching and learning are met with considerable resistance.

I find faculty development to be a viable option for leaders of liberal arts colleges who wish to improve the teaching and learning that occur at their institutions and who want to help faculty find more satisfaction in their work as teachers, advisors, scholars and colleagues. I believe that we have learned a great deal over the past five years that enables faculty development practitioners to be successful in their work at liberal arts colleges. In this chapter I intend to convey some of these learnings. I will first present some of my own biases about the appropriate goals for a faculty development program, then will share with you some of the learnings from my colleagues in liberal arts colleges. I will conclude by making use of these learnings in the design of a hypothetical faculty development program at "Exemplar" College.

Purposes

I believe that any organizational leader, whether in a college or corporation, must be concerned with not only the convening goals of the organization (production, quality of education, financial solvency) but also with the personal and professional growth of the members of the organization. People work in organizations to meet a variety of needs other than just those for security. Herzberg and his colleagues have shown us that an organization which meets lower order needs (security, pleasant work environment and so forth) will be able to reduce job dissatisfaction. Job satisfaction, on the other hand, requires an organization's responsiveness to higher order needs (sense of accomplishment, clarity and significance of mission and so forth). (55) I believe that when an organization is sensitive and responsive to the higher order needs, it will prosper.

I also believe that faculty development *per se* is only one aspect of the solution to the complex institutional problems that now face the liberal arts college. If this type of college is to survive and even flourish, then faculty development must be interrelated with other aspects of a comprehensive institutional renewal program. These other aspects involve reflection as well as action, research as well as development.

Faculty development must be responsive and contribute to the growing body of literature about adult development. (56, 66) During the coming decade, we must learn much more about the ways in which faculty members (as well as other adults) learn and grow if the liberal arts college is to be responsive to the full range of potential students and social contexts.

Faculty development practitioners must be prepared in the near future to help faculty confront changes that will range from the mundane to the profound. In the area of instruction, for instance, at least five different levels of change will soon have to be confronted in the liberal arts college as well as in most other higher education institutions. (see Table One). These multiple levels of change are required as a result of decreasing enrollments, changing student interest and needs, increasing instructional costs and increasing faculty enrichment.

Level one change will be minimal: a faculty member will alter one segment of a course or will try out a new instructional method. Typically, a faculty development facilitator can consult on the design of this segment, provide a setting in which the faculty member can safely test out the new method (workshop, teaching laboratory, colleague support group) or offer diagnostic feedback about the nature and effect of the new segment or method. The faculty member will need little if any release time, money

Table One

Five Levels of Instructional Change for Faculty

Level of Change	Nature of Change	Consequence of Change	Resources for Change		
			Institutional	Faculty Development	
One	Change in one segment of a new course or Use of new instructional method	Faculty member experiences new challenge: renewed, interest, excitement, performance anxiety	Mini-Grants ($50-500) Mini-Sabbaticals (1-2 weeks) One-time "experimental" courses	Short-term design consultation Instructional design and methods workshops Teaching laboratories	
		Faculty member must learn some new content and skills	"Error-embracing" environment and reward system: tolerance of temporary increase in error rate of faculty member	Instructional innovators support group Classroom diagnosis Peer consultation	
		Faculty member likely to temporarily experience some failures, student dissatisfaction and confusion.			

Two	Change in the design of an entire course *or* Use of a new instructional strategy	Faculty member often changes image of self (role): becomes instructional designer or manager rather than information-giver. Temporary feeling of no longer being valuable to students. Faculty member is temporarily more busy, than less busy. Faculty member is likely to temporarily experience some failures, student dissatisfaction and confusion	Release time (one month or one course) Equipment Content-Consultation "Error-embracing" environment and reward system	Long-term design consultation Instructional innovators' support group Peer consultation Organization development (department)
Three	Faculty member changes primary teaching responsibility to new area within same discipline *or* Faculty changes to new interdisciplinary program (making use of knowledge in current discipline)	Faculty member must redefine role in discipline Faculty member must learn new content Faculty member must learn new instructional methods and designs Faculty member is temporarily very busy Faculty member is likely to feel temporary rejection from some colleagues in discipline Faculty member is likely to temporarily experience some failures, student dissatisfaction and confusion	Sabbatical (at least one year) Books, content, consultation, instructional materials Money for conferences, travel, visits to other programs, etc.	Long-term course design consultation Instructional diagnosis Instructional design/methods Instructional innovators support group Life and career planning Organizational development (department)

Four	Faculty member changes discipline: begins to teach in a new field	Faculty member must redefine self and life purpose	One or two-year sabbatical	Help faculty acquire knowledge in new field quickly and effectively
		Faculty member must learn new field (and integrate with previous field)	Financial support for new agencies and institutes for retraining and renewing faculty	Help faculty integrate new knowledge and instructional methods
		Faculty member must learn new instructional and research methods, designs, and language	Safe environment for faculty member to try out new discipline on campus	Organizational development (inter-departmental)
		Faculty member is likely to feel overwhelmed for extended period of time	Support of faculty in new discipline for new colleagues	Supportive counseling to faculty member and family
Five	Faculty member changes to a profession outside higher education	First major institutional shift for many faculty	Development of skills and attitude matrix	Career planning
		Variable consequences depending on nature of shift	Collection of information about manpower needs outside of higher education	Supportive counseling to faculty member and family
			Match up faculty matrix with high demand fields	

*I wish to thank Charles Swanson of California State University at Fresno for his initial formulation of this model of faculty change.

or personal support for this change effort.

At level two, the change becomes more significant. The faculty member redesigns an entire course, begins a new course or embraces an entirely different strategy of instruction (for example, competency-based) which may involve learning many new methods. This faculty member almost inevitably will need some release time or help in reworking current courses. Typically, one month during the summer, or three hours release time during a semester or quarter, will suffice for this level two effort. An instructional development facilitator can provide significant assistance in this redesign. Faculty usually can complete this type of change with minimal disruption to their personal or professional life, but without some external assistance (consultation, release time, money, equipment), this level of change rarely occurs in a constructive manner. Typically, a faculty member will become burned out after an unassisted level two change.

The third level of change is being confronted by liberal arts colleges that are involved in major curricular reforms. This level involves the faculty member's shift to a new area of instruction in her discipline. A psychologist, for instance, might leave the area of physiological psychology to begin teaching in a new program on adult development and aging. This level of change usually requires some resources that are not available to the faculty development facilitator (for example, books and resource people in the new area of instruction); the college must be willing to grant some release time and money if this level of change is to be successful. Witness the disasters which usually befall major curricular change when faculty receive no assistance to initiate and sustain this change.

The faculty development facilitator can be of considerable service to the faculty member in helping him through this transition. The facilitator can provide advice on alternative instructional methods and feedback on the faculty member's performance in teaching the new course. More importantly, the facilitator can assist the faculty member in redefining his new place in the discipline, through life and career planning seminars, workshops on interdisciplinary teaching or the creation of faculty support groups (made up of faculty members undergoing similar changes).

The fourth level of change is profound for many faculty, yet may become quite common in liberal arts colleges (and many other colleges and universities) during the next two decades. Faculty in programs with severely declining enrollments will change disciplines in order to teach in new fields or fields with rapidly increasing enrollments. Faculty members in philosophy, for instance, may have to begin teaching English Composition. Sociologists may have to begin teaching organizational theory in the business department. The changes in area of expertise will usually not be extreme (for example, a history professor is not likely to have to teach mechanical engineering), but they often will cause significant stress in the faculty member who is uprooted from his discipline or department. Level four change will require one to two years of paid sabbatical, apprenticeships or mentorships and consultation with the receiving department or school.

Faculty development facilitators again will be able to help faculty manage the significant transitions associated with this level of change. The support structures noted for level three change (for example, life planning) are even more important for level four. In addition, short-term supportive counseling may be required. Practitioners can be of assistance in helping faculty identify compatabilities between their present skills and aptitudes and those required in the expanding fields of the college. A matrix of skills and aptitudes can be constructed to make compatible matches more likely.

Level five change represents the most significant transition for faculty. Most adults in our society have been involved in at least one major institutional transition in their lives: they left school and got a job or became homemakers. Many faculty, on the other hand, have never left the educational institution since they began attending school at age four or five. Thus, the prospect of leaving the collegiate institution is particularly stressful for faculty — though the level of stress will vary greatly depending on how different is the institutional setting to which the faculty member is moving. Many research and development laboratories or private practices closely resemble the life style of higher education setting and may not represent a radical shift.

A college or university must determine what its responsibilities are for preparing a faculty member to leave the institution. Some higher education leaders find that this type of support makes practical sense as a means of encouraging "dead wood" to leave the college, thereby leaving room for the recruitment of more innovative, more stimulating and often less expensive young faculty members. Other leaders believe that the institution should assume some responsibility for helping a faculty member get a job for humanitarian reasons: if the faculty member has committed his allegiance and attention to the college for several years, then the college is obligated to assist him in finding new work. Others, however, believe that a college or university is not responsible for job-retraining. In California, for example, there are laws which prevent this type of support for career change in public institutions.

Learnings About Faculty Development in the Liberal Arts College

Over the past five years there have been not only some important new learnings about faculty development in the liberal arts college but also new ways of sharing these learnings; for example, the POD Network and the Faculty Development Newsletter. Lance Buhl will talk about the use of consortia to share learnings about faculty development in Chapter Seven. In addition, several national agencies have set up programs in which faculty development practitioners can learn from others about how faculty development is conducted to meet diverse and complex faculty needs. The Society for Values in Higher Education conducts such a program for liberal arts colleges (Project for Institutional Renewal, Jerry Gaff, Director), as has the American Association for Higher Education, through its regional program (1974-1975) and its project with the National Endowment for the Humanities (Cricket Levering, Director).

The largest national project in faculty development has been conducted by the Council for the Advancement of Small Colleges (CASC) through a one-year grant from the Lilly Endowment (1974-1975) and a two-year grant from the W.K. Kellogg Foundation (1975-1977). In the latter program, forty-five faculty, called "on-campus consultants" (OCCs), from small liberal arts colleges throughout the country received training in a variety of faculty development practices at four national institutes. Some of the areas to which the OCCs were exposed were: instructional diagnosis and improvement, student evaluation of instruction, course design and reform. All of the OCCs also were trained in the use of consulting skills and provided with information regarding grantsmanship, futuristic curricular planning and evaluation of faculty development programs. The institutes became close and enriching learning communities. OCCs shared successes and failures and provided important interpersonal support during times of personal and professional change.

The OCCs received copies of the two volumes of *A Handbook for Faculty Development*, (7) written by Steven Phillips and me for this program, a series of three to four on-campus consultations with a "mentor" (A nationally known faculty development consultant), and attended periodic meetings of all OCCs in a geographic region. Additional money was provided for regional group members to plan, implement or attend workshops, set up interinstitutional exchange programs or attend other major CASC activities. Following a four-day training program on "Illuminative Evaluation," (91) ten of the OCCs also visited twenty-eight of the participating CASC colleges to evaluate and consult about faculty development.

While many benefits can be identified from this program, (26) one of the most important was the insights gained by the OCCs about how faculty development can be implemented in the small liberal arts college. These insights have been shared with me by the OCCs through the twenty-eight illuminative evaluation reports and responses to a "Faculty Development Practices" (FDP) Questionnaire. Thirty of the OCCs completed the FDP questionnaire, as did six other practitioners of faculty development at non-CASC colleges.* Following are some of the most important learnings gained from these reports and questionnaires, (26) as well as from other writings in the field, (7, 48, 101) and my own work with more than one hundred liberal arts colleges.

Structure

For the most part, faculty development in the liberal arts college seems to be jointly-owned by faculty and administrators. Faculty have major, but not exclusive, influence over planning, conducting activities and evaluating the faculty development program on their campus. Administrators have some influence in these areas, and have major influence (sometimes exclusive) concerning the budget for faculty development programs.

Programs that tend to be more administratively owned have the advantage of usually being more solidly based in terms of money, room and other resources. Administrators often are able to get external funding for a program and are able to give the program credibility and visibility through participating in its activities (as did Richard Gross, then dean and now president of Gordon College, in starting a professional growth contract program). (126)

Faculty ownership, on the other hand, allows — even forces — a faculty development program to be immediately responsive to the needs of faculty; it also provides a channel for the emergence of a new type of faculty leadership. People who are involved with faculty development (unlike those involved in many other faculty committees) tend to be or become interested in teaching and learning, as well as equitable faculty personnel

*I wish to thank these six respondents for their cooperation. I must preserve their anonymity and the anonymity of the 30 OCCs who responded to the questionnaire.

policies and the professional growth of faculty. Such concerns are important, yet often neglected, by academic administrators and other faculty leaders.

Typically, in its early stages, a faculty development program is not "owned" by anyone, other than perhaps the founder or director of the program. Administrators often are uninvolved because there is not yet a concern about either money or program coordination. Faculty are uninvolved because they do not yet see any benefits from the program. One hard-pressed faculty development practitioner has observed that faculty are "willing to participate as long as no work is required" and that administrators are "very cooperative as long as no money is required."

There need not be anything wrong with initial ownership of a program by the person who runs it. The faculty development practitioner meets her own professional growth needs through the program. She makes use of faculty development resources to improve her own teaching or administrative skills, makes contact with interesting people from other disciplines and colleges, develops strategies for implementing innovations that she wants to see on campus and moves up the ladder of faculty governance or academic administration. In many instances, the most successful faculty development programs have been started and sustained by individuals who have made extensive use of the program to meet personal and professional goals.

This condition is to be encouraged rather than condemned, for the faculty development coordinator is practicing what she preaches and is gaining something more from the program than just the gratification that comes from helping other faculty members. A variation on this condition is often successful: a small group of faculty form a self-help group, which is designed specifically to meet the needs of the participating members. This group may expand in size and/or may gain formal status, but only under the stipulation that all participants continue to benefit personally and professionally from the experience.

My own recommendation is that faculty development in a liberal arts college be clearly and consistently viewed by both faculty and administrators as a faculty-owned operation. Even more than in large universities, the liberal arts college administrator must be sensitive to infringement upon the prerogative of faculty members in the area of teaching and learning — for this area is central to the task of faculty at liberal arts colleges. As Sikes and Barrett (101) have observed, a faculty development program:

must grow out of faculty action. Administrators can decree changes in parking areas, or deans can change schedules, and faculty generally will comply. But changes that require commitment and acceptance if they are to work cannot be dictated; much of the commitment is generated from faculty involvement in the creation and implementation of their development program.

While the role of administrators is important at early stages in a faculty development program (and at all stages as long as the administrator holds the pursestrings) faculty must be actively involved in the planning and implementation of the program. Those faculty who are most actively involved should find that their own personal and professional needs are being met by the program.

Relation to Institutional Development

Faculty development on most liberal arts college campuses appears to be primarily directed toward the needs of individual faculty members; it therefore has not focused on institutional issues. In many cases, however, OCCs and faculty development practitioners at other liberal arts colleges have indicated that their program is now, after two or three years, beginning to extend into other areas and to link with other campus programs. This extension results in part from increasing credibility that is assigned by the campus to both the faculty development program and the people who are running it. Furthermore, since these colleges are small, many of the faculty and administrators who are actively involved in the campus faculty development program are also actively involved in other program activities; consequently, there is personal as well as programmatic integration of concepts and activities.

The relationship between faculty development and curricular reform is perhaps most interesting and complex. In several CASC colleges (for example, Eureka College and Acquinas College), an active faculty development program has helped to create a demand for curricular reform. At several other colleges (notably Alverno College, Sterling College, Davis and Elkins College, Mars Hills College, Central College and St. Olaf College), the opposite has occurred. Curricular reform has provided an impetus for faculty development: as a result of significant curricular changes, the faculty have felt the need for new resources to help them adjust to the instructional changes that are required by the new curricular structure.

At several colleges, faculty development has been linked in a highly productive way to institutional planning and research. This linkage has often occurred as a result of the influence exerted by an external consultant like Arthur Chickering, Jack Lindquist, Richard Meeth or Harold Hodgkinson. Hartwick College, for instance, participated in the Strategies for Change Project (68, 93) at the same time it was participating in the faculty development program of the College Center of the Finger Lakes (CCFL). (7) Many of the same faculty and administrators participated in both projects. As a result, the research, planning and organizational change emphases of the Strategies project were closely related to the instructional improvement and personal development emphases of CCFL.

In the future, other linkages between faculty development and various campus activities can be anticipated. As administrative and staff development activities become more prevalent (as they probably will in the next two to three years), we can expect a rather natural interrelationship to grow between these activities and those being offered to faculty. Firmer connections also should be established between faculty development centers and the resources that are found in student counseling departments, teacher education programs, development offices, institutional research offices, admissions and recruitment offices — to name but a few.

Staffing

At most liberal arts colleges, faculty development has become a people-intensive enterprise. While monies are occasionally spent for new equipment, most of the funds are allocated to salaries and benefits or to release time for faculty. Even voluntary donations to a faculty development program usually take the form of work rather than materials or money. The issue of staffing is therefore a central consideration in the design and implementation of any faculty development program. We will consider three different types of staffing arrangements: full or part-time staff, voluntary staff and external consultants, then briefly discuss the recruitment and training of staff.

At the liberal arts colleges we surveyed, only two have full-time faculty development coordinators (University of Puget Sound; Azusa Pacific College), while two others have a half-time released faculty member (Regis and Hartwick Colleges). Each of these institutions has received substantial external funds. In most instances, liberal arts colleges report that faculty development is being conducted by faculty (or academic administrators) who hold full-time appointments outside faculty development. Jerry Gaff's description of the status of faculty development in 1975 still seems to hold true in liberal arts colleges: most faculty development activities are provided through voluntary service. (48) Those colleges that do release faculty or hire staff rely on "soft" money from foundations.

In discussing the advantages and disadvantages of full or part-time staff for a faculty development program, the FDP questionnaire respondents provided many valuable insights. With regard to advantages, the respondents noted that part or full-time staff legitimize and institutionalize a faculty development program. A part or full-time coordinator can give the program greater visibility, provide better program coordination, sustain more meaningful activities and find more time to seek external funding. A part or full-time coordinator frees up faculty, so that full-time faculty need not devote time to voluntary services for other faculty, but can instead attend to their own professional growth or to other campus issues. By providing at least a half-time secretary for faculty development, a college can also release faculty from time-consuming and frustrating but essential clerical duties related to scheduling, workshop arrangements and so forth.

On the negative side, most college leaders believe they cannot afford a part or full-time staff. Second, such a person might be labelled an "administrator," "outside expert," or even "meddler," and hence, might lose or never gain credibility with the faculty. If the coordinator is not teaching full-time, he may cease to be an effective model for other faculty and/or may tend to become preoccupied with busy work and the hierarchy of the institution. Furthermore, the faculty may tend to lose their initiative as "self-developers"; they increasingly may rely on the specialized expertise of the coordinator, rather than on their own very real ability to help each other.

Several advantages were frequently noted in our questionnaire responses on voluntary staff. Most importantly, voluntary services by faculty tend to increase faculty ownership for the program. Volunteerism represents "grass roots" support for faculty development. It also ensures that program activities are being geared to the needs of faculty; otherwise, the volunteers will discontinue their support. As a result of participation in a faculty development program, volunteers become better informed and more committed to the program. They tend to become more trustful of their colleagues, having shared both strengths and weaknesses with them. Volunteers are more likely to motivate other busy faculty because they themselves are busy. Those providing services are self-selected. If they are effective and interested people with status on campus, they are more likely to be useful to other faculty. In short, volunteers can be low-cost, effective resources to faculty. A group of volunteers sometimes can accomplish much more than one or two full-time staff members.

On the negative side, volunteers rarely have enough time to do an effective job They are usually already heavily committed and then must choose between faculty development and other important activities (including their own teaching). Because they are hard-pressed, volunteers rarely can give this program high priority. Consequently, support is usually shallow (even though widespread) in an all-volunteer program. Another problem relates to perceived or real "expertise." Faculty volunteers are rarely trained in the skills and methodologies of faculty development. They must receive that training, or the campus must be willing to put up with services of variable quality. Any on-campus consultant will experience the problem of being "a prophet in his own land" — this problem is compounded by volunteerism.

Use of Consultants

The volunteer is a "special," often nonrepresentative, person who can provide valuable services to a program that relies exclusively on the volunteer, however, the program will usually remain mundane, under-supported and responsive to only a small percentage of faculty needs. Some colleges have, as a result, made use of external consultants to help create interest in and/or extend their voluntary faculty development services.

Several advantages have been cited by respondents to the FDP questionnaire concerning the use of external consultants. The three advantages most frequently mentioned are objectivity, credibility and expertise. The external consultant is able to look at campus problems and resources from a dispassionate, outside perspective. The consultant can often confront issues that are too "hot" for internal resource people to handle. The external consultant carries weight. She brings sophisticated skills and contacts to a liberal arts college which often is geographically isolated from similar institutions. Perhaps more importantly, she is a prophet from another land. Faculty want external expertise if they are going to give up precious time. The external consultant is often able to motivate, excite or inspire faculty. She is often a "safe" confidant or a supportive mentor or trainer. The respondents generally agreed that an external consultant is particularly appropriate if no internal resources are available, if an internal resource can be trained in the use of a technique, or if short-term, highly focused impact is desired.

Conversely, the external consultant is often detrimental to the development of campus resources and a sense of self-reliance. Members of the campus community may become dependent on the consultant and assume that he or another consultant is needed to solve all campus problems. The external consultant often will lack sufficient knowledge of the campus and may find himself side tracked by superifical problems. The effects of an external consultant are transitory ("hit and run") if there is no follow through.

External consultants often "start with two strikes against them." Many faculty and administrators negatively react to outside experts — especially if the expert offers "instant or pet solutions," "says nothing new" or is not "successful in actually *doing* what he/she encourages others to do." One particularly disillusioned practitioner at a CASC college noted that most consultants "come to learn from us . . . then go back and write their books or get paid to talk about our successes and problems at other places."

Consultants play many different roles. Perhaps the most frequently filled role is that of the external expert. In the CASC colleges, two quite different conclusions were reached by respondents concerning the use of the consultant as expert. Several OCC's argued for the early use of the expert or advice-giver. Such a person can help in the planning process and can establish credibility for an idea or program activity. Conversely, a consultant may be of use to a campus "only after a [high] degree of mutual learning and trust has been reached." In general, it appears as if a consultant as expert will be most effective if: 1) he comes from a similar type of liberal arts college (making the inter-campus exchange programs particularly valuable), 2) he has been given sufficient time to learn about the campus before becoming an active resource, and 3) he is being "legitimately" brought in to offer new ideas and insights, rather than to confirm the opinions of those bringing him in.

A second type of consultant, the facilitator or clarifier or problem-analyzer, was also controversial. Such a person does not bring answers but brings skill in helping campus members find their own answers to their own concerns. Some questionnaire respondents indicated that excellent results have been achieved through the use of this type of consultant. The faculty who are exposed to the facilitator/clarifier/analyzer tend to feel ownership for the solutions that are generated and are more likely to implement and follow through on these solutions. Other respondents are much more pessimistic about this approach: they say consultation of this type is "consistently a flop" or of "limited success." Faculty do not seem prepared for this style of consultation. The expert who gives answers is as familiar a consultant role as it is a teaching model. Furthermore, facilitation takes more time than most colleges are willing or can afford to give the consultant, although, in the long run, continual reliance on outside experts rather than the development of internal problem-solving expertise is most costly by far. In general, it would seem that facilitative consultation is most appropriate in advanced or "mature" programs that have already established credibility. There is some irony in this conclusion, for facilitative approaches to consultation are often offered as entry level activities: the consultant "helps the client to help himself" or "helps the client to identify what his problem really is." Here, consultants face the same problem as do faculty in their teaching: shall we give the answers and get on with it or help students learn how to develop their own answers.

A third model places the consultant in the role of evaluator, judge or status-giver. Several practitioners have remarked that this mode of consultation is particularly appropriate at a very early point in a faculty development program. It is often useful to ask an external consultant from some esteemed location to place his seal of approval on a program or strategy. Several respondents, however, noted that this type of consultant is usually received graciously (especially if a potential source of funding or accreditation) and then quickly ignored. If the consultant, as evaluator, is collaborative or "illuminative" in her approach, then this form of consultation is veiwed by many respondents as being quite valuable. The approach here is to help faculty generate and use evaluative information they respect, not to pass judgment from afar.

A final style of consultation is consistently viewed in a positive manner by respondents to the FDP questionnaire. The consultant serves as trainer, mentor or model. If there is a clear need for training, then an external consultant will be accepted and effective in his role. Many of the forty-five participants in the CASC program indicated that their "mentor" has provided a vital and highly successful service to their own professional growth. The mentor was an experienced faculty development facilitator who worked closely with a few OCCs in each region. Those mentorship relationships that did not work tended to be caused by an incompatability in the values or interpersonal styles of the mentor and either the OCC being served by the mentor or the campus community of the OCC. Those mentors that have been particularly effective in working with OCCs have tended to be quite eclectic in their use of consulting practices: advice-giving, facilitative, evaluative, even therapeutic.

Table Two

Consultative Roles and Goals

Consultative Roles	*Appropriate Consultative Goals*
1. *Expert*: advice-giver, "Wise Old Man," idea generator	1a. Obtain new/more information b. Validate current information or opinions
2. *Advocate:* promoter, crusader, salesman	2a. Convince others of an idea, strategy or goal b. Obtain information about a particular idea, strategy or goal
3. *Judge*: evaluator, certifier, overseer	3a. Determine the success of a program b. Convince others of the success of a program
4. *Negotiator*: broker, mediator, conflict-resolver	4a. Resolve a problem b. Prevent the occurrence of a potential problem
5. *Trainer*: model, teacher, coach	5a. Increase capacity of current staff to provide certain services b. Reduce the reliance on external consultants
6. *Facilitator*: clarifier, gate-keeper, friend	6a. Improve the way in which current program operates or problems are solved b. Begin a new program in an effective and enjoyable manner
7. *Diagnostician:* observer, analyst, describer	7a. Find out what is wrong with current program or process b. Anticipate potential problems
8. *Catalyst*: starter, energizer, visionary	8a. Help get a program off the ground b. Invest a program with new excitement
9. *Designer*: planner, assessor, path-finder	9a. Develop an effective program b. Develop a process for continuing review and renewal of program
10. *Controller*: reward-giver, punisher, agenda-setter	10a. Insure that a program is given adequate consideration b. Insure that a program is implemented

All four styles of consultation seem to be appropriate in certain settings and at certain times. It is essential that the person who is recruiting the consultant be explicit about the role to be played and goals to be attained by the consultant. Table Two contains a description of ten consultative roles and associated goals which a client may find useful as a general checklist. An explicit consultative contract is particularly valuable in establishing roles and goals. See an excellent example of such a contract in Lance Buhl's Chapter Seven. It is also essential that the consultant and client remain in close contact during and after the consultation in order to determine if mid-course corrections in style, content or goals are needed, and to define what is being or has been learned from the consultation that can be helpful in setting up future consultations.

I would suggest that expert consultation can be particularly helpful at an early stage in a program, provided the consultant is given enough time to learn about the institution but does not take over the program or foster dependency. A facilitative style is appropriate when a program is mature. This type of consultant can help an individual or organization clarify purposes, identify internal resources or resolve interpersonal conflicts but is not appropriate when used with a new program unless the campus is already accustomed to or prepared for this type of consultation. Evaluative consultation can be effective when a program needs to acquire increased credibility or when the faculty development practitioner or committee is prepared to re-examine the program's directions and achievements (for-mative evaluation). Finally, the role of consultant as mentor or trainer is potentially of greatest value if a campus is willing to allow one or two of its faculty or administrators to first benefit from these services and then convey them to others.

Recruitment and Training of Local Facilitators

The use of external consultants will in large part depend on the current expertise and background of the program staff (paid or voluntary), which in turn is dependent on recruitment and training activities associated with the program. Several important factors relate to the issue of recruitment and the ingredients essential for effective training. It is essential that a staff position not be viewed simply as an "administrative job." Even if a faculty member is hired full-time as a faculty development practitioner, she should retain faculty status and continue to participate in faculty activities. At large universities, a full-time specialized staff generally will be acceptable to the faculty. This is not the case at a small, liberal arts college. As noted by the FDP questionnaire respondents, the faculty development facilitators did not feel they were held in high regard by the liberal arts college faculty. Status is not her reward. She must be actively involved in the program and derive personal benefit from it. If she is involved only in the planning and coordination of faculty development activities, then she will soon be labeled "paper-pusher" or bureaucrat and will lose credibility. Practitioners also should teach part time or at least assist with courses being taught at the college. A faculty development team or committee should keep these factors in mind when recruiting, selecting and defining a job description for the program director.

Since most faculty members who would be interested in working on a faculty development program at a liberal arts college have no formal experience in providing this type of service, some training is usually appropriate. Given that faculty development is no longer in its infancy (though probably not past adolescence), it would be foolish not to benefit from the learning of others. I would suggest five steps in a training program for a new practitioner. First, the trainee obviously should be provided with the basic literature in the field; Jack Lindquist has identified this literature for the field of faculty development in Chapter Two. Perhaps this volume should be added to this list.

Second, I would encourage the trainee to attend an intensive, residential training program for consultants and/or trainers of at least two weeks duration, which can be split into several sessions. This program might specifically focus on faculty development practices. This kind of workshop has been conducted by CASC, the NTL Institute and the POD Network. Alternatively, the new practitioner might attend a workshop that would introduce him to more general training and consultation practices. Such a program is offered by the NTL Institute, University Associates (LaJolla, California), and the Gestalt Institute of Cleveland. While these latter programs are of high quality and provide participants with a valuable, general perspective, they are not directly oriented toward higher education.

A new practitioner might set up his own training program through a consortial arrangement. Five or more colleges can jointly hire a consultant to work with one or two new practitioners from each campus; Lance Buhl presents in Chapter Seven a model for that training. Regardless of how it is arranged, the intensive training experience is valuable not only as a vehicle for the rapid acquisition of new knowledge and skills, but also as a meeting place for new practitioners who are experiencing similar career changes and are confronting comparable professional and organizational challenges.

Third, I would suggest that the trainee establish an ongoing mentoring relationship with someone who already has considerable experience in the field. Usually such a relationship is more for collegial sharing than formal training, but it can accelerate learning at a low cost, as we discovered in the CASC program. The mentor should periodically visit the trainee's campus to work alongside of and talk with the new practitioner and to help him select appropriate program strategies and design successful faculty development activities. The trainee might periodically visit the mentor's campus (if the mentor is located on a campus) or visit another campus with the mentor. The mentor serves not only as an invaluable source of new ideas, skills and perspectives for the facilitator when he has started his new job, but also as a personal model and source of essential support and encouragement during particularly difficult times.

Fourth, the trainee should have access to faculty development resources (instruments, designs, exercises and so forth), such as are found in the two volumes of *A Handbook for Faculty Development* (7) and in the handbooks and related resources of University Associates and the NTL Institute. These materials should be used selectively, and they should be modified and tailored to the specific faculty population being served. Furthermore, if possible, the new practitioner first should observe someone else using these resources (A workshop trainer, a mentor or a colleague on another campus), or should use the materials in a safe and noncritical setting (for example, among friends on the faculty or the faculty development team). Though the new practitioner should be encouraged from the start to develop new materials and become an active and creative contributor to the field, a great deal of time will be lost and many failures will be experienced if the practitioner does not make some uses of resources that are already available in the field.

Finally, an effective training program should involve the formal linkage of the new practitioner to other practitioners and resources in the field. The trainee should join the Professional and Organizational Development (POD) Network and probably the American Association for Higher Education. He should also become familiar with and make himself known to appropriate national and regional information clearinghouses: NEXUS (American Association for Higher Education), ERIC (Washington, D.C.), the CASC National Consulting Network and The Resource Center for Planned Change (American Association of State Colleges and Univer-

Table Three*

		Structure	Process	Attitude
Focus of Intervention	Individual	*Instructional Development* Consultation and training on course design, curriculum reform and educational technology *Organizational Development* Evaluation of faculty Faculty reward system	*Instructional Development* Classroom observation, diagnosis and training Training in interpersonal and small group skills Training in out of class skills associated with faculty roles	*Instructional Development* Promotion of alternate instructional methods Discussions about teaching Values Clarification *Personal Development* Life and career planning Counseling
	Group	*Instructional Development* Curricular and course design consultation Interdisciplinary and team teaching *Organizational Development* Departmental reorganization Use of space and time	*Instructional Development* Discipline or department centered instructional training programs Peer observation and feedback *Organizational Development* Group process observation	*Instructional Development* Knowledge utilization Departmental/divisional retreats *Organizational Development* Team-building Support groups
	Institutional	*Community Development* Communication and support networks *Institutional Development* Research and development center *Faculty Development* Program governance	*Community Development* Intergroup negotiation *Institutional Development* Implementing development programs *Faculty Development* Program planning and implementation	*Community Development* Community Building *Institutional Development* Development of support for change *Faculty Development* Generating program support
	Meta-Institutioal	*Meta-Development* Funding Establishment of formal networks and consortia	*Meta-Development* Define and clarify new change oriented professions Continuing education for educational change agents	*Meta-Development* Publication of books, periodicals, etc. Demonstration projects Cooperative research projects

*Source: William H. Bergquist and Steven R. Phillips, *A Handbook for Faculty Development*, Volume II (Washington, D.C., Council for the Advancement of Small Colleges, 1977), p. 9.

sities). Through these formal or informal relationships and contacts, a faculty development practitioner can help ensure that he will keep up to date on this new and still growing field.

Activities

If one broadly conceives of faculty development in terms of its use to faculty as professionals, persons, members of organizations and members of a community, then a wide and extensive set of services are within its preview. In Table Three, Steve Phillips and I have listed and attempted to categorize many of these activities. In this section, I will specifically focus on those activities which are most commonly found in or have been found to be most effectively provided through a faculty development program.

Diagnosing the Need to Improve

A resource that is to be found in virtually all liberal arts colleges that have inaugurated faculty development programs is an instrument for the evaluation of teaching. In most instances, these instruments are used for the evaluation of instruction by students, though in several instances faculty use them to evaluate themselves or their peers. The student evaluation instruments which have been most commonly used are IDEA (Center for Faculty Evaluation and Development, Kansas State University), TABS (Clinic to Improve University Teaching, University of Massachusetts), Cafeteria (Purdue University) and SIRS (Educational Testing Service). The first two of these instruments are recommended for a faculty development program, since they provide effective bridges between evaluation and development. The Cafeteria procedure is recommended if a college or individual faculty member wishes to build a student evaluation instrument that is tailor-made to a unique set of needs.

The instructional diagnosis and improvement process which was first developed at the Clinic to Improve University Teaching (University of Massachusetts) and has been refined at the University of Rhode Island (Glen and Bette Ericksen), McGill University (Chris Daggett) and the University of Puget Sound (Steve Phillips), is being used with increasing frequency at liberal arts colleges. It employs TABS as its student evaluation of instruction instrument. Faculty development facilitators find this process provides them with more detailed, descriptive and systematic information about a faculty member's performance in the classroom than they can gather in any other way. Furthermore, the "clinic process" helps a faculty member formulate a program for improvement of his instruction.

This diagnostic-improvement process could readily be applied to other aspects of the faculty member's professional life (for example, advising or committee leadership) and could be effectively coupled with a professional growth contact. This service is certainly among the most valuable and promising that have been developed in the faculty development field. Its increasing acceptance and use by practitioners is indicative of its value.

Introducing Teaching Improvements

Concern for the improvement of instruction is also frequently expressed through workshops and consultation on both traditional and non-traditional instruction methods. Many faculty development practitioners offer workshops or symposia on such topics as: "how to organize a lecture," "leading a discussion" or "formulating instructional objectives." These sessions on traditional methodologies are usually well-received, though many are attended by faculty who don't really need the information or skills and are avoided by faculty who clearly need help.

One of the most important learnings during the past five years in the field of faculty development concerns the focus of these methodologically-oriented services. Faculty must be provided with information and skills training that directly relate to their current concerns as instructors. As a rule, they first want to do better what they are already doing, rather than learn how to teach in some new way. The faculty member who is a poor lecturer, for instance, usually wants help with his lecturing, rather than help in learning how to set up a Personalized System of Instruction, even though a poor lecturer ultimately might benefit more by selecting one alternate instructional approach. Faculty development programs which only offer services on nontraditional methods rarely win acceptance from faculty who can benefit from these services. Most practitioners first should offer workshops and seminars on traditional issues (lecturing, discussion, grading, course organization) before moving on to nontraditional approaches to education.

Accumulated experience in faculty development also leads to the conclusion that one to three hour sessions on instructional methodologies can be useful in raising new interests and challenging outmoded assumptions. Luncheon seminars, colloquia series and "mini-versities" which offer in a workshop setting brief exposure to a wide variety of alternatives are some of the more effective interest-raising approaches. These short-term sessions, however, rarely provide faculty with sufficient time and resources to actually initiate new activities in the classroom. Behavior change requires that faculty participate in longer (usually residential) workshops with follow-up consultation or in ongoing weekly group meetings that last for at least one term. Too few liberal arts faculty development projects have developed this depth of assistance.

Instructional Design

Only a few liberal arts colleges are currently providing services in the area of course and curricular design consultation. Most of this work is being done by practitioners trained at the Center for Instructional Development at Syracuse University (see Claude Mathis' description of this program in Chapter Four: Joseph Durzo at the New Hampshire Consortium (see Lance Buhl's description of this consortium in Chapter Seven) and Sigrid Hutchinson (now at Syracuse University) through the Council for the Advancement of Small Colleges and St. Benedict College. Using a similar model of design consultation, Jim Holsclaw at Azusa Pacific College asks faculty to identify instructional problems and needs, to analyze the setting in which the instruction will take place (assessment of student characteristics, conditions surrounding the problems or needs and relevant resources) and to organize and manage an appropriate instructional program. Course design workshops have been conducted at Pacific Lutheran University and Regis College, during which faculty receive consultative assistance in designing experimental mini-courses (Pacific Lutheran) or full-courses (Regis). In these workshops, faculty have been exposed to several different design principles, (7) as well as nontraditional curricular models. At Regis College, faculty diagnose their own instructional setting, through a student learning style questionnaire, videotapes of their classes and student evaluations.

Talking About Teaching

Virtually all the liberal arts colleges which are surveyed in the FDP questionnaire offer activities that encourage faculty to talk about their teaching. In some instances, this may mean setting up a lounge in which faculty can meet informally and talk. At other colleges, periodic seminars are held regarding some educational issue, or faculty attend a yearly retreat where the educational goals and practices of the college are discussed. These types of activities, while valuable and relevant to professional development, usually do not probe the more personal dimensions of a faculty member's professional life, as do the extended workshops that have been held at the University of Puget Sound and with the College

Center of the Finger Lakes. During these week-long workshops, (7) faculty reflect on, discuss and write about various aspects of their lives as teachers and learners. Faculty often interview each other and/or are interviewed by the staff prior to the workshop. Faculty discuss educational values and philosophies, rationales and instructional practices, compatibility between espoused and practiced educational values, alternative "paradigms" for the classroom and so forth. These discussions often will continue after the faculty return to campus.

Personal and Professional Growth

Life and career planning (7) has not yet been provided by many liberal arts colleges, though about one half of the respondents to the FDP questionnaire indicated that this procedure soon will be used on their campus. Professional growth contracts are also becoming more common on liberal arts college campuses. At Gordon, one of the first colleges to develop and implement this process, faculty (and administrators) survey their own professional strengths, weaknesses and goals, then formulate plans for further professional growth. Together with a professional growth committee, the faculty member makes a commitment to this plan; the institution, in turn, through the committee, makes a comparable commitment in terms of money, release time, on-campus resources, and so forth. (126) A similar model, called "enhancement of subject matter," is offered at Azusa Pacific College. This form of life planning may soon become the most popular and effective basis for organizing and sustaining a professional development program.

Interpersonal skills training is offered on infrequent occasions by colleges with faculty development programs. Some colleges offer short on-campus workshops on communication or advising skills. Others offer two to three day off-campus workshops on small group leadership, decision making, conflict management or problem solving. Still other colleges offer one-to-one counseling for faculty who experience interpersonal problems in conjunction with their teaching or advising of students.

Personal growth counseling and workshops are perhaps the most controversial of faculty development practices, yet more than half of the respondents indicated that some type of personal growth experience for faculty takes place on their campus. I suspect that much of this activity involves informal and valuable discussions between a faculty development facilitator and her faculty clients. At a small liberal arts college which is religiously-oriented, the personal growth activity may be closely related to the spiritual life of the faculty member. At other colleges, the personal growth component may relate to the physical domain of the faculty member's life: exercise, recreation, physical examinations. During 1976-77, Azusa Pacific College offered both spiritually-oriented retreats, on such topics as "How to be a Christian College" and "How should we then live," and a variety of consciousness-raising activities related to physical fitness, including a "Faculty Physical Fitness Activities Inventory" and a "stress test" to detect cardiac problems.

Organization Development

Most faculty development practitioners recognize the need for organization development activities as part of a long term and comprehensive faculty development program. Very few of these practitioners, however, are now employing the methods associated with organization development: management development, team building, training and consultation on decision making and conflict management, or structural technical consultation. (47)

Management development is being offered to faculty by only two of the CASC and two of the non-CASC colleges in my survey, and these arrangements are highly informal. Typically, these services are provided to department or division heads or to faculty who are moving into administrative positions. A particularly effective training program is now being offered by CASC through Main Event Management (Sacramento, California). By means of economic devices and the careful selection of 152 principles, the staff of Main Event Management acquaint academic administrators (and faculty) with the theory and practice of personnel management in a manner that facilitates the retention and use of this information on a daily basis. Given that faculty, like administrators, must work through other people (secretaries, clerical staff, students) to get a job done, they can benefit from this program as well.

Team building is the most commonly-used organization development tool, according to the FDP questionnaire respondents. Facilitators work with academic departments or the entire institution to help these groups work more effectively together. Though few facilitators have been formally trained, or even exposed to, team building procedures, they sit in with a group to provide helpful suggestions on the organization or operation of the committee, or help the group organize a retreat. Formal team building activities were provided to CASC colleges by external consultants in its first (Lilly-funded) faculty development program. Faculty development committees were provided with team building assistance while planning for faculty development activities at both a national institute and regional follow-up meetings and to the Project on Institutional Renewal Through the Improvement of Teaching in its first summer workshop. In the latter case, teams later reported this experience to be a major factor in sustaining their work into a second hard year.

Team building activities have also been conducted at several of the regional meetings of the OCCs (most notably in the Southern region under the mentorship of Carol Zion). Through its involvement in both the Strategies for Change project (Jack Lindquist) and the College Center of the Finger Lakes (Bonnie Buenger-Larson), Hartwick College has received team building assistance from external consultants. Both Lindquist and Buenger-Larson worked with various departments and program staffs at Hartwick to help faculty more effectively solve problems, accomplish goals and enjoy their relationships with each other.

Training and consultation in the use of decision making and conflict management processes are used by only a few liberal arts colleges. At Hartwick College, faculty committees make either formal or informal use of process-observation and survey-feedback techniques that have been learned by committee members who attended Strategies for Change or CCFL Faculty Development workshops where these techniques were introduced. Steve Phillips provides similar training and consultation services at the University of Puget Sound, as does Walter Sikes (Yellow Springs, Ohio) at several different liberal arts colleges.

In general, we can expect organization development activities to increase as faculty development practitioners gain experience, greater credibility and begin to assume new leadership roles in the institution. The new linkages between faculty development and comprehensive institutional development (8) programs also will engender new interests in the acceptance of organization development services. At both Messiah College and Hartwick College, for instance, new information about the institution enabled faculty not only more effectively to determine the direction of faculty and organization development activities but, perhaps more importantly, to demonstrate the need for and create interest in these activities. In the near future, we can anticipate much more frequent and extensive interaction between institutional research, institutional planning, organization development and faculty development. Certainly, the many learnings gained by faculty development practitioners about the dynamics of the college, as well as the credibility that they have established as helpers and consultants, will qualify many practitioners for this expanded role.

A Sequence of Activities

From my own experiences with faculty development programs at liberal arts colleges, I would strongly suggest that practitioners begin with activities that are reflective and consciousness-raising, rather than prescriptive or remedial. These initial activities should also be free of jargon and pretension. Discussions about teaching — especially in retreats or intensive workshops — are valuable start-up activities, as are in-depth interviews with faculty about their teaching and career. Professional growth contracts are also of interest and value to the liberal arts college faculty and provide one way of moving a faculty development program beyond talk into action. At the early stages, I would suggest that faculty evaluation and development be kept separate, though over the long term they must be interrelated.

Once the credibility of a faculty development program has been established, I would urge a practitioner to give serious consideration to the use of intensive one-on-one consultations with faculty. The instructional diagnosis and improvement process that was developed at the University of Massachusetts or the course design service that is provided by the Center for Instructional Development at Syracuse University can be of value to faculty in a liberal arts college. An integration of these two forms of consultation would provide even more effective consultation. I recommend these services because they involve skills that can be readily learned (training programs are available at the University of Massachusetts and Syracuse University to prepare practitioners) and because they have been found to have immediate and positive impact on the quality of teaching and learning. Furthermore, at a small liberal arts college, virtually any faculty member who wants to make use of this type of service can receive adequate consultative assistance from a one or two person staff.

Finally, I would suggest that at an early stage in the design of a faculty development program, consideration be given to the personal and organizational development aspects of faculty development. I do not suggest that these services be offered at the start of a program but only that planning for their use begin at an early point. These services are not readily found or created on a small college campus, yet when they are finally wanted, the demand is often immediate and persistent.

Financing

Of the thirty CASC faculty development programs which were surveyed by the FDP questionnaire, nineteen are totally supported by institutional funds, two are supported by more than fifty percent institutional funds, while another five are supported by less than fifty percent. Five of the colleges receive no institutional support (four of these have no funds). Typically, a CASC college spends between $2,000 and $4,000 per year on faculty development (not counting volunteer time), though these figures may be somewhat inaccurate given the unclear distinction at most colleges between faculty development and curriculum development, conference travel, sabbaticals or library acquisitions. Liberal arts colleges seldom gather together all their traditional developmental monies, then put them in a pot with this new $2,000 to $4,000 to make a significant fund for a systematic plan of professional development. But they should.

Most of the colleges that spend more than $4,000 per year on faculty development have an external grant that usually at least matches the contribution of the college. Public yearly support (primarily HEW Title III at CASC colleges) for faculty development ranges from $3,000 to $5,000, whereas private foundation support ranges from $30,000 to $100,000. Most colleges with private foundation support commit between $3,000 and $20,000 to receive between $10,000 and $80,000 from the foundation.

Given that so little money is currently provided in the liberal arts college for faculty development, several issues must be given some attention: 1) what are the human costs associated with a low dollar program that relies on voluntary assistance, 2) how can a faculty development program be designed to minimize both human and monetary costs, and 3) what program goals can one realistically expect such a program to achieve?

The issue of human costs is critical to the survival of faculty development at the small liberal arts college. If the individuals who lead and provide services through a faculty development program are not given any release time for their work, are primarily benefitting other people rather than receiving benefit themselves, and are adding their faculty development responsibilities to a burdensome set of other institutional responsibilities, then the human costs are considerable. Furthermore, these costs tend to contradict the very purposes of faculty development. I have heard many voluntary faculty development facilitators speak of the severe restrictions in their own personal growth as a result of devoting primary attention to the growth of other faculty. Frequently, faculty development practitioners (as well as other isolated innovators) become burned out after a few years, becoming the disillusioned critics of the very field that once held so much promise for them.

The human costs and disillusionment can be reduced, without increasing monetary costs, through the use of one or more strategies. First, work in the area of faculty development can be equated with work in other institutional service areas (committee chairpersonship, departmental leadership, student activity supervision). Faculty development facilitators should be excused from one or more of these major assignments—though we must realize that the problem often resides with the facilitator: he must decide to give up something if faculty development is a priority.

Second, faculty development activities can be directly related to teaching responsibilities. Students can be given academic credit for assisting the faculty member with faculty development activities (interviewing faculty, classroom diagnosis and feedback, data analysis and so forth), while the faculty member can receive credit for teaching these students. A faculty member can get one course "release time" this way, and the students can obtain an excellent social science or pre-professional education, using the college as a "field placement." Faculty also can use some of the "release time" during a sabbatical to learn about and provide faculty development services.

Third, by setting up consortial arrangements with other colleges, the costs for external consultants can be shared and joint projects can be initiated which will reduce expenses for equipment, printing, program administration and so forth. One college might sponsor a specific event which would be of interest to faculty at neighboring colleges, then charge a small registration fee to these other faculty and thereby defray some costs.

Fourth, the instructional support budget for the college can be re-examined to determine if some of the money can be diverted to faculty development activities — since faculty development is a form of instructional support. Typically, some of the money being used for audio-visual equipment, movies or technicians can justifiably be reassigned on at least a temporary basis to faculty development activities that will help faculty to make more effective use of these resources. One sabbatical a year reserved for faculty development can provide a staff to facilitate faculty renewal *on* the job.

Fifth, residents of the local community are often willing to provide administrative and support services to a faculty development program. In small communities — where many liberal arts colleges are located — there are often highly trained and knowledgeable spouses of faculty who cannot obtain meaningful work in the community and find most voluntary community services to be uninteresting or irrelevant. A training program can be set up to enable these people to become classroom diagnosticians, course design consultants or program administrators. This training can be particularly effective if these people already have had advanced education in such fields as psychology, anthropology, social work and education. Not only will the spouses find this type of work to be challenging and relevant to their own personal concerns about teaching and learning, but can also provide them with new, marketable skills.

Numerous other strategies for the provision of low cost faculty development services could be identified. These five should suffice, however, to demonstrate that faculty development can be provided, even under conditions of severe financial constraint, if college leaders are willing to explore nontraditional sources of people, funds and time. Nevertheless, even with exceptional creativity and good fortune, there are limits as to what can be accomplished through a low-cost faculty development program. The goals for such a program must be realistic.

First, one cannot expect such a program to be active for more than three or four years with the same leaders. Sustained attention to faculty development eventually requires material rewards. A three or four year program should not be discounted, for much can be accomplished during this period of time. A long-term voluntary commitment, however, is unrealistic, for volunteers may either burn out or become interested in other problem areas. Either keep leadership rotating, with all the accompanying repetition in training and discontinuity in thrust, or establish a permanent position for faculty development.

Second, a low-cost program cannot provide sustained, intensive services for individual faculty members, nor can it be of much value to a department or other administrative unit that must solve complex, organizational problems. Volunteers rarely have sufficient time, expertise or motivation to provide this type of demanding service. A voluntary program must primarily serve as a catalyst: faculty will be encouraged to begin their own self-improvement project, or a department will be directed toward resources (people, books, designs) that it can use to address its problem. Beyond this point, the individual faculty member or department must take the initiative.

Third, a faculty development program that is run with small financial commitments will rarely contribute to the overall development of the college as an educational institution. Without the long-term commitment of financial resources to the improvement of teaching and learning, based on reconsideration of institutional priorities, a college will rarely be able to improve significantly its educational climate or processes. A low-cost faculty development program can assist some individual faculty members in the improvement of their teaching — and for this reason is definitely worthwhile — but by itself can rarely impact on teaching and learning in general at the college.

Evaluation

Few evaluations of faculty development had been conducted in the liberal arts colleges that we surveyed. Even those colleges that have received grants from federal agencies or private foundations generally have not requested (or received) funding for evaluation, nor have they done much planning about evaluation. Twenty of the thirty CASC respondents to the FDP questionnaire indicated that they currently have not adopted any procedure for evaluating their faculty development programs, other than the illuminative evaluation which was conducted by CASC. Four other CASC OCCs noted that their programs are being informally evaluated by the dean, president or a review board, and this is probably also true of the twenty OCCs who indicated that no evaluation was being performed. One of the OCCs mentioned that her CASC mentor had been an important source of "formative" evaluation, while six other OCCs described "in house" evaluations, like those described above. Probably the most elaborate of these is being conducted at Azusa Pacific College. Jim Holsclaw and his colleagues developed a set of program goals, then asked members of the faculty to identify "indicators" for each goal — that is, observable behaviors or cues that will help the staff determine whether or not progress has been established which reflects the current status of the college. Activities to be undertaken to reach each goal have also been identified. The program will be evaluated by examining the extent to which each of these activities has helped to move the college (as determined by the indicators) from its current status toward the desired goals.

In the future, we can expect foundations and individual colleges to be increasingly concerned about program evaluation as funds for faculty development become increasingly scarce: practitioners will have to demonstrate program impact in order to sustain financial and institutional support. A variety of approaches to program evaluation are appropriate for faculty development. Steve Phillips and I identified seven such approaches in the second volume of our *Handbook for Faculty Development.* (7)

In brief, the first of these approaches, "historical-descriptive," relies on systematic and objective reconstruction of the past history of a program. The "measurement-correlational" approach requires the accumulation of quantitative information to determine the extent to which variations in one program factor, for example, student rating of instruction, correspond with variations in other factors, for example, hours of consultative assistance. The "quasi-experimental" approach yields flexible designs for comparisons between the impact of the program and the impact of control conditions.

The "developmental-intensive" approach requires the study of program impact on a specific faculty member or department, while "action-research" produces information about the program for its continuing improvement which is based on the identified needs and interests of the program staff. "Illuminative" evaluation determines the nature of and reasons for program impact through the use of interviews, observations and review of documents, questionnaires, instruments and so forth. Finally, "consultative" evaluation yields not only information for program improvement (as do action-research and illuminative evaluation) but also provides the program staff with specific recommendations concerning alternative program directions, potential program resources and so forth.

Each of these approaches is appropriate in certain settings, depending on the time and money that is available and on the purposes for which the evaluation is being conducted. The historical-descriptive, measurement-correlational and developmental-intensive approaches generally take less time and money than do the other approaches. Action-research, illuminative and consultative evaluations are most likely to yield information and insights that are immediately useful to the program staff, whereas the quasi-experimental and developmental-intensive approaches are of greatest value when trying to convince other people of the worth of a program (the quasi-experimental approach appeals to the head; the developmental-intensive appeals to the heart).

A Hypothetical Example: *Doing Faculty Development at Exemplar College*

One way to summarize these thoughts is to describe the way I would begin faculty development were I a professor in a small college. Here is my story:

Exemplar College is a cozy little liberal arts school nestled in the hills of a sparsely populated region of the Eastern United States. Approximately twelve hundred students are attracted to Exemplar each year because of family pressures (a "safe" place for our child), a periodically successful basketball team, a "good" academic reputation, small size and reportedly "comfortable" relationships between students and faculty. Several years ago our rather traditional curriculum at Exemplar had been challenged, though not changed, by several administrators and some faculty who wanted Exemplar to be more responsive to the career interests of students, and by some faculty who wanted the general education (core) program expanded and the courses offered through this program improved.

I am a tenured, associate professor in the Department of Psychology and have been at Exemplar for seven years. I have become interested in faculty development as a result of observing the effects on my own classes of poor teaching among my colleagues. I saw students come to my course who had been turned off, overworked, under-stimulated or even humiliated by other members of the faculty. I came to the painful realization that what happened in other classrooms was my business, for it was affecting what was happening in mine. I was also dissatisfied with my own teaching. I felt that I was in a rut and had lost contact with the excitement (as well as anxiety) associated with my first years as a college teacher. Faculty development also intrigued me because of my professional interest in human development and institutional change. Lastly, I was convinced that the pressures for curricular change which were then impinging on the campus needed to be accompanied by effective faculty development. If we were to change the curriculum we also needed to change teaching practices and course designs; otherwise the curricular reform would remain on paper.

At the beginning of the fall semester four years ago I contacted the academic vice president and president about my interest in faculty development. The president seemed to be preoccupied, but the academic vice president expressed considerable support for my interest. She said she also was concerned about the probable effect of anticipated curricular changes on the morale and effectiveness of the faculty. She thought that I should form some sort of planning group and work through the faculty senate to set up a program. After several days of deliberation and budget review she found $3,000 for the year that she could provide for expenses associated with travel, secretarial services and supplies. If the program was working by the end of the academic year, and seemed to have the support of most faculty, then she indicated that another $3,000 might be available next year.

With $3,000 in hand, I was confronted with the task of starting a faculty development program. How was I to win faculty support? How should I determine what to do? How would I know if the program had been successful and how would I demonstrate this success to others? How would I find or develop the resources to meet faculty needs?

I soon realized that I needed to acknowledge four realities: 1) I didn't have much money to work with, 2) I didn't have any release time and was already very busy, 3) I needed to initiate a program which would meet both my personal needs and the needs of my colleagues and 4) even though I had won the respect of many of my colleagues, some were certain to resent the intrusion of a psychologist and his jargon into their peaceful, disciplinary lives.

I formulated and acted on five strategies that reflected these realities. The first strategy enabled me to find some time to begin and maintain the faculty development program. I tied in my faculty development activities with two of the courses that I was currently teaching. While there are many disadvantages to being a behavioral scientist when starting a faculty development program (jargon, lack of credibility), one advantage is that it directly relates to the subject matter being taught (for example, educational psychology, human development, organizational theory, interpersonal relations, sociology of small groups and organizations, and community development). I would mention, in passing, however, that I have since observed clever faculty development practitioners in other fields (history, engineering, literature) who have also been able to relate faculty development to their courses (for example, study of values, historical methodology, systems analysis).

As a second strategy, I brought together a "self-help" group of six faculty who wanted to work on their own professional development. I didn't care that these people were already good teachers and were not the faculty with whom I was annoyed. They were colleagues who were not afraid to examine new ideas ("early adaptors" in diffusion-of-innovation theory), were interested in teaching, and were vaguely dissatisfied, as I was, with their own teaching. We used this group as a supportive place in which to develop professional growth contracts and to test out new ideas and actions (for example, trying out a new simulation in the group before using it in a class). Members of the group agreed to engage in an intensive week-long workshop (see strategy four below) and to meet for three hours each week. In order to find time to do all of this additional work, we each cut down on our other committee work by one-third for one year. We dropped off non-essential committees and took on less work in the committees of which we were members ("early adaptors" also tend to be "over-committers").

In addition to working on our own professional development, we met as an *ad hoc* planning committee on faculty development. Our planning meetings were held once a month and took the place of one of the weekly meetings of the self-help group.In addition,we did some team building as a planning group during the intensive week-long workshop. As one of our initial activities, members of the planning group interviewed two other faculty members about their strengths (resources that can be useful to other faculty) as well as needs. By beginning with an assessment of strengths, we were able to avoid the justifiable defensiveness that comes with being asked by a colleague to identify problems and weaknesses. We used the information about both strengths and needs to plan for future faculty development activities. The goal of the planning group was to draft a proposal by the end of the year, with accompanying documentation and first-hand experiences by the group members, which was to be submitted to the faculty senate for deliberation.

The third strategy that I employed was to plan and implement an intensive week-long workshop on faculty development. A sample model for this type of workshop is described in Table Four. I brought in an external consultant to help me with this workshop. This consultant had experience in conducting intensive workshops at the University of Puget Sound and at the College Center of the Finger Lakes, was widely conversant with different aspects of faculty development (instructional, personal and organizational development), was effective in working over a long period of time with individual faculty members and was comfortable with working on personal issues as they related to professional performance. I invited the support group to the workshop, as well as several members of the faculty at Exemplar and other neighboring colleges (see fourth strategy). The workshop was conducted for about fifteen people at a rustic retreat location.

This type of workshop was essential to the life of the faculty development program at Exemplar, for it had a significant impact on participating faculty — the kind and extent of impact that kept them committed to and involved in faculty development. Even if a faculty member could not point to even one or two tangible, personal impacts from the workshop (most participants could), they returned to campus with a new appreciation of faculty development and its potential use in the improvement of teaching and learning at Exemplar. The participants were hooked and were ready to gain from further activities. Without that initial intensive event, there would have been no core of committed faculty. This core was needed to sustain the program at its onset.

I now had the interest of several colleagues on which to build next steps. My fourth strategy was actively to seek out contacts with neighboring colleges. An informal consortial arrangement was established involving: 1) inter-campus exchange of human expertise ("prophet from another land") and physical resources, 2) joint sponsorship of costly activities (such as the week long workshop), and 3) inter-campus colloquia about teaching and learning (to reduce parochialism). In setting up this consortium, I talked to Gary Quehl (president of CASC) about the use of consortia for professional development activities.

My final strategy was to seek out external funding for the program. I held this off until late fall so that the planning group did not wait for external funding before doing anything. I strongly urged the planning group to design a highly distinctive and focused program if we were going to submit it for funding to a national foundation, or a more general and comprehensive program if we are going to submit a grant to a local or regional foundation.

I found that these five strategies can be employed during the first year of the program with a budget of $3,000. Much of this money went for the intensive week-long workshop ($2,000), paying for consultant fees and travel, and some for the room and board expenses for the participants and consultants. Some of the $2,000, however, was covered by faculty coming from other colleges to the workshop. A portion of the remaining $1,000 went for secretarial services (preparing the grant proposal, announcements or formal invitations for the workshop, materials). The remaining money went for supplies (for example, video tapes, copies of instructional diagnostic forms and student evaluation forms) and the travel of two of the team members to local conferences on faculty development, teaching and learning and curricular reform.

Where were we at the end of one year and where were we going from there? I, as well as other members of the support group, had gained much from that year. Through our growth contracts, workshops and support group meetings, most of us had tried out several new instructional methods (simulations, role playing) or designs (self-pacing, audio-tutorial modules) in our classrooms. All of us were somewhat more aware of our attitudes about and values associated with teaching and learning and were somewhat more congruent in our espoused (theory-in-mind) and practiced (theory-in-action) beliefs about education.

Several of the support group members confronted some personal stress and career change associated with this re-examination of attitudes and values. For these faculty, the support group and workshop activities were of use in life and career planning. Other participants in the support group confronted some resistance in their academic departments to the new instructional innovations. While no formal organization development activities were implemented during the first year, the support group members provided observations and suggestions to these faculty about their departments and the resistances they were encountering.

I found that by the end of this first year, some other faculty were curious about — even interested in — the program. We were in a position to extend the program to other faculty. We also had established a firm base of continuing support for the program. The dean continued to provide money in recognition of our documented accomplishments — based on professional growth contract reports, workshop evaluations, interview data and so forth. External funding was unfortunately not obtained, but mechanisms for interinstitutional sharing of resources and expenses had been established. Most importantly, there was a commitment on the part of those people who had planned the program to its survival, for the program had met their needs. Other faculty would be more likely to become involved in this planning and implementation process if they believe that it will also be of immediate value to them.

During the second year, I encouraged a second support group to form and suggested (but did not insist) that they make use of resources and learnings from the first year members. My own support group continued to meet, though less frequently. I also planned for and/or provided a variety of short-term faculty development services for faculty who had not been involved in either support group (as well as those who had been involved). Program planning was in the hands of faculty from both support groups, subject to the final approval of the faculty senate. Most of the actual planning was done by very small groups (two to three members) with occasional checking and definition of program goals in a larger meeting.

During the second year, and throughout the third and fourth years, I suggested that the support groups (especially the first) begin to confront the large, pressing problems of Exemplar College: curricular reform to meet career-training needs, revision of the core curriculum and so forth. I anticipated greater campus visibility for the faculty development "group": a loosely organized, *ad hoc* network of faculty made up of members of both support groups and a few interested others had been established. This group periodically met to discuss, take stands on, and map out strategies for specific educational policies or programs.

Members of the group also were available to consult with departments on organizational development or individual faculty members on instructional diagnosis and course design consultation. Through our consortium, I lined up "mentor" relationships to provide us training in these areas. By the start of the third year, these consultative services were formally established. I obtained approval for an ongoing practicuum in higher education (three credit hours per semester) for five to ten junior or senior students in the social sciences, education and other pre-professional programs (law, medicine, business, nursing). These students were trained in and assisted with the instructional diagnosis and design consultation services. I also recruited five members of the local community (three are faculty spouses with advanced degrees) to assist with these services. Much of the $3,000 from the dean was used during the third year to send these students and community volunteers to national and regional training programs in these consultative areas. I encouraged the students and volunteers to develop their own professional growth contracts and to form a support group in order to maximize their learnings from the practicuum experience.

At the end of the fourth year, the program is now at a turning point. It could be discontinued in favor of a new approach to the improvement of teaching and learning (for example, a program for retraining faculty in new disciplines). Alternatively, the program could be integrated with another campus program (for example, a new institutional research project). The faculty development program could also be rejuvenated if I, other members of the original support groups or new faculty would like once again to reduce our commitments for one year, to develop a professional growth contract and to learn and develop as professionals and persons. If I could be involved in such a renewal process on frequent occasions, then I would be able to provide better service to my students and colleagues. I also would find more meaning, creativity and enjoyment in my work. This would continue to make faculty development an important part of my life and the life of Exemplar College. But whatever happens, I know we have accomplished much in these four years and now have several skilled and committed people ready to carry on the work toward significant improvement of this college.

Table Four

Sample Workshop Design

Duration: One Week

Focus: Instructional Development (Secondary emphasis on personal and organizational development)

Day & Time	Activity	Brief Description*
Wednesday	Orientation to Workshop	Review Workshop Design
Evening	Informal Social Period	Review Rationale for Workshop
Thursday		
Morning	Discussion Session: Role as a Teacher	Respond to question: "Who Am I As A Teacher?" (I, p. 208)
	Short Theory Session: Teaching Styles	Presentation of a taxonomy of six different teaching styles (I, pp. 20-22)
	Discussion Session: Teaching Styles	Small group discussion on implication of ideas from theory session.
	Micro-College Planning	(I, pp. 255-257)
Afternoon	Micro-College	Concurrent presentations by staff and interested participants on topics chosen by entire group.
Evening	Skill Training Session: Helping	Theory and practice in establishing a helping relationship. (I, pp. 213-233; II, pp. 194-217)

Friday		
Morning	Discussion Session: Roles as a Learner	Participants reflect on their own learning processes in a variety of settings
	Role Play: Student Learning Styles	Presentation of six different learning styles. (I, pp. 28-31)
	Short Theory Session: Student Learning Styles	
	Micro-College Planning	

Afternoon	Micro-College	Actual teaching in a video-taped laboratory.
	Teaching Laboratory	(I, pp. 105-109; II, pp. 180-198)

Evening	Skill Training: Problem-Solving	Presentation and practice in using a variety of problem solving techniques. (I, pp. 180-198)

Saturday		
Morning	Discussion Session: The Influence of the Institution on the Classroom	Use of problem-analysis to assess nature of institutional influence; Individual assessment, plus small group discussion
	Micro-College Planning	

Afternoon	The Dilemma of Power	A simulation on power and systems**

Evening	Free	

Sunday		
Morning	Exercise: Small Group Decision-Making and Conflict Management	Consultation and brief theory session. (I, pp. 157-179)
	Micro-College Planning	
Afternoon	Micro-College	
	Teaching Laboratory	
Evening	Skill Training Session: Decision-making	Use of Decision-Making games, plus theory (II, pp. 159-193)
Monday		
Morning	Discussion Session: Reflecting on Planning for the Future	Use of Life Planning Exercises modified to specifically focus on teaching. (II, pp. 218-265)
Afternoon	Teaching Laboratory: Preparing for Return Classroom	Participants provided with opportunity to try out new teaching methods
Evening	Discussion Session: Preparing for Return to Significant Other People	Reflection on personal learnings from workshop, how to convey these to spouse, children, friends, and so forth.

| Tuesday Morning | Workshop Evaluation: Interviews | Participants interview each other regarding significant learnings from workshop; particularly, what did each participant learn about the way he learns, how to continue the type of development begun at this workshop. |
| | Workshop Evaluation: Questionnaire | Evaluation form given out to participants. |

---

*References in parenthesis refer to page numbers of descriptions for specific activities in either Volume one (I) or two (II) of Bergquist and Phillips *A Handbook for Faculty Development* (Washington, D.C.: Council for the Advancement of Small Colleges, 1975, 1977).

**Simulation is available from William Bergquist c/o Council for the Advancement of Small Colleges, Washington, D.C.

4

The University Center

by Claude Mathis

Claude Mathis is the veteran of this group; his Northwestern University Center for the Teaching Professions has been going strong since 1969. He is a Texan, with a B.A. and M.A. in psychology from Texas Christian University and a Ph.D. in educational psychology from the University of Texas. He has been a professor of education at Northwestern since 1956 and currently is associate dean of the school of education as well as director of the center. Claude has been very active within the Big Ten and nationally as a leader in efforts to improve university teaching. He is widely published on the subject.

This chapter combines a review of descriptive studies regarding university services for teaching improvement with many practical tips and issues to consider when developing or renewing such a program. The diversity of services recommended in this chapter are well worth considereing in any setting. So is Mathis' stress on the student as the principal reference point for teaching improvement services. If such services do not work for students in their quest for learning, they are hard to defend.

Introduction

The development of higher education in the United States has followed the same departures from logic found in most democratic institutions. The discontinuities in the arguments about the liberating mission of the liberal arts versus the practical vocationalism of the land grant model, the availability of higher education as a privilege or a right, and the relationship between mass education, years of schooling, and income are all captured in the ambivalence with which higher education either embraces teaching as an ultimate solution, or tolerates the notion as a blemish to be endured. Nowhere do all of these seeming inconsistencies merge more reluctantly, and yet more creatively, than in the system of tensions known as the modern American university.

Anyone who spends enough time at a university, either as a faculty member or a student, to become aware of the special culture of the institution soon learns that universities are not like other higher education institutions. Universities have faculty who are identified with a broad range of fields far beyond those historically classified as the liberal arts and sciences. Despite recent evidences of interest in improving teaching, universities are dedicated to a model of education which emphasizes research and scholarship. The presence of graduate programs and the use of graduate teaching assistants to provide much undergraduate instruction is a further distinction. The student population in a university is usually more diverse than can be found in other postsecondary institutions. Also, universities have a governance structure which is more complex, generally more bureaucratic, and less informal than most other institutions.

Many additional distinctions could be made between the university and the community college, the undergraduate liberal arts college, and other types of postsecondary institutions. (79) Teaching in a university, and attempts to improve it, represent role expectations for faculty shaped by a number of forces which must be taken into consideration in designing Centers or programs. These forces are:

1. *The reward structure within universities*—In most universities the reward structure does not directly support improving teaching. Universities do not discourage teaching, but neither do they reward commitments to teaching as generously nor as effectively as rewards which are distributed for research and scholarship.
2. *The use of graduate students as undergraduate teachers*—Most universities with extensive commitments to graduate and professional training use

teaching assistants in a variety of instructional roles. This is both a source of variety in undergraduate instruction as well as a frequent cause for concern on the part of those being taught.

3. *The existence of many faculties rather than one faculty*—Universities represent a wide range of disciplines and professional specialties in their educational programs. The demise of general education within universities has led to much pressure on the undergraduate programs in professional schools. Most students do not attend universities to seek a liberal education, regardless of what the public relations staff may indicate to parents. This range of efforts in university programs leads to the department being a powerful element in shaping the values and attitudes of faculty members. Departments represent boundaries which are much more difficult to penetrate at the university level. Most disciplines and professions tend to feel that their solutions to effective teaching represent the "one best way." Each department usually has its favored best way.

4. *The presence of undergraduates in a graduate environment*—The commitment to scholarship and research by the university can lead to a system of priorities which favors graduate programs rather than undergraduate teaching. Undergraduates may find themselves accommodating to the graduate nature of the institution rather than staff members accommodating themselves to undergraduate needs. For example, subtle differences exist between teaching libraries and research libraries, yet the function of a library in most universities is for the purpose of doing research.

5. *Faculty identification with disciplines*—Faculty in universities are more inclined to identify with their disciplines nationally than with their institutions locally. The nature of their commitment to research and to the importance of national visibility tends to influence the way time is spent. If teaching has a lower priority, then efforts to improve teaching are given less time.

The improvement of teaching in a university may employ strategies and efforts which will be effective in one institution yet ineffective in another. No general model has yet emerged to solve the multitude of problems associated with generating and maintaining effective teaching in as complex a setting as a university. During the past decade, however, many universities, both public and private, have made some commitment to the examination and improvement of teaching in a way which they feel best fits the demands of their own cultures. The remainder of this chapter will consider some solutions and generalizations which are important for the development of programs to improve teaching in a university context.

Studies of University Centers

Several studies have been reported in recent years which contain useful data about attempts to improve teaching in universities. One such investigation was completed by Robert Moats at Northwestern University in 1975 and reported on efforts to improve teaching at ten major universities in the United States. (84) The universities involved in the study were University of California at Berkeley, Cornell, The University of Michigan, The University of Minnesota, Northwestern, Stanford, Syracuse, The University of Tennessee and Vanderbilt. The information from these universities was collected during the 1974-75 academic year. During the short period of time between then and the writing of this chapter, several of the programs have changed significantly, and one has been abandoned by the faculties which it served. Nevertheless, the general observations of the report are worth considering. Four major objectives were cited by the center and program directors at these institutions as being the most frequent stimuli for efforts: 1) The centers and programs were initially established to serve as advocates for the educational interests of *undergraduates*; 2) The design and implementation of *instructional innovations* represented the major program effort; 3) The initial strategy which was used to begin the process of improving undergraduate instruction was to *increase faculty awareness* and involvement in the examination and improvement of teaching within the context of course offerings; and 4) A high priority of the centers and programs was the *evaluation of teaching* for self-improvement. I have italicized the major focus of each point to draw attention to the major themes which dominate university programs.

When asked to comment on the major problems within their own institutions which limited the ability of centers and programs to address the improvement of undergraduate teaching, the directors enumerated three primary concerns. First, the major retardant to instructional improvement efforts in these university settings was the confluence of two traditions in higher education — the dominance of research as a traditional value and the autonomy of faculty, as represented by disciplinary and departmental identities, in viewing teaching as a process which is amenable to "outside" help. Second, the presence of graduate programs and the use of graduate students in undergraduate teaching stimulates an academic conservatism which influences many undergraduates in universities to be less than receptive to nontraditional learning experiences. Third funding was frequently uncertain. In those institutions where university funds were committed to the center or program, the issue was that of maintaining and competing for a general pool of funds which has now reached a steady state. Other directors indicated a concern about the uncertain future of outside funding for teaching improvement efforts. Outside funding often is used for specific projects. Attempting to improve teaching within a university through the use of funds earmarked for specific projects calls for academic legerdemain not frequently found in those trained to be scholars.

A more recent study completed by Bette Erickson at the University of Massachusetts reported information from twenty-seven centers and agencies in universities throughout the United States. (35) Approximately one-third of these efforts represented programmatic attempts to improve the attitudes, knowledge and skills of faculty members through the evaluation of teaching, the examination of values and attitudes about teaching, and the dissemination of knowledge about higher education. Nearly one-half of the centers and programs emphasized improvement through the development of teaching materials and individual course planning. Instructional design represented their primary commitment, and media, graphics, and the production of materials the major methods.

A third study by James McMillan, also reported in 1975, surveyed thirty-five public and private universities in the United States identified as having some center or agency for the improvement of teaching on their campuses. (73) McMillan found that the primary purpose of the agencies was to influence faculty to improve their teaching. The agencies were usually located within the central administration of the university, with an average of two to four full-time equivalent staff who spent most of their time in research and development functions and in providing instructional services to faculty. About half the agencies provided grants to faculty for instructional innovations, and the most visible service included workshops, consultations with individual faculty, courses and instructional design, and seminars on teaching. Media and technology played an important role in the activities of the agencies. Many of the agencies indicated that staff worked with departments in analyzing and developing curricula and in the evaluation of teaching by students. Most of the agencies reported some form of published dissemination such as newsletters and articles about innovations in teaching.

   The agencies viewed themselves as being primarily service organizations for the faculty. Most of the units reported that they responded to contacts initiated by faculty rather than "reaching out" to them. The terms "low key," "let them come to us," and "respect for faculty initiative" tend to describe the dominant posture of these agencies in their relationships to faculty.

   Such a passive picture seems to reflect the need of the agencies to maintain credibility by working only with those faculty who are motivated to seek help or who need help the least. Also, these agencies judged their success in terms of apparent changes in faculty as reported by faculty. None of the agencies reported any interaction directly with students either as informants about the need for instructional improvement or as evidence that change had taken place. Only four of the agencies indicated that changes in student achievement were part of the evaluation of their efforts.

   One clear conclusion from these studies is that centers and programs are not living up to their potential by only raising the consciousness of faculty and assisting those who are already effective. One wonders at the logic of developing programs to improve undergraduate teaching without including undergraduates as a basic source of information. Systematic efforts to prepare graduate students for their teaching responsibilities should be a part of the center's efforts. Identification and remediation strategies which are not personally demeaning should be attempted for those faculty who are obviously ineffective in their teaching. Evaluation strategies should go beyond using the opinions of faculty as the major data base. Centers should be less timorous about risk-taking and more venturesome in their efforts to influence change.

Three Approaches to Improving Teaching

   Three general strategies often used by universities to improve the quality of education are instructional development centers, faculty development programs and centers for the study of higher education. Jack Lindquist briefly discusses each thrust in Chapter One, but they bear re-examination here because of their prevalence within universities. By far the most prevalent of these strategies is described by the term *instructional development*. This approach views the classroom as the central focus of change. Instructional improvement results from effective interaction of teachers, methods and students in a classroom. The instructor is the agent for delivering specific methods of instruction so that student learning takes place. The classroom becomes the entry point for the application of specific methods of instruction. The instructional development approach, in its purest form, emphasizes systematic course design, curriculum development, instructional technology, the application of audio-visual media in teaching and a systems approach to the analysis of the relationship of instruction to learning outcomes. The Center for Instructional Development at Syracuse University and the Educational Development Program at Michigan State University are outstanding examples of the application of instructional development strategies to the examination and improvement of teaching.

Established in 1971 and reorganized in 1973, The Center for Instructional Development at Syracuse University represents a major investment of university funds in an attempt to influence curriculum innovations which extend beyond the single course to the design, production and evaluation of integrated curricula sequences. Michigan State University initiated its Educational Development Program in 1965. Its conception has resulted in a comprehensive program, supported by university funds, which includes course development, clinical approaches to the improvement of teaching, media services and instruction television networks.

Another general approach to improving teaching in universities is the *faculty development* model. Faculty development differs from instructional development in that the faculty member becomes the major focus of attention and the point of entry into the examination of teaching and learning. Whereas the instructional development approach focuses on the activity of teaching, the faculty development approach may or may not be directly concerned with the act of teaching. Faculty development is concerned with the many roles faculty have in the institution they serve — not just their role as teacher. While instructional development deals more with the performance of the teacher in an instructional situation, faculty development is more humanistic in its approach and views effective teaching as resulting from the satisfactions which faculty derive from their personal identifies as well as from the roles they have as representatives of their institutions or as teachers in the classroom. Examples of programs with a faculty development emphasis are the Center for the Teaching Professions at Northwestern University, the Center for Improving Teaching Effectiveness at Virginia Commonwealth University, and the Center for Effective Learning at Cleveland State University.

A third strategy for the improvement of teaching in a university setting is the center whose major function is *to study* the field of higher education and disseminate the results. Such centers also work with faculty in a variety of ways but central to their philosophy is the importance of treating higher education as a legitimate subject for experimental investigation. The Centers for Higher Education which were established at Columbia University, The University of Michigan and The University of California at Berkeley were developed from a commitment to treat higher education as a legitimate topic for investigation and to develop a systematic body of knowledge about higher education through publications programs and other means. The Center for Research on Learning and Teaching at The University of Michigan and the Consulting Group on Instruction Design at the University of Minnesota represent two excellent examples of research and development efforts focused on teaching and learning, in which the research function is a high priority for the time of those involved in the programs.

No one center or program represents a pure version of these approaches. Any productive effort to improve teaching should have elements of all three solutions visible as part of the total strategy for impact. The wide range of faculty interests and disciplinary approaches to teaching in universities demands that some solutions for improvement be sought through the application of instructional design principles. Other solutions are best obtained through concentration on the person of the faculty member and his or her values about teaching. Research is essential because it contributes to the understanding and improvement of programs and because it helps staff maintain parity with faculty colleagues.

Centers do tend, however, to have a "personality" which reflects a general dominance of one approach over others. This usually results from the emergence of a philosophy about teaching which is based on the values and attitudes of those who staff the center, from the nature of the mission of the institution and the values associated with the way the mission is made operational and from the reinforcement of early successes in the history of the center. Most centers begin by doing what the staff can do best. If this leads to success, an individual identity begins to be formed which helps to shape the future. The nature of funding for centers also influences individual programs by forcing the center to become what its grants and contracts from outside sources dictate, or what the expectations of internal sources of funding demand. For example, a center which must demonstrate specific successes each year in order to compete for university funds may find it more advantageous to follow the path of instructional development since this strategy has the potential for effective management of short-term outcomes. The application of a specific method in a number of classes during one academic year represents a manageable project which can be evaluated to generate information about the success of the method.

The faculty development approach, on the other hand, is more difficult to manage for purposes of accountability. Changes in values and attitudes in faculty members are difficult to evaluate, and short-term effects are elusive at best. A faculty development philosophy tends to emerge as a dominant force in those centers in which the values and attitudes of the staff are less concerned with immediate accountability. Evaluations of faculty development approaches tend to emphasize more unobtrusive measures of accountability and are based more often on long-range indications of change.

The approach which emphasizes research about teaching leads from strength when applied in a university setting because of the emphasis on research in universities. The major difficulties with this approach are convincing the university administration that teaching is a legitimate subject for research and collecting appropriate experimental data when one's colleagues are the subjects. Strange are the principles of inclusion and exclusion which operate among academicians to determine what is a legitimate topic for research and what is damned as unworthy. Teaching, for many reasons, is often relegated to the latter category. This may be changing, however, as witnessed by the many journals now available for reporting on research and development in the teaching of specific disciplines.

Purposes

Any center which develops programs to examine and improve teaching eventually must come to terms with what is meant by "good teaching." My best advice is to recognize the indeterminate nature of goodness and to seek its meaning in the careful analysis of the teaching of those faculty who are themselves particular examples of goodness. Evaluating those specifics against a statement of craft such as that offered by Eble or against summaries of research on teacher effectiveness represents one way of testing the valudity of these examples. Using questionnaires and other response forms which faculty fill out can be another useful way to develop a profile of factors thought to contribute to effective teaching. Several of the forms in *A Handbook for Faculty Development* are thoughtful instruments which can be used or adapted depending on the information needed. (7)

One important distinction which should be made in defining good teaching or the object of improvement is between training and education.

Most academicians view themselves as educators rather than trainers; yet many of the methods and techniques used in the classroom, especially those involving technology, are more useful for training functions than for the accomplishment of broad educational goals. Training emphasizes the needs of particular systems and involves preparing learners to perform specific tasks in those systems, to fit into the machine and help it run smoothly. Training is evaluated in terms of the contribution the program makes to the objectives of the system. Instruction describes the activities of persons who control training efforts. Education is generally not thought of in terms of the demands of a specific system. The goals of education involve learnings which attempt to prepare people for the many systems of a society. The worth of an education is assessed by the growth and development of the individual learner. Teaching is more frequently used to describe the activities of those who educate.

Figure One presents some examples of decisions about learning which are arranged around the essential parameters of training and education on the one hand and efficiency and effectiveness on the other. The examples suggest that all training does not involve decisions about efficiency, just as all education does not aim for effectiveness. Extending these four categories with your own examples may help to identify the complexities of the teaching-learning process in the university. Universities attempt effective training along with efficient education in their quest for the best fit of cost with quality. Each example also represents a potential problem for the center, one which must be solved in terms of student needs and relative cost. Low cost options are offered by training-efficiency solutions, while high cost options are represented by education-effectiveness solutions. Individualization of learning options and student satisfaction generally follow a reverse pattern.

Different disciplines have different demands for determining the balance between education and training. Among the many significant ironies of academe is the frequent observation that those disciplines which espouse education with the greatest vigor are themselves significantly involved in training as the dominant method for seeking the goals of education. Persuading faculty to attempt new approaches to teaching should involve the recognition that successful inducements in one discipline may be failures in another. Each discipline must ultimately develop its own mechanisms for improving its own teaching.

Just as there are many roads to travel toward the goal of effective teaching, there are many definitions of the goal itself. Rewards for effec-

Figure 1

EFFICIENCY	
1. Organizing intact classes for large numbers of students where retention of information is the primary objective.	1. Large lecture sections for introductory general education courses.
2. Developing an instructional program in which maximum exposure to content is done in a minimal amount of time.	2. Organizing a curriculum around fixed units of time for teaching and a hierarchical concept of knowledge.
3. Designing instructional objectives which specify minimal competencies.	3. Limiting course registrations without providing equitable student access.
TRAINING	EDUCATION
1. Designing instructional objectives which specify levels of competency beyond the minimal.	1. Providing students with some degree of self-determination about sequence and structure of educational programs.
2. Providing for individual choice in methods used to attain objectives.	2. Rewarding a wide range of teaching styles and educational methods available for students.
3. Flexible scheduling of training sessions to allow for diagnosis and remediation.	3. Student-centered learning which emphasizes individual growth and development.
EFFECTIVENESS	

tive teaching therefore should be based as much on one's willingness to try to improve as on the attainment of a successful outcome. In essence, the purpose of a teaching improvement center is to stimulate and assist efforts to improve, whether in training or education. The criterion of program success becomes the number of people who are making sincere efforts to improve along lines reasonably consistent with recognized teaching effectiveness factors.

Structure

The studies of instructional development agencies in universities cited earlier in this chapter all found that the dominant organizational plan for a comprehensive teaching improvement center in a university was one which placed the agency under the supervision of someone in the central administration, usually the academic vice president or the provost. This arrangement is almost universal for comprehensive centers. Special use centers, such as those involved in medical education, may be under the supervision of a dean or a sub-unit of the larger structure. One exception to this general rule for comprehensive centers is the Center for the Teaching Professions at Northwestern University, which is part of the School of Education. The director of the Center is an associate dean in the School of Education with responsibilities for the direction and administration of the Center. The relationship of the Northwestern Center to the School of Education was one which the central administration felt to be important because it indicates sponsorship by the one faculty on campus who should know the most about how to teach effectively.

Teaching improvement centers or programs should be positioned in the line of authority within the university in a way which permits the director to have direct access to the person responsible for budget allocations. In addition, its position should be one which can be interpreted by the faculty as attributing importance to its mission. Most faculty tend to judge the worth of institutional commitments by how close an academic enterprise is to those who fund it. If the money filters through several authorities before arriving at its final destination, then what it pays for must not be very important.

If the center or program director reports to a vice president, this latter person should be the person responsible for the day-to-day operation of the academic affairs of the university. Some institutions have administrative responsibilities divided so that all center directors report to the vice president of science and research. To include a center for the improvement of teaching in this arrangement is to completely misinterpret its mission on the campus. It is vital to the success of such centers that they be viewed by both faculty and students as having a logical place high in the academic organizational chart.

Ownership

An essential objective during the first year for teaching improvement staff is to acquire "ownership" of the program. This means making the center an active force for shaping educational policy in the university as opposed to reacting only to the directions which filter down from above. Occasionally, the administrative officer to whom the center director reports may be tempted to push the center in directions which might solve his or her immediate problems; in the long run this might be detrimental to the center's credibility. Center staff should be prepared to argue against inappropriate directives. They also should be willing to give logical advice about educational quality before problems get out of hand. A specific example of a request which was not in the best interest of one center in a larger university involved having center staff render opinions about effective teaching for those faculty who were being considered for promotion and /or tenure. The vice president for academic affairs asked the center director to develop a program of observation and diagnosis which he in turn would ask the candidates to submit to. The staff of the center successfully argued against such a program even though honoring the request would have meant a larger budget. This successful defense of the center from the imposition of direction from above has contributed greatly to the view on campus that the center is owned intellectually by those who are directly involved in its programs and not by an authority removed from its activities.

The ownership of a program by a director and staff is best obtained by visible evidence of competence, by advice which is sound and in the best interest of the educational efforts of the university and by an identification with faculty as the ultimate source of authority. This identification should begin early in the first year, and can be initiated by using selected faculty members on advisory boards, by discussing the mission of the center with appropriate university committees and the faculty senate, and by submitting annual reports to the faculty. An inventory during the first year of faculty resources is another method for developing early relationships to faculty. Noonan describes the kinds of questions which should be asked. (88)

Structural Power Levers

Any strategy for improving teaching in the university should take account, first, of the leverages of power which can be used to initiate faculty involvement in the process of change. A pragmatic analysis of the structure and distribution of power should precede any decisions about organizational structure. While the allocation of power within most universities may appear similar to organizational charts, the internal exercise of this power is different for each institution. In some institutions, deans are the Colonels of the academic army; in others the departmental chairperson is essential for stimulating change. Although it may appear illogical, the president or chancellor and the chief academic office (vice president or provost) may have the least power to implement academic change. They may order it, but they cannot make it happen. Faculty, administrators, students, and alumni all have a share in the allocation of power, and they attempt to exercise it according to their perceptions of how much they have. Generally the faculty either wins or delays, depending on the issue at hand. For this reason, any assessment of political leverage should take account of faculty opinion leaders.

Time spent in analyzing this society is not time wasted. The same techniques used by the behavioral scientist to assess social class are useful in this context. Faculty members who are willing to evaluate the importance of their colleagues are valuable informants. Accurate perceptions result from the use of a wide range of sources of information with relevant data cross-validated through more than one source. Center staff should be expected to spent time away from their offices and in the academic departments. Staff should have personal skills which allow faculty to relate to them and "open up" about the institution. Competency in interpersonal skills is essential for success in any venture which depends on "friendly persuasion" for its energy.

Links to Departments

At the university level, the most meaningful and potentially rewarding decisions about the educational activities of the institution are usually made at the departmental level. Departments in universities are quite powerful in determining whether or not university policy about the quality of education will become a reality. Departments have been both damned and defended as the most effective way to organize instruction in the university. While the sanctity of departmental ownership of a discipline has been breached in many instances (environmental studies, urban affairs, communication studies and biomedical engineering, to mention a few), the department in a university represents a basic decision making unit. This places it in a position of obvious importance to influence educational change.

In most universities the department should become the point of impact for instructional improvement. This means that any center with a university-wide commitment must be sensitive to the many languages which departments use to converse about higher education generally and teaching specifically. Department chairpersons are important power brokers, especially if they represent disciplines held in high esteem. Center directors would be well advised to call upon department chairpersons to find out what the center might be able to do for the department, rather than for the purpose of telling the chairperson what the center is going to do for the university. A successful director is a person who is willing to spend time in the "field" to attract the attention of faculty. Calling on the department chairperson in her own office rather than asking the chairperson to come to the director's office represents to some an insiginficant element in planning for the success of the center, yet such small acts recognize the implicit power which will eventually determine the credibility of the center.

Center Advisory Committee

Advisory committees are one strategy for recognizing the power structure. The appointment of an advisory committee for a university center permits a forum for the many voices of scholarship in the university to articulate their ideas about teaching. An advisory committee also provides an opportunity for explicit evidence of the wedding of research competence and effective teaching. The appointment of those faculty who are the best models of the teacher-scholar and who have among them some of the "power brokers" in the various faculties, provides evidence that the center should be taken seriously by the university community. This advisory committee should be appointed by the chief administrative officer of the university, if possible, in order to communicate the approval of those in formal command. To be certain that the committee only *gives* advice will keep the center from becoming a projection of the sometimes idiosyncratic vision of each member of the committee. The center director would be wise to accept more advice than he rejects, however, at least until credibility has been established by performance.

Staffing

One does not need a large staff to accomplish center objectives. Centers do not expend time equally with every faculty member in the institution; nor are acitivites spread equally throughout the university. A small staff can accomplish much, even in a large institution, by a selective and carefully planned application of efforts. Few centers have more than four full-time staff members, including secretarial and clerical staff. Graphic artists and media specialists represent the most frequent non-academic staff in large, public university centers. Many agencies consist of the director, a full or part-time co-director, a secretary, and part-time persons with special skills. Many university centers would not be able to operate effectively without student help, especially graduate student assistance through internships and other arrangements.

The Center Director

The director of a center is a critical appointment, since program development will reflect the values and attitudes of the person who is given initial responsibility for the center. The desirability of having someone from within the university who has the confidence and support of his colleagues is an important consideration in appointing the first director. Someone from within the university will know the infrastructure well enough to minimize the amount of time needed to become acclimated. The director's position will be more secure if he is also a tenured member of one of the faculties within the university. Directing a center carries with it certain risks which those competing for promotion and tenure should not be asked to assume. The improvement of teaching involves development activities which are highly applied and offers little opportunity for the completion of the type of experimental research or traditional scholarship which is frequently prized by promotion and tenure committees. Tenure provides some protection for a director if the enterprise fails because of inadequate funding or unsound conceptualization. With tenure, in most instances at least, a director will have a place within the university to return.

The director's task will be less difficult if he is both a productive scholar and an effective teacher. The image of the scholar-teacher in the context of the university is the role model which has the greatest probability of success with university faculty. The director should be an example of what is valued in the wedding of teaching to scholarship. The director's task would also be simplified if he is not over-committed to a particular orthodoxy of salvation for those who are less than effective in their teaching. The director should be able to relate comfortably to the many disciplines and professions seeking the services of the center. This calls for a degree of tolerance and eclecticism not shared by all university faculty.

The selection of a director is a decision of sufficient importance to require time, the involvement of advice and counsel from faculty and other members of the university community, and a clear assessment of the personal skills needed for success. Centers for the improvement of university teaching should not become a haven for the dispossessed within the university. Unfortunately, the temptation is sometimes very strong to appoint as director someone who is among those displaced persons in the university who, at the moment, have nothing to do. An effective director usually will be someone who will find it difficult to take the assignment because of the commitments which he already has to a wide range of activities in the institution.

Other Center Staff

Staff skills, of course, must reflect the nature of the programs offered by a center; however, the disciplinary identities of staff are important considerations when a center's efforts involve the total university. The most frequent source of staff for teaching improvement agencies are the disciplines of education and psychology. Educational psychologists are a major force in instructional development, and higher education and the behavioral sciences represent identifiable forces in those centers which emphasize a faculty development approach.

A different approach to staffing would be to involve faculty from many fields of study who are knowledgeable about teaching in their disciplines and who can communicate with their colleagues in their langauge. Instructional development and faculty development may be best served by preparing faculty to perform an educational function in their own fields rather than to anticipate salvation from a central hive of psychologists and professional educators. Psychologists particularly suffer a credibility gap in their relationships with other disciplines in which consultant help for improving teaching may be needed. This is especially true of the relationship between psychology and the humanities and arts. Faculty in a department of English may be totally mystified by conversations about teaching which are liberally laced with references to reinforcement, behavioral objectives and performance outcomes. Any staffing pattern which provides for the involvement of a wide range of disciplines in teaching improvement programs would support the idea that each discipline and department can assume responsibility for its own teaching improvement efforts.

In selecting staff, the director should have specific job qualifications in mind before inviting someone to work at the center. An interest in teaching and an ability to get along with people is not enough. The person should be able to articulate a logical philosophy about teaching and translate a stated position into specific teacher behaviors. To the extent possible, staff should represent different points of view. The director must avoid the temptation to replicate his own values in staff appointments. If staff are to serve a wide range of needs, they should have a wide range of skills. Staff members need to be tolerant of each other's intellectual commitments; it would be pointless to have someone who is an expert in humanistic encounter and someone who is an expert in programmed learning spend all their time arguing with each other about the primacy of their approaches to teaching.

A systematic staff development program should be instituted as soon as the director has one companion. Regular staff meetings with parity of participation are one way to establish positive morale from the beginning. Staff should feel an identity with the center which makes it theirs; the pronoun "we" should dominate staff consciousness rather than the pronoun "I." Staff efforts will be diluted if the faculty "prima donna" system is transplanted to the center. Developing effective team commitment is one of the primary leadership challenges for the director.

Probationary periods for staff are advised as one way of avoiding the inevitable mistakes which occasionally occur in making appointments. Often neither the director nor the new staff member can anticipate a problem until "on-the-job" reactions begin to appear. During the probationary period, new staff should be evaluated by observing them as they work with faculty in several disciplines not their own. During the probationary period, the director should be especially helpful to the appointee so that this time is a fair test of the skills of the person.

Supplemental Staff

Many centers depend upon volunteers for a number of staff functions. Quite often students, both graduate and undergraduate, are willing to spend some time on activities in the center in return for the informal relationships and learnings which develop from contact with both paid staff and clients. Student interest is one reason for including an educational function in the mission of the center. If paid staff are themselves faculty members, they can offer courses, seminars, internships and independent study opportunities as part of the center's commitment to the improving of teaching. Doctoral students often become involved in dissertation problems as part of the research and development function of the center. Centers with budgets of under $100,000 and a comprehensive mission are never able to have available the paid staff necessary for taking advantage of the opportunities which the problems of a university offer.

Several approaches to supplementing regular staff are possible. We use undergraduate workstudy students at the Center for the Teaching Professions, especially in the media area. We also have developed a media talent pool of students on campus who have audio-visual and media skills. Before being listed in this talent directory each student must undergo a demanding evaluation of the skill or skills for which the student wishes to be listed. This roster has the endorsement of the center, and the students are hired for specific jobs by the departments, public relations, and other offices within the university. To become a member of the media talent pool is a sign of distinction among students. Paraprofessionals from the community can also be a source of useful talent. Very often, retired school teachers can be called upon to take on specific responsibilities, at modest cost, for a day or two during the week. The Center for Learning and Development at McGill University has been one of the most successful programs in using paraprofessionals well.

Activities

Most centers have a program structure which emerges from necessity rather than from reason. Planning for the mission of the center can save time and minimize risk if the planning is flexible enough to accommodate the occasional serendipitous opportunities which always occur. Rather than describe the various programs which are in operation at different university centers, I would like to present a rationale for a comprehensive program structure and provide some different examples for the program elements. This program structure closely parallels the plan which was implemented through the Center for the Teaching Professions at Northwestern University. Many other university centers, however, have their own variations of the strategies used in the Northwestern model. In fact, the many variations of this basic program which are now in operation throughout the United States attest to the validity of the rationale.

Nearly all centers design their efforts to match the objectives which were articulated at the time the basic plan of the center was presented for funding, either to the university administration or to an outside funding agency. For example, the Educational Development Program at Michigan State University started from six goals which emphasized the following in relationship to the improvement of *undergraduate* education:

1. The identification of major problems in the area of curriculum, the learning and teaching process, and the use of faculty, financial, and physical resources.
2. To stimulate and conduct research that would suggest solutions to identified problems.

3. To undertake projects and studies that would give promise of improving both the quality and the efficiency of the undergraduate program.
4. To support and provide service to groups interested in experimentation with new procedures and methods in learning and teaching.
5. To facilitate implementation of faculty and administration approved solutions to problems.
6. To identify and communicate progress in research, experimentation, and implementation. (30)

These objectives are typical of those who direct instructional development agencies in universities. Note the emphasis on undergraduates, the curriculum, procedures and methods of teaching and quality and efficiency in the teaching-learning process.

Other centers which are committed to a faculty development approach might have a statement of goals which is general and less detailed in the identification of specific areas of concern. For example, the objectives of the Center for the Teaching Professions are:

1. The improvement of the teaching of prospective teachers and prospective members of the faculty in a variety of fields at Northwestern University.
2. Involvement with other educational institutions and professional organizations to help them improve their teaching programs.
3. The establishment of a model for similar centers at other universities throughout the world which have continuing responsibilities to improve the quality of the education they offer. (80)

These objectives, of course, could have led to an instructional development solution. That they did not at Northwestern University is more of an indication of the values of the faculty in a private university than a lack of faith in the instructional development approach to improve teaching and learning. The center's commitment to the implementation of the three general objectives presented above has resulted in the articulation of a philosophy and style which has identifiable components. The faculty development approach assumes that effective teaching results from much more than attention to curriculum development and/or the mechanics of classroom behavior. Also, the improvement of teaching goes beyond specific intervention strategies at an individual or a departmental level even though the individual and the department are the points of initial impact. At least four general types of intervention can be identified which call for different strategies to influence change in the teaching behaviors of faculty. These are: 1) graduate preparation of future faculty members, 2) assistance to first year faculty, 3) programs for faculty in mid-career, and 4) efforts to redefine the meaning of professionalism. Each of these should be discussed in some detail.

Graduate Preparation of the Future Faculty Member

Very little has been done to prepare the new Ph.D. for the teaching responsibilities which will inevitably become a major part of a career in higher education. Most Ph.D. candidates have nothing in their graduate programs which is even remotely related to preparation for college teaching in their disciplines. In some form, preparation for college teaching should involve a systematic effort to prepare the Ph.D. candidate for teaching responsibilities in a manner which makes the preparation a viable part of the doctoral program.

Preparing doctoral students for teaching responsibilities, although not yet common, has recently become more acceptable than it has been in the past. The traditions of the Ph.D. as a research degree have become less rigid, largely due to the demands of graduate students themselves, and many departments now recognize their responsibility to help graduate students prepare for academic careers which will involve teaching as well as research.

Harvard University has initiated a program for teaching assistants through its Office of Instructional Research and Evaluation, which brings faculty and students together for seminars on teaching. Video-taping of classroom performance represents a central element in the process. The Center for Learning and Development at McGill University offers seminars for teaching assistants in response to an endorsement by the faculty of the principle that teaching skills include student motivation, discussion skills, lecturing skills, evaluation, instructional design and audio-visual teaching. The center plans to develop self-instructional packages on these topics to be available to graduate students as a "drop-in" resource.

The Northwestern Center has developed a "Seminar on College Teaching," which is part of the curriculum of the graduate school and is available to departments for the purpose of introducing advanced graduate students to the methods, strategies and problems involved in teaching at the college level. This course is listed as a general graduate school course, which means that it does not have departmental ownership. In this way a graduate student in any department can take part in seminar activities without having the course appear on the transcript with a specific departmental affiliation. As a general graduate school offering, the course is on an equal basis with the courses used for research activities. At the time the seminar was established, only the University of Utah had a university-wide programmatic experience for teaching assistants to help them prepare for their future teaching responsibilities. This concept was expanded at Northwestern to include all graduate students interested in teaching. The reward to the graduate student is the credit received toward the degree for participating in the seminar.

Many institutions now have similar courses in their curricula. A notable example of a departmental program for helping teaching assistants in a specific discipline prepare for their course assignments is found in the department of psychology at The University of Michigan, where Wilbert McKeachie instituted a comprehensive and much copied effort. This program uses the resources of the university, especially of the Center for Research on Learning and Teaching.

During its first year at Northwestern, departments offering the Ph.D. were cautious in exploring the potential of the "Seminar on College Teaching." By the beginning of the third year, however, the seminar was available to students in all the academic departments, either as a course taught within the department or as one offered by the center, and each department had approved it for major credit toward the degree.

A sample outlined for the "Seminar on College Teaching" is presented below. The course has brought together graduate students from different disciplines, who thus have the opportunity to educate each other about the demands of their fields of study. This, together with the participation of effective teacher-scholars throughout the campus, provides richness of content which is often pursued beyond the limits of the course.

"Seminar on College Teaching"

This seminar will be concerned with the issues and practices of teaching in higher education. The seminar will contain two concurrent components: 1) seminar discussion on the nature and directions of college teaching, and 2) individualized conferences and practicum experiences for teaching skill development. Discussion sessions will be led by Center staff and distinguished resource persons, and are intended to acquaint prospective college teachers with the philosophical and institutional issues attendant to the profession. Practicum sessions will focus on preparation of a format and materials for an undergraduate course and simulated teaching experience.

Objectives:

The seminar is designed to satisfy a number of learning objectives for participating graduate students. Its general objectives include the ability of students to:

1. Recognize the relationships between the three elements of effective teaching:
   a. learning objectives
   b. teaching strategy
   c. evaluation procedures
2. Understand the psychological principles attendant to effective teaching, including human learning, interpersonal relations, dimensions of classroom achievement, the role of affect /emotion in learning, and so forth.
3. Relate the results of research on college teaching to instructional design and development in his or her respective discipline.
4. Discern those student characteristics which have the greatest influence on college teaching and how teaching must consider student traits in addition to learning requirements.
5. Engage in careful self-analysis about the decision to begin a career in college teaching, commitment to the task and a definition of the personal qualities which qualify him or her for the role.
6. Recognize the role of teaching in higher education in relation to complementary faculty responsibilities, i.e., research, advising students, community services, consulting, and so forth.

Seminar Topics:

The College Teacher: Roles and Responsibilities
Instructional Design and Development I: Objectives
Instructional Design and Development II: Teaching Strategies
Instructional Design and Development III: Evaluation of Students and Grading Procedures
Psychological Foundations of Teaching — Theory
Reseach on College Teaching
The College Student
The Technology of Teaching
Evaluation of College Teaching
The Institution of Higher Education: Future Directions
Presentations of Projects

The Initial Year of a Faculty Member's Appointment

Most colleges or universities have no in-service experience for a new faculty member designed to ease her entrance into the educational life of the university campus. Usually no formal assistance is available for making the first year a successful teaching experience. Yet the first year in a new environment can be crucial in determining the satisfactions to be received from the years beyond the first.

I am not aware of any university which requires *all* new instructors and assistant professors to undergo some form of in-service training before they are turned loose on students. Many universities, however, do provide some incentive to a new faculty member to help her become more proficient in classroom performance. The most frequent method is the availability of a venture fund or an instructional improvement budget which can be allocated to beginning faculty for specific teaching improvement projects. The usual pattern, however, for general socialization to the culture of a particular university is for the beginning faculty member to learn "on-the-job," usually from those in the department who are willing to take the time to talk

Centers for the improvement of teaching can help the beginning faculty member develop a conceptually sound approach to teaching and the education of undergraduates. Formal activities, such as workshops for beginning faculty and "drop-in" seminars, can be helpful for the career development of those who participate. If the center can become the agent for administering funds made available to new faculty for the improvement of teaching, then some consistent effort can be made to coordinate the projects and bring together involved faculty to talk about their ideas for improving teaching. The center then to some extent controls the direction of instructional innovation by selecting those projects which fit a specific instructional model. Some control over the objectives for improvement at Michigan State University is exercised by the Educational Development Program through its ability to award instructional improvement funds. Another strategy is for the center to become involved with faculty after the funds are made available to the faculty member. The center then can become a resource which helps the faculty member get effective return for the dollar.

The strategy used by the Center for the Teaching Professions at Northwestern involves variations of these two approaches. The center has awarded funds for the improvement of teaching to beginning faculty members, and the staff also has contributed time to helping faculty members develop projects which are funded from other sources in the university. The procedure used to award support is typical of most centers. Faculty members are encouraged to submit brief descriptions of what they wish to accomplish to the staff of the center. This negotiation proceeds through individual conferences with the faculty so that opportunities exist for the development of alternative suggestions. The staff member assigned to monitor the project follows the development of the activity and is available to provide assistance at any time. After the worth of the project has been clearly delineated, a funding partnership with the department involved is negotiated so that the total cost of the project includes funds from the center as well as support from the instructional budget of the university. For example, one professor proposed the use of center resources to develop a film series for the history department which would be required of students and open to the public. Each week a different faculty member from the department introduced the film and directed the discussion after the film was shown. Participants from the community were actively involved. Center staff helped develop the sequence of topics, locate suitable film and advertise the venture to the broader community. The center also helped design an evaluation system. The history department provided funds to rent the films, and the center provided consultation, some coordination, and the expertise to show the films. Risk capital for instructional improvement should be recognized as a legitimate concern of the regular budgeting process of the University; therefore, the use of center funds to encourage partnerships of support is an inducement to budget other funds for educational development.

The Middle and Later Years in Faculty Careers

After a faculty member has acquired tenure, a full professorship and a good salary, attitudes about self and role change; the incentives which were important when an individual started may no longer keep her productivity high at the mid-career point and beyond. Helping the older faculty member remain productive, especially with regard to teaching, becomes a critical necessity for the effectiveness of higher education. The mid-career crisis for many faculty members should be recognized for what it is — a need for new directions in teaching and scholarship, as well as a quest for new experiences in the context of an already well-established professional commitment.

Programs for faculty during mid-career or beyond are becoming significantly more important, since the average age of faculty is increasing each year. One does not have to project far into the future to envision a faculty who are, on the average, fifty years old and teaching undergraduates in the same institutions where they started their academic careers. Both age and decreased opportunities for movement from one institution to another can create a lethal combination of factors deadly to the maintenance of interest and productivity in teaching and the process of education.

Many universities are becoming aware of this need for mid-career programs. For example, the Center for Program Development at Northeastern Illinois University has established a program for tenured senior faculty members which will support efforts to help these faculty members become more proficient with various aspects of alternative learning. "Faculty Fellowships in Nontraditional Teaching" are awarded each year to senior faculty who are given release time to attend seminars, meet with nontraditional students, and study methods for learning outside the classroom. (129)

On many campuses the need to reallocate resources has resulted in some faculty having to face the possibility of pursuing other careers outside of academe or of retraining for different responsibilities in their own institutions. Faculty who are in need of retraining are often older, tenured professors. Illinois State University has approached this problem by establishing a Professional Development Center. The goals for the Professional Development Center include helping faculty respond to new program development made necessary by the need to reallocate existing personnel resources; to respond equitably and creatively to the need for staff reduction; to assist in developing and coordinating policies and resources for the most effective utilization of faculty; and to develop a model for a Professional Development Center which may be of help to other universities. These general program goals, together with specific objectives for individuals, are being implemented through educational leaves, workshops, individual counseling and coordination with other campus resources. (132)

The appointment of senior faculty as center associates or faculty fellows is one way of establishing a relationship with the center without placing the faculty member in the position of seeking remediation. The Faculty Fellow Program at Northwestern is one example of a way for faculty members to become more closely associated with the center and with each other throughout common interests in teaching. Faculty Fellows are experienced teachers who have already demonstrated a commitment to creativity and change in their teaching. Their association with the center provides an incentive for renewal activities and for a regular interchange of ideas about teaching. Each Fellow is given a small amount of money as risk capital for instructional innovation. Faculty Fellow projects have included the development of a national system for the evaluation of teaching, an automated piano laboratory for teaching beginning piano students, computerized lessons on dental materials for continuing education courses, a language for computer-assisted instruction, and self-instructional programs in obstetrics and gynecology for third-year medical students.

A center director must be sensitive to the political realities of appointments such as these, however. To pick your favorite "star" without reckoning with campus opinion may be more alienating than productive. Extensive advice should be sought for such appointments.

Another strategy for bringing both junior and senior faculty together is the faculty "self-teaching" seminar.' The Center for the Teaching Professions has sponsored these seminars since 1973 and has been involved in the publication of three books from papers generated by participants. The evaluations of the seminars indicate that participants were attracted to the prospect of interaction among colleagues and graduate students from different disciplines. Each seminar has a theme; the preparation of position papers about the theme was suggested because of the high value of scholarship among the group. None of the faculty who participated was given release time for the purpose, yet they met together for a full quarter, one afternoon each week. The royalties from the sales of the three books come to the center to support additional faculty self-teaching seminars.

Redefining the Meaning of Professionalism

Nearly all college professors have a primary definition of their roles which results from an identification with their disciplines. Professorial associations are frequently the major reference groups for defining professional behavior in specific disciplines. Professional associations and learned societies thus can do much to help improve teaching in higher education by emphasizing excellence in teaching as well as in scholarship. Professional associations and learned societies are only beginning to accept responsibility for helping their members become effective teachers as well as contributing scholars.

Centers for the improvement of teaching can do much to facilitate the demand for help in improving instruction from the associations by encouraging members to request such help directly from their particular associations. The link between the disciplines in a university and these associations is a strong one because most associations are organized to represent one discipline. Centers can also provide some support for associations that are attempting programs. For example, the Center for the Teaching Professions at Northwestern University has developed working relationships with a number of professional associations with this objective in mind. Committees on teaching have met at the center from the American Political Science Association, the American Board of Pediatrics, the American Philosophical Association, the Philosophy of Education Society, the Association of Departments of English and the American Psychological Association. The American Sociological Association is using publications from the Center in its Sociology Teaching Project, and a joint project to improve teaching in the field of the philosophy of education has been conducted by the Philosophy of Education Society and the American Philosophical Association in association with the center.

Financing

The budgets of university centers for improving teaching range from a few which expend over $600,000 a year to those spending less than $50,000. Michigan State University annually spends over $2,000,000 to support its Educational Development Program, while the University of Tennessee claims excellent results on less than $50,000. Clearly, it is hard to determine how much to spend without considering the purposes of individual centers.

Here at Northwestern, we have managed to implement the program I have just described on an annual budget of about a quarter of a million dollars, allocated as follows:

Salaries for Professional Staff	$63,000.
Secretarial	15,000.
Administrative Assistant	11,500.
Student Assistants	10,000.
Employee Benefits	14,300.
Equipment Purchase and Rental	20,000.
Production of Materials	10,000.
Visiting Associates and Auxiliary Faculty	45,000.
Travel	20,000.
Release Time Faculty and Other Professionals	35,000.
	$253,800.

The basic central staff costs are less than $100,000, but the energy, expertise and ownership put into the program is greatly extended by line items for student assistants, visiting associates, faculty released time and faculty travel.

Several university centers, such as Northwestern's, were initiated under grant funding. Grants certainly can provide a helpful boost, but major centers such as those at Michigan State and Syracuse were supported from the beginning by hard university dollars. Even if grants become available, it is wise to build into them a commitment by the university to pick up support on a gradual basis over the grant period, as we have done at Northwestern. Although it often is hard to find university dollars in these days of scarce resources, the argument for improving teaching by in-service development through stable staffs and the success of established programs have been compelling enough that new university centers such as those at the University of Texas, Austin, the University of Wisconsin, Parkside, and Ball State University have been started primarily on university funds.

One ready ally for obtaining budgetary allocations from the university are students, who are becoming increasingly active in making their presence felt at budget time. This is especially true for those institutions where tuition charges are high. Students are learning how to relate costs to quality and are beginning to make demands for an increase in quality as costs go up. Center directors would be wise not to ignore these concerns, since centers for the improvement of teaching are critical staging areas for the kinds of examinations of quality which students seek. The Associated Student Government at Northwestern has recommended that a portion of the 1977 tuition increase be made available to the Center for the Teaching Professions to support programs for improving the quality of teaching in the undergraduate programs of the university.

The nature of the budgeting process in most universities is such that "add on" money is quite important, for once money has appeared as a line item in a budget, it tends to stay there. The problem is getting it there in the first place. Departments are a powerful stimulus for attracting "add on" monies for educational improvement, since departments are the arena in which dollars get translated into programs. For example, a department chairperson in chemistry is more likely to get money to upgrade laboratory instruction — especially if students are complaining — then would a center director alone who might see the need but be removed from the locus of application. Working closely with departmental chairpersons to identify specific activities of benefit to individual departments is a useful expenditure of staff time. These activities then can form the basis of requests for additional university funding. The usual strategy is to ask for money to accomplish objectives which would be of benefit to a number of departments rather than limiting objectives to the needs of a specific department.

Center directors should know how to state their case in the most persuasive manner possible. Students again become useful allies, since the most persuasive reason for improving teaching is that it improves the quality of education and has a salutary effect on student learning. Any evidence to substantiate this observation is valuable data to accompany a request for university dollars.

An example of a university commitment to educational development is the Educational Development Fund at the University of Minnesota (25). It represents a model for the allocation of funds to venutres for improving the quality of education. During 1970, the Board of Regents of the University of Minnesota approved a program of support for educational development recommended by the university senate. The program is supported by setting aside instructional funds and establishing an all-university mechanism to review proposals for support by the fund. The plan calls for the fund to build gradually to a level of 3% of the University's instructional budget. A committee of seven faculty members and five students was appointed at the time the fund was established to assume responsibility for recommending expenditures. The plan calls for the allocation of the fund in equal shares to departments, colleges and the university at large. The availability of the funds at the University of Minnesota has influenced, and will continue to influence, the commitment of the university community to innovative methods and models of instruction and education as a means of improving the quality of education. The many agencies and groups at the University of Minnesota whose mission is the improvement of teaching benefit from such a funding policy. Many universities now are paying for programs through a similar percentage allocation of instructional funds.

Evaluation

While attempts have been made to classify the various kinds of university programs to improve teaching, no systematic guidelines exist which relate program elements to impact. Bruce Francis has suggested a three-stage sequence of program functions which suggests evaluation foci (see Figure Two), but few centers have a comprehensive plan for evaluating such functions. (43) Yet evidence of impact has a direct relationship to future funding. Higher education may not be able to afford in the future shotgun approaches to the improvement of teaching. The more we know about the effectiveness of strategies and techniques under specified conditions, the more we will be able to conserve resources and at the same time accomplish our objectives.

James McMillan points out that making decisions about alternatives requires useful information which only evaluation can provide. In the context of instructional development these decisions involve both process (the ongoing methods of the agency) and product (impact and accomplishment of objectives). Each calls for different evaluation strategies and data gathering techniques. (74) Much can be learned about evaluating effective teaching from a study of the literature on job analysis. For example, the Critical Incident technique which uses factual descriptions of instances of job related behaviors characteristic of effective and ineffective workers is a useful tool for identifying those behaviors which contribute to success in teaching. (42) The ideal evaluation plan is one which treats change or reform as an experiment which has methodological rigor built into the process of reform. (13) An excellent discussion of evaluation components in instructional development programs is contained in a publication authored by faculty and staff at Syracuse University. (33)

Personal Reflections

The experiences which accumulate as any program grows are, of course, not the same for everyone. Both the context, the faculty and the program staff produce a different mix of elements which uniquely influences the outcomes. Some heuristic hindsights seem to have validity, however, as cautions for those who might venture into the unknown. The following represent the answers to the question, "How would we have done it differently?" for one program in which I have been involved for the past eight years.

At the beginning insist on a contribution of university funding along with outside support rather than starting with a budget which is totally from "soft dollars." Most seed money grants obligate the university to "pick-up" funding at a time several years removed from the initial start-up grant. Much can happen to the fiscal affairs of a university in a three- or four-year span. The best intended obligations at the beginning can become obsolete quite rapidly in the present economic climate of higher education. Matching funding from the beginning allows the university to spread out

Figure Two

Program Elements	Stage One Consciousness Raising	Stage Two Focal Awareness	Stage Three Subsidiary Awareness
Speeches Conferences Workshops Materials	Use of nationally-known speakers Large-scale conferences Discussion of importance of and need for instructional improvement Discussion of controversial issues in faculty development	Workshops on specific teaching practices and skills Micro-teaching to diagnose and discuss individual weaknesses Observation by and consultation with master teachers Workshops to develop evaluation techniques and devices	Workshop to train faculty as consultants Weekly or monthly seminars on teaching Libraries of periodic publications on teaching and higher education Annual faculty retreats, summer institutes
Evaluations of Instruction	Questionnaires on individual goals and faculty development Student-run evaluation programs Pilot projects to test reactions and general interest Results which are confidential and experimental	Diagnostic evaluation devices Tests of faculty reaction to specific item content and wording Statistical analyses to validate and standardize procedures Trials of new evaluation devices, administration systems, and feedback procedures	Diagnostic devices primary but appropriate for personnel purposes accepted Reliable, efficient collection, processing, and feedback procedures established Student Evaluations used as ONE among several inputs
Policy, Program and System Changes	Establish position of Dean for Instructional Improvement Faculty-Senate resolutions on teaching effectiveness Funding of studies of evaluation and new instructional systems Funding of conferences on instructional improvement Funding of master-teacher awards	Provision of outside consultation services to faculty Provision of grants to improve teaching for individuals or groups Testing of alternate instructional systems Testing of alternate reward systems for teaching improvement	Establishment of developmental contracts for faculty Establsihment of moderate teaching awards for large numbers of faculty Acceptance of teaching improvement as grounds for sabbaticals, promotion, and tenure

*Francis, J. Bruce, "How Do We Get There from Here? Program Design for Faculty Development," *Journal of Higher Education* 46(6), 1975, 728.

its obligation over a longer period of time, and it gives the program a greater sense of security for developing long range plans for efforts within the institution.

A strategy of starting with faculty members who are already "winners" may be the shortest road to credibility, but it too often leads to a commitment of all staff time to making the good better, rather than to helping the poor and mediocre become good. Some time at the outset should go to the faculty member who seems to have consistent problems in the classroom. The trick is to develop credibility and at the same time begin to work quietly with those cases which are the difficult challenges, but in a way which does not overshadow what staff is doing "up front." Programs should be developmental, but remedial needs should not be ignored.

Faculty development programs all too often begin by trying to do too much. The temptation to be "all things to all faculty" is very much with any program in its beginning stages of development. The belief that by chasing all "rabbits" one will catch a few is a deceptive strategy when one considers the amount of effort spent in chasing those that should have been recognized as elusive, or in catching those that might better be ignored. A selected and well planned set of beginning initiatives lays the groundwork for expansion at a later time, especially if staff are engaged in on-the-job training. Being able to say "no" to faculty requests at the outset is preferable to stimulating expectations for a wide range of program efforts which have to be retrenched selectively at a later time because of overcommitment of staff time.

The best time to think about evaluation is before you begin whatever it is that needs to be evaluated. Evaluation strategies are too frequently initiated after the fact of an event, thus robbing the program of valuable information which, with a little foresight, could have been obtained with minimum efforts. One staff person should be charged with the responsibility of being the evaluation "conscience" of the program. The value of videotaping segments of program elements in order to recapture critical incidents for evaluation and analysis at a later time should not be ignored. Both videotape and voice recording can be helpful in this respect, but their use must result from advance planning.

Attempting to initiate a faculty development program in a university with part-time staff is difficult at best. Sustaining the initial successes with part-time staff is attempting the impossible. If one's time is split between traditional faculty responsibilities and innovation, then some responsibilities are usually shortchanged at the expense of the others (or the staff person works full-time at two jobs, probably doing neither well). Full-time commitment is essential for quality. If program staff are themselves faculty members, one solution is to rotate staff from program involvement to regular faculty responsibilities on a three- or four-year cycle. This maximizes faculty involvement in program activities, provides an opportunity for new thinking to be applied, and eventually provides a nucleus of faculty who are responsive to faculty development needs "out there."

Those professionals who make a career of faculty development programs must ever be mindful of the continually changing nature of the constituency which programs are designed to serve. Any program which is over ten years old is now relating to many faculty who were not at the institution when the program was initiated. If this constituency is being ignored, then the program has identified with a subset of faculty and has maintained this identity by relating only to these who were the initial recipients of the program efforts. This, of course, is a group which gets smaller every year. A ten-year difference in both the chronological and career age of a faculty member can be responsible for significant value differences. Program directors and staff must constantly be alert to listening to *all* faculty for clues about faculty development needs. Initial success tends to encourage staff to hold on to that which was successful. This applies to programs as well as faculty. The discovery that informants are no longer informing us about the real world of the faculty is but one bit of evidence that success can be as dangerous as failure. Both can alienate faculty development programs from the community to be served. The only difference is that the failure is perhaps more immediate.

Involving undergraduates from the beginning, both in the planning of center programs and in implementing activities, should have high priority. Undergraduates are the direct beneficiaries of whatever improvements in teaching the center can initiate; they certainly should have a voice in the direction of these improvements. Including undergraduates in planning functions not only keeps lines of communication open to an important constituency, but also provides an opportunity for the center to educate students about the process of learning. Undergraduates can be actively involved in a number of ways. Students can be included on advisory committees. They can be asked to participate in planning groups to develop strategies for specific improvement activities. They can be used as informants about problems in educational programs. If the student government on a campus is organized into task forces, those students who are concerned with academic issues and educational problems would be likely candidates to include on center committees.

One reason some center staff resist the inclusion of students in planning and evaluation is that students are a transient population and staff must spend time in helping students "rediscover the wheel." As soon as one group of students is trained to understand the mission of the center, they graduate and a naive group comes in which requires the same initiation. Center staff should accept this responsibility willingly, since student involvement is as much for the educational benefit of the students as it is for increasing the effectiveness of programs. Center staff should never lose sight of their educational responsibilities. They are themselves teachers as much as they are agents for helping others improve their teaching. One major problem in the organization of centers is that staff become distant from students and lose their sensitivity to the constantly evolving changes in values and attitudes which students have about themselves and their education. To think that students today are like they were in the late 1960's and early 1970's is to court disaster in educational planning. Staff must be kept consistently in touch with the consumers of our efforts.

When centers are first established, the tendency is to start with programs which improve the educational functions of the university outside the center. Such terms as "service function," "stimulate improvement," "react to faculty needs," and "support departmental planning" all suggest a posture which makes the center stand apart from active participation in the education offered by the university. Professional staff in the center should teach; the center profits if this teaching can be offered by the center and in its own facilities. Some centers offer courses for graduate students; very few, if any, offer courses for undergraduates which help them become more enlightened consumers of the education which the university provides for them. Such a course might involve an introduction to the idea of the university, how to evaluate the quality of education, what to look for in a good course, what is "the liberal arts," how to take advantage of what a university has to offer, and how to begin planning a career. Guest lectures and consultants are quite useful for such a course. The initial plans for a center ought to include a mechanism for offering courses for credit through an approved unit of the university or the center should be approved by the appropriate university authorities for offering a curriculum through its own organization. Such approval usually guarantees that professional staff who teach these courses will have appropriate academic credentials and parity with faculty in academic departments.

Place more emphasis on instructional development at the beginning of planning. Starting a center requires that some assessment of faculty needs serve as a basis for program development. If one starts with the needs of the liberal arts faculty, the need to "play down" instructional development soon becomes apparent. As time passes one learns that many of the questions which finally get asked are related to instructional design problems. By the time this subtlety is diagnosed, staff positions may be committed to persons who are effective with faculty in helping them identify problems and becoming aware of values and attitudes which relate to these problems but who have no specific design skills for seeking practical solutions. One staff person, from the beginning, should be a practical, hands-on-hardware-design specialist who is more concerned with the mechanics of the teaching-learning alliance in specific courses than with the beliefs, values and attitudes of the faculty member.

5

Staff Development for the Community College

by Chester Case

Chet Case has had a wide variety of teaching and administrative experiences at the high school, community college and university levels. His undergraduate degree in history is from Reed College, and he also has an M.A. in history from the University of California-Berkeley. His Ph.D. in higher education also is from Berkeley, where he later served as a supervisor of teacher education. He presently is Professional Development Facilitator at Los Medanos College and has been active on the west coast as well as nationally in helping establish staff development programs. In perhaps the best way to learn just what a professional development facilitator does, several interns per semester work directly with Chet on the Los Medanos campus.

In Chapter Five, Case discusses the virtues of a teaching improvement program unit and officer. He also argues the importance of a staff development "curriculum" which aids not only continuing faculty but new faculty, part-time faculty, administrators and classified staff. Chet offers a number of suggestions for designing such programs, and many of these tips once again are as pertinent in universities as they are in community colleges.

Introduction*

If one looked no further than the public pronouncements of prestigious community college bodies — and the hopes pinned in rhetoric by movement spokespersons to staff development — surely the conclusion would be that the community college is a veritable snug harbor for staff development. The American Association of Community and Junior Colleges in 1973 pronounced staff development "top priority." Staff development was heralded as a means by which community colleges could respond to the heavy demands brought by the advent of "new students," changes in instructional technologies, and the pressing need for institutional resilience. To foster staff development on a national basis, the AACJC in 1976 lent its support to the development of a national network of community college staff development persons. This nation-wide project was headed by Dr. Carol Zion of Miami-Dade Community College, a long-time pioneer in community college staff development. She was assisted by eight community college staff development specialists, serving as regional co-directors. This work culminated at a national conference in October, 1977. There, staff development persons from community colleges across the country created the Council for Staff, Program, and Organizational Development. Roland Terrell, Director of Staff Development for Florida Junior College, was elected as the first President.

Further evidence of the kind of role staff development can play in community college affairs is found in the five-year plan proposed in 1977 for California's community colleges by the state-wide Board of Governors. Staff development is mentioned in the plan's back-up position papers as a means to attain goals such as basic skills in education, mastery learning, reaching the "non-traditional student," delivering counseling services, multi-cultural teaching and learning, to mention several. One position paper proposed staff development as an end in itself, advocating that statewide resources be brought to bear to "develop developers" for local campuses. (15)

There are a number of aspects to the community college which support the concept of staff development. The community college is self-

*My colleagues at Los Medanos College, particularly Charles C. Collins and John I. Carhart, have been wise counselors and keen thinkers and are very much represented in these pages. I wish to thank them, staff development colleagues throughout the nation, and especially Thelma J. Scott of Los Medanos College who bore the brunt of the research and did the case studies.

consciously, and by design, a teaching institution. This is the premiere aspect favorable to staff development. If an institution proclaims its distinction to be excellence in teaching, then it follows that efforts to sustain excellence will be compatible with institutional aspirations. Faculty are not expected to do university-type research and are spared the rigors of the "publish or perish" regimen, but they are expected to teach well.

Another favorable attribute stems from the relative newness of community colleges as institutions. They have recently arrived on the post-secondary scene and their increase has been rapid. There is a vigorous, continuing dialogue on goals, philosophy, mission and proper design. Many institutions have, in effect, created their own goals and mission, remain self-conscious in their efforts to fulfill their institutional aspirations and perceive in staff development a means to do it.

In contrast to the modern multiversity with its diffusion of authority and the liberal arts college with its traditions of faculty governance counter-poised against administration, the community college, generally speaking, has a greater degree of centralization of control. Hence, the essential element for successful staff development programming is more accessible: the backing of the organization's authority system, and that which flows from the backing, the allocation of adequate resources.

Certain aspects of the community colleges' operation virtually mandate staff development — and this is a factor favorable to staff development activities. For instance, employment of technical specialists from commerce, industry and the professions as part-time instructors in the vocational programs that constitute so large a proportion of the instructional programs, forces the issue of training in basic techniques of instruction. Despite the large and growing ranks of part-time instructors new to community college teaching, too few colleges have progressed as far as Portland (Oregon) Community College and Burlington Community College (New Jersey) in initiating programs for the training of new, part-time instructors in curriculum development and instructional strategies.

This is by no means an exhaustive list of favorable factors, but it should suffice to point up the compatibility of the concept of staff development with the institutional characteristics, ideology and practices of the community college. At least these are the way things *should* be, given the ideals of the community college. Yet, there are relatively few fullscale programs in operation. In conducting a doctoral study of staff development, Don Bass asked a jury of persons knowledgeable in the field to identify community college programs. He told me only some 50 were so identified, which is a small number considering the total of community colleges in the United States and Canada. (5) There are some exemplary programs, and Terry O'Banion describes them in a book called, *Programs that Work.* (89) My own program is fully presented in *Professional Staff Development: A Community College Model.* (14) Reports of three colleges' staff development efforts are included in Appendix C. I am not claiming that these three are representative or exemplar; they are simply examples of staff development efforts at varying stages of development, in different settings, with differing patterns of organization and emphases. Geography was a factor in selection. All three are Northern California colleges, relatively near Los Medanos College and thereby accessible for visiting. The reader should find these brief reports a helpful counterpoint to the generalizations made in this chapter.

Still, these programs represent positive action in a small minority of community colleges. Why so few programs? Apparently there are formidable unfavorable forces capable of nullifying the favorable aspects of staff development.

Unfavorable Factors in the Community College Setting

The community college's proud myth of teaching excellence bears within it a factor unfavorable to staff development. This factor is revealed in the logic of an instructor's comment to me at a staff development planning workshop, "If staff development is to make me an excellent teacher, and I am already an excellent teacher, then I don't need development." Unfortunately development can take on a negative, almost remedial, connotation and arouse potent resistance from erstwhile clientele. When it is imposed on clientele in what amounts to an affront to competence and professionalism, it can become what Sue Brock, coordinator of Faculty Development at St. Mary's Junior College in Minneapolis, deplores as the "We have it; you need it" approach.

The history of staff development on any campus is extremely important. What has happened before — successes and/or failures — will have an important bearing on what follows. Any staff development effort is sorely handicapped by a legacy of unsuccessful projects designed as answers to such monumental problems as declining enrollments, elevation of the morale of a whole staff, the setting and embracement of a new set of institutional goals, the introduction of a new (and probably expensive) instructional technology. Unfortunately, a number of colleges have prejudiced potential clientele against broad scale staff development by ill-conceived, manipulative staff development efforts.

Another unfavorable factor is the belief that staff development is expensive, that it drains away scarce resources far out of proportion to benefits accrued and that it requires a massive apparatus of personnel and shifts in the organizational structure. This is a way of saying that there is not yet available a conclusive, persuasive way to verify the value return to the college of investment in staff development efforts. Still, unfavorable aspects at any given college may well be only those basic "givens" of complex organizations: resistance to change, competition for resources, and prior commitments — as well as misunderstandings, aversions, and animosities (real and imagined).

Local Readiness for Staff Development

How can we determine the readiness of our particular college for staff development? I would ask the following sets of questions:

Authority: Who has the authority? (Take into account both the formal and the informal authority system.) Is there any base of authority that could champion a staff development program and "shelter it"? Who can say "yes" or "no" to requests for money? What bases have to be touched to get FTE's for staff development work? Who could veto a project? Who on campus could influence opinion, pro cr con, on a subject? What has collective bargaining brought into the picture? Is faculty development a faculty right?

Resources: What is available in terms of local expertness for the implementation of staff development? What is available in terms of money, released time, energy from faculty and administrators? What is available in the form of support services, technological assistance, equipment and materials?

History: What already has happened at the institution in respect to staff development? Have there already beene needs identified and met with one or more programs? What was the "image" and the aftertaste of previous staff development activities?

At what stage is the institution in its development? Is it at the beginning? Is it "stagnating"?

Is it seeking renewal? What has been the record of innovations at the institution? What is the receptivity to innovation and change?

Institutional goals and Commitments: Are the goals and commitments of the institution articulated? Are they widely known? Are they shared? Are they capable of moving people to action? Are they binding? Are they in process of change? How closely does the formal match the informal?

Social System: In the social system of the college, what norms exist that might support participation in staff development? What incentives work? How do people earn prestige and status?

This line of inquiry can be conducted as a variant on the notion of "action research" discussed by Lindquist and Buhl. It yields a kind of snapshot of the institution, a status report on "how things are." From this base of knowledge, the next step can be launched. The next step is needs assessment.

Needs Assessment

From needs — individual and institutional — derive goals. Goals are translated into objectives and program activities. Programming hinges on needs assessment, and thus the process requires a good deal of attention.

How can institutional and individual needs be ascertained? In the jargon of today, they can be ascertained by the application of "needs assessment" techniques. Varieties of these techniques can be sorted into categories of naturalistic, survey, and deductive. The staff development person ought to study these approaches and then put together a combination that works for his specific college. I lean toward an eclectic approach in needs assessment, not ruling out any useful approach. I do recommend, though, that there be a central person in the process of assessing needs, preferably the staff development person.

The naturalistic needs assessment approach operates on the assumption that individuals know what they need and, given the opportunity, will express and act on those needs. Thus, the strength and extent of needs are, in effect, assessed and accommodated at the same time by an invitation to faculty to apply for incentive grants for self-designed projects — or college personnel are invited to design personal growth plans. Still another variation is incorporated in De Anza College's management development program. Individual managers maintain a vita which expresses the needs of the individual in terms of career development. In aggregate, the needs of individuals are taken to be institutional needs. On the basis of individual needs, program activities are designed. Also, individuals set goals to be attained by individual means. This process meshes with the management evaluation process. It is expected that individual managers will "read" institutional needs and taken them on as individual needs.

Survey needs assessment is essentially a market survey. An instrument, open-ended or forced-choice, is administered to a prospective clientele. Respondents are presumed to know their own needs, which are inferred from the choices and/or rankings made among proposed activities. This approach is widely used and many effective instruments have been developed. (8) One problem with this survey approach is that it tells what respondents like, but does not tell what they will actually commit themselves to do. Another problem is that institutional needs are not assessed directly but only inferred from aggregated individual choices.

Deductive needs assessment calls for the deduction of needs. In this approach, more than others, the work of a careful and sensitive analyst is required. One type of deductive assessment might be called a "discrepancy approach." The goals of the college, its mission and its commitments to what *should be* are compared to describing *what is*. Needs are revealed in the discrepancies between *what is* and *what should be*. Available documents (goals amd mission statements, accreditation reports, or study-committee findings and surveys) are useful sources of information. One well-conceived and sophisticated survey instrument for measuring this kind of discrepancy is available in the *Institutional Goals Inventory* developed by the Educational Testing Service. (61)

Staff development needs can be deduced as well from the theory and experience related to the developmental patterns of adults in general — and college personnel in particular. An illustration of this can be drawn from the Los Medanos College experience with the new-faculty program. Successive annual groups of new faculty displayed what might be termed a "migration of need" during the course of the year-long program. The three-stage migration was as follows: 1) immediate, here-and-now entry needs, 2) needs for role taking, consideration, self-appraisal, and 3) needs to explore philosophies, values and practices of education, both personal and institutional. *A priori* program planning, however, posited an early need to examine philosophical issues. When this proved to be in error, program changes were made to better synchronize program content and participant need.

Another variation of this approach to needs assessment is to deduce needs from assumptions about the needs of humans in organization settings in general and community college settings in particular. For instance, persons new to a demanding role, such as instructor or division chairperson, need a humane and intentional socialization process. Mid-career faculty professionals need stimulation and affirmation of worth. Humans in organizations need to participate in decision making and formulation of policy that affect them in their work. As the several examples show, assumptions are laced with value assertions.

The survey approach to needs assessment program planning follows verification of need, thus building in a high probability of program acceptance. In the deductive approach, program planning follows *presumed* need, thus courting risk of non-acceptance. Basically, deductive approaches are more prescriptive and replete with value judgments; hence more risky. Someone, well supplied with data, intellectually honest, skillful in analysis, and sensitive to the institutional setting and the community, hazards a conclusion, "What this college needs is . . ."

Sooner or later, it seems to me, a mature staff development program will lean heavily on deductive needs assessments. It is because of this I recommend that the staff development person become a close and sensitive observer of his college — that he becomes, in effect, an instrument of needs assessment. It takes an accumulation of knowledge, skills and experience to be able to walk the tightrope between felt need and prescription — and to come up with program activities that mesh institutional and individual needs, that are well accepted, and that show a satisfactory payoff.

In my own case, for instance, I have come to view staff development for community colleges as not just "instructional development" or "faculty development," although these activities are important. It is beginning to address the development needs of five somewhat distinctive clientele: 1) new faculty (few in number these days, but ever present and very strategic for development activities), 2) experienced faculty (a large and perhaps the central group), 3) part-time faculty (a clientele in great need and eager for attention) 4) management (a relatively compact and definable clientele with a built-in need and an acceptance of development activities in the realm of management skills) and 5) classified staff (the secretarial and business personnel, paraprofessionals and technicians, buildings and grounds workers — next to part-timers, the most overlooked but also potentially receptive and appreciative group). Three other potential clientele, heretofore largely uncultivated, easily could be added: students, governing boards and advisory committees.

I think it is wise to think in terms of inclusive staff development, covering at least the five major clientele, for each group can promote the learning opportunities of students. The clerk at the registrar's window, the maintenance person supervising work-study students, the financial aids director interviewing students, and the faculty member in the classroom all are part of the community college's opportunity to help students learn. Although I will not address staff development services for each client in this chapter (another publication tackles that assignment), (15a) I hope you keep this conception of total staff development in mind.

Very broadly, in the community college as in complex organizations in general, staff development aims at two sets of goals that are mutually supporting but separable: 1) goals oriented toward the "product" of the college; that is, relating to the learning opportunities for students, and 2) goals oriented toward the work force; that is, toward maintaining and advancing the ability of the work force to perform necessary work.

Some Approaches to Selecting Needs

As a staff development person, how do you go about choosing from among the needs of your institution those for programmatic attention? Establishing priorities and setting sequences is a complex business that blends pragmatics and theory. My recommendation for this business is to think big, but start small. Think of the program as extending over time, with room to take up needs in sequence. Make a kind of grand design with the whole institution as the arena, but let the design be flexible. And in the meantime, be very pragmatic. The beginning program should especially go after needs that translate well into staff development goals and interesting program activities. The pragmatic touch here is to select needs that are valid and can be acted upon with a high degree of potential success. In staff development, success breeds success; the ripple effect is the very best way to transmit good news.

Several of the basic needs facing all community colleges can be translated into low-risk, high-payoff program activities. A beginning program might well address one or more of the following needs:

1. The need for new faculty, full and part-time, to be oriented to the college.
2. The need for instructors new to community college teaching to be "inducted" into their new profession.
3. The need of experienced faculty to relate to one another across teaching fields on matters of educational concern.
4. The need for classified staff to increase their skills in interpersonal relations, problem solving and conflict-management.
5. The need for management to explore techniques for time management.
6. The need to familiarize personnel with support services.

Carol Zion combines theory and pragmatics in what she refers to as the "shoe pinch" approach to needs selection; where the shoe pinches, it hurts — and that is where the need exists. The veteran staff development person will keep a steady lookout for "shoe pinching" but will also move the program steadily along in accordance with the evolving, long-range and large-scale needs of the institution and its personnel — as Zion and her associates have done over the years at her college. Program activities at Miami-Dade have addressed needs in areas of curriculum development, communications, interpersonal relations, orientation of classified staff— just to mention a few. Currently, the program is dealing with needs related to organizational role clarifications and management skills development. Among the ongoing staff development needs likely to be met by mature programs such as Miami-Dade's may be mentioned the following:

1. The need for mid-career counseling and planning, with options for re-training in teaching areas and strategies.
2. The need to review and re-appraise institutional purposes.
3. The need to respond to institutional changes brought by demographic shifts in the attendance.
4. The need to update curriculum and instruction.
5. The need to counteract alienation and fragmentation.
6. The need to provide for career paths for classified staff.

I have said a great deal about needs and their relationship to staff development because I think too little is usually said. Goals derive from needs; needs breed goals. Goals indicate what a program activity *intends* to do; needs have to do with *why* the program is being conducted. I recommend a heavy investment of time and energy in needs assessment at the outset of a program and a continuing attention to needs assessment during the on-going program.

Viewpoint in Staff Development

Viewpoint is a combination of such aspects as definitions, theory, values, opinions, premises and manifestoes of "the way it ought to be." Program viewpoint is more the spirit than the letter of the program. Shaping program viewpoint are a number of converging influences including the "givens" of the program's charter, values indigenous, administrative and faculty persuasions, the college's organizational climate, and not the least, the personal values, skills and professional stances of the program's staff. In an important way, viewpoint shapes how staff development will be conducted in respect to mood, tone and commitments.

Parts of the viewpoint are tangible — as in the statement of purpose and goals of the program. Other parts are less concrete and have to do with the tone or spirit of the program. The tenor of a program might be instrumental and tightly focused, for instance, on the implementation of a particular instructional strategy. Or it may have the humanistic flavor, slanted toward personal development and the realization of human potential.

A staff development person needs to be very concerned with program viewpoint. All activities occur in the context of the viewpoint and, spoken or not, the viewpoint is prologue to whatever activities are mounted. The sounder the viewpoint, the richer it is in theory and experience, the more informed and realistic it is for the institutional setting, the more elevated the program will be and more likely to become an on-going function of the college.

Viewpoint is expressed when premises are articulated. The premises from which De Anza College derived its overall staff development program are that the staff should:

1. be responsible to the comprehensive needs of the staff;
2. assess needs of staff prior to creating in-service activities;
3. place emphasis on personalization, individualization, and more active participation of the college's total personnel; and
4. make maximum use of a diversity of training and support activities and resources.

At Los Medanos College, an "Improvement of Instruction" plan for experienced faculty was developed. The plan featured the design by the individual instructor, in concert with colleagues, of a personal professional growth plan. The plan begins with this statement which reflects program viewpoint:

1. Professional and personal development is a career-long process. This is natural and desirable. Across a career in education, a person's interests, needs, and goals will evolve in patterns that are partly unique to the individual and partly common to other professionals. A basic intent of this improvement of instruction plan is to provide a means by which the college and its resources may facilitate the attainment by the educator of a worthwhile professional and personal goal at whatever point in a career she may be.

2. Individual differences among educators are a strength and a valued resource to the college. Because of individual differences among educators as individuals, and because any one educator in a career will have changing goals, the improvement of instruction plan must be flexible and be capable of offering options for individualization.
3. An adequate plan for the improvement of instruction requires adequate support. Necessary for the operation of an effective program for the improvement of instruction is the commitment by the college of resources in terms of personnel, funding, incentives and governance.
4. The improvement of instruction plan is an integral component in the college-wide, comprehensive program in staff and program development. The improvement of instruction plan set forth here assumes the existence of a broad program serving the faculty, staff, and administrators of the college.
5. All educators are potential participants in the improvement of instruction plan. The plan should be broad and inclusive and should offer opportunities for development to faculty members and administrators other than those regular faculty members who must meet the biennial requirement for evaluation and participation in improvement of instruction.

As a program evolves, certain problems in definition will be encountered. One troublesome definition is that of "Development" as distinguished from normal professional work. This can be a key distinction, particularly when the issue involves policy or contract stipulations on personnel rights and/or obligations. Everything the professional does is not development. But where to draw the line? An attempt was made to make distinctions between varieties of professional work in an individual project plan for new faculty at Los Medanos College. Here is a portion of the plan:

> As to focus, the project should have to do with professional development. But, what is professional development? The concept is hard to pin down. It needs to be defined in a larger context. The project should not be some workaday professional activity, nor should it be an activity undertaken to maintain professional competencies. In the preceding sentence, three overlapping zones are implied. Sketched out and fitted with examples, these zones illustrate the continuum inhering in professional activity from I. Workaday, to II. Maintaining, to III, Development.

Schematically, this is:

Professional Activity	Workaday	Maintaining	Development
Evaluation of student work	Scoring and grading student papers	Item analysis and renovation of an objective exam	Investigating the implications of Mastery of Learning
Instructional strategy; leading discussions	Preparing discussion topics and leading discussions	Recording a discussion (audio or video for analysis) of teacher-learner verbal interaction	Designing and initiating a discussion series based on small group dynamics
Curriculum Development: Independent learning	Setting up and conducting conferences to help leaners define objectives	Evaluating systems for keeping track of individual projects	Researching the psycho-social concommitants of independent learning

Structure

Staff development needs a structural framework to give it organizational coherence, continuity, accountability and longevity. There are several ways to structure staff development, ranging from the virtual nonstructure of the *ad hoc*, episodic approach to the institutionalized program.

An Argument for Program Status

My own preference is for the institutionalized program. Most colleges, however, do not have a staff development program *per se*. They have an aggregation of activities, some as venerable as the sabbatical leave and the fall orientation session, as well as the familiar one-shot guest speaker, workshops, seminars, incentive grants for innovation and the like. Some colleges have persons or committees that do staff development work but not within a framework of a program. In common practice, the term program is used loosely.

There are advantages of the program approach to staff development, such as the visibility and durability the program acquires. By being visible, the program becomes testimony to the college's commitment to development. The program has a much better chance of merging, over time, into the regular operations of the college or becoming a part of the expected and predictable institutional environment. Also, a program can be evaluated because it has stated purposes, implements activities and has outcomes. Because a program has a propensity to perpetuate itself, it will provide a basis for both long-range and short-range planning. The program basis supplies a way for dealing with the inevitable (and desirable) necessity of providing for a succession of staff development goals.

The advantages do not altogether cancel out the disadvantages. In some circumstances the program approach probably would not be the best way to proceed. Instituting a program in some colleges could be a major undertaking which would lead into political thickets from whence staff development might never emerge. It could be just too big a step to take at one time to line up key persons, find resources, set up and staff key roles and intrude upon the accustomed "ways of doing things." Also, it could be a disadvantage from the viewpoint of misdirecting scarce and provisional early energies into a lot of work on what to do, rather than doing.

Organizational Patterns and Linkages

One organizational pattern for staff development is event-centered. This is inescapably episodic in nature and provides little basis for systematic planning and program building. Typically, an administrator or faculty member or a committee would be assigned the responsibility for putting together the event, such as a guest speaker, a workshop, or a retreat or convocation. This approach can work well for an occasional, well-placed event. It has a property of self-renewal, since it starts *de novo* with each event. Moreover, costs are low; but the lack of continuity, fragmentation of efforts and lack of accountability are serious handicaps for any serious staff development effort.

A staff development effort on a given campus takes a giant step beyond the *ad hoc*, episodic event centered approach when it is accorded program status and is ensconsed in an organizational unit well articulated with the college's process of planning, budgeting, accountability and decision making. My preference is for the position-based organizational unit, for it has the advantage of having a direct line to the president and a role that is clearly staff, not line. An advisory committee can work closely with the staff development facilitator and can, on many occasions, take on functions in the program such as seminar leader, peer evaluator, coordinator and the like. Yet, structural arrangements, such as the position-based pattern, should not contrive to so specialize and isolate staff development that the sense of clientele "ownership" is dampened. "Ownership" as discussed elsewhere is a vital ingredient for program vitality. Yet there is a practical limit to ownership — and that is at the point at which the staff development facilitator's professional functions and discretion are impaired by too tight a control by a clientele or committee.

Staffing

The basic issue in staffing development is to provide for the delivery of staff development facilitator position as the pivot for staff development for this, but I advocate the establishment of a full-time, well-supported, staff-development facilitator position as the pivot for staff development efforts. There are advantages and disadvantages to this approach. Among the disadvantages are: cost of salary, problems of justifying the position, the danger of the program becoming a one-person show bearing all the limitations and quirks of the leader, difficulty of finding a qualified person and disruptions to routines.

But, in my opinion, advantages overwhelmingly outweigh the disadvantages. Since the position is full-time, stable and has a future, the person in the position has a reasonable time period to sharpen and acquire necessary competencies. Having a familiar person in an accepted office helps personify the program, which heightens program visibility and opens up accessibility to potential clients.

Some considerable preparation is necessary to become proficient in staff development work. Staff development is becoming a professional specialty with an emerging, though eclectic, body of knowledge and skills, role attributes and normative strictures of its own. To motivate persons to undertake the necessary preparation, there needs to be some tangible payoff, such as the prospect of a full-time position with some reasonable assurances of longevity.

If you were to ask me how to test a college's readiness for a really serious staff development program, I would respond, "Find out how ready and willing the college is to making a serious commitment to a workable staff development position." Can the funds be found? Can the potential value returns to the college of the costs of the position be visualized (and found to be good)? Can the organizational structure accommodate the sure-to-follow activities of the incumbent? Are the personalities and styles of key managers and influential faculty compatible with the operation and impact of the position?

In my own experience as Professional Development Facilitator at Los Medanos College, the following attributes of the position have proven to be of great value in rendering the work of the staff development possible.

1. It is full-time.
2. It bears adminstrative rank, pay, prerogatives at mid-management level.
3. It is a *staff* (not line) position.
4. It reports directly to the president.
5. It is a "practitioner" position, as distinguished from a coordinator, broker-type of position.

The Work of a Staff Development Specialist

If frequent conversations with staff development colleagues from throughout the nation had not taught me that what I do is very close to what others do, I would hesitate to offer my own experience as Professional Development Facilitator at Los Medanos College as representative of the staff development facilitator's work. There are important differences, of course, stemming from background and experience, personality, values, skills and talents, and perception of the role; but there are also striking similarities.

I am sometimes asked, "Now, just *what* do you do?" Then comes the deluge. There is no end to what a person in my position can get involved in. Colleagues in similar positions corroborate my experience. A big problem is not what to do, but what not to do. Here is a list of activities sorted out by clientele and selected to depict the range of activities:

1. *Faculty:*

All faculty:	Assessment of instruction (in-class observations, surveys, consultation on curriculum design, conferencing on professional and personal issues and problems.
New faculty:	Plan, direct, and implement seminars and workshops for the Kellogg Program.
Experienced faculty:	Consult and confer on individual professional growth plans.
Part-time faculty	Orientation sessions and teaching techniques classes.

2. *Management:*	Chair Management Development Committee
	Chair weekly management meetings
	Plan and conduct informational and/or skills sessions
3. *Classified Staff:*	Plan and conduct orientation sessions, seminars, and workshops
	Consult on the development of a classified staff association
4. *Students:*	Help plan retreats, orientation and training sessions for students in governance roles.
5. *College as a Whole:*	Set up training sessions for interviewing committees.
	Write "think" pieces and working papers.
	Plan and implement curriculum development projects.
6. *The Profession:*	Participate in planning staff development conferences.
	Write papers for advocacy.
	Maintain correspondence, host visitors, disseminate materials.

At Los Medanos College, patterns have emerged that suggest the kinds of work in which a staff development person will get involved; these include planning and implementing, managing, teaching, consulting (inside the college), consulting (outside the college), conferring with individuals and participating as a citizen of the college. Some of the work is in structured situations and some is in informal situations, as the opportunity presents itself; some is with groups and some is with individuals.

There are some kinds of work that I think would compromise my position and damage credibility and trust. High on the list of this kind of work is the evaluation of personnel for promotion or retention and the adjudication of claims on release time or funds (such as travel and conference monies or innovative grants). I try to steer clear of these kinds of work, but many staff development colleagues find them a part of their duties.

Locating and Recognizing the Facilitator

Where do you find staff development persons, and how do you know one when you see one? How are staff development persons developed?

These are the key issues in staffing the staff development program. One view is that the potential supply of staff development facilitators is virtually limitless, since the essential functions of that role are so much akin to what education is all about — teaching and counseling. I agree, up to a point. There is on every college campus a cadre of persons who are potential staff development facilitators and not all are instructors or counselors; one outstanding practitioner, Karen Foss of Seattle Central Community College, is a classified staff person.

Yet, the word *potential* should be stressed. It is common practice, for instance, to draw candidates for staff development from the ranks of outstanding teachers and counselors. But that which makes for excellence in teaching and counseling is not necessarily that which makes for excellence in staff development work. Even for the most promising candidate, a transitional experience is highly advisable.

As more and more staff development specialists take to the field, patterns suggestive of desirable traits, skills and knowledge are emerging. Some suggestive insights were provided by surveys taken at two community college staff development conferences. (10) In attendance at the conferences were chief administrators (presidents and deans), faculty members, classified staff persons and staff development persons. They were asked to give their choice of desirable traits, skills and knowledge and then sort their choices into the categories of "most important," "essential" and "useful."

As might be expected, there were some variations among the responses. Yet the choices of traits did cluster around credibility, openness, trustworthiness and commitment to program and clientele. Traits considered desirable included enthusiasm, perceptiveness, practicality, acceptance, flexibility. Optimism is mentioned, along with determination and persistence, energy and non-aggressive assertiveness. As for skills and knowledge, there were again variations between responses, but a clustering again occurred. Ranking high are skills in communication, group dynamics, interpersonal relations and coordination. Mentioned, but less emphasized, were knowledge of learning theory, instructional development and research skills.

Questions on experience and background were not asked but I expect these would come up: teaching experience and experimentaion in curriculum design, instruction and evaluation (for credibility with instructors), work in group process, in developing skills in communication, in faculty organization and/or management (to get a feel for "getting things done"), and some considerable seasoning in the environment of learning institutions. Community colleges would probably hold out for community college experience, but I am not sure that it is indispensable so long as there has been varied experience in environments of learning and so long as the person is a "quick study."

In my mind's eye, I see the qualified candidate — man or woman, faculty, classified or management — as a person who is interested in and comfortable with people, something of a visionary with a good sense of reality, ready and able to work with and for others with considerable subordination of self, an optimist with strong interests in how people learn.

Developing the Staff Development Facilitator

There are two points at which the staff development facilitator can profit from transitional developmental experiences; at the point of entry to the specialization and at a "second wind" point of career. It would be highly desirable to have available an institute or center where persons chosen to be staff development specialists by their college could go for training. Except for the very few universities that offer work in staff development, or allow graduate students to do their research in staff development, there is virtually nothing available. Los Medanos College, with the support of the W.K. Kellogg Foundation, is attempting in a small way to fill this void. Beginning in Fall, 1977, the college will host three interns in staff development per semester. These persons will have been sent by their home campus to improve skills and background in staff development work and to acquire a variety of experiences. The program is designed along the lines of an internship.

Colleges employing or seeking to develop local talent as staff development specialists might want to consider the prospective curriculum of the Los Medanos College program. The fourteen-week program, which will engage the intern full time, will cover a great deal of territory, including

1. practice and mastery of the "tools of the trade," theories and practice in curriculum design and instructional strategies, analysis of instruction, group process, instruments for data collection;
2. assessing needs stating goals, program design, implementation and evaluation;
3. communication, oral and written;
4. self-awareness, values, impact on others, communication traits;
5. study of the work of a staff development specialist, expectations of

administration and clientele, deferred gratifications and lack of closure, deprivation of accustomed reference groups, marginality and loneliness;

6. consideration of professional ethics and practices, confidentiality, impartiality and equity in provision of services;
7. collection of resource banks consisting of design models, exercises, reaings, an the like; and
8. familiarization with other programs.

Staff development specialists should be their own best customers and seek to counteract two of the more troublesome effects that "go with the territory" — over-exposure and burn-out. A fact of life for the staff development facilitator is over-exposure. One knows when one is over-exposed; the bag of tricks is depleted. At this point, the specialist needs to get out into the society of other staff development people, to recycle the needs assessment procedures, to undertake a course of training — or learning — that will result in new competencies. Another option is to move to another campus, but such lateral mobility at this time is scarcely a realistic possibility given the current scarcity of staff development specialist positions.

Another fact of the staff development facilitator's life is "burn-out," when the huge energy and emotional drain of full-bore functioning depletes the reserves and fatigue sets in. Burn-out is particularly baneful as it inhibits the spontaneity, the invention, the sensitivity of perception that is necessary for proper functioning. As in the case of over-exposure, antidotes for burn-out are a change of scene, a working through of the state of things with kindred souls and a personal re-grouping of energy and focus.

Other Approaches to Staffing

There are, of course, ways to accomplish the essential work of staff development other than through a full-time facilitator. One way is to open up a partial position and fill it with a faculty person on reassigned time. Though this approach can be a practical intermediate step between no staff development person and a full-time person, it has built-in problems. One problem is the person's inevitable division of time, attentions and energy. Program scope will be constrained by the limited amount of time available for development and implementation. I know of one person in such a position, whose continual refrain is, "So much to do, so little time." Frequent turnover is likely to be the fate of such positions.

Another approach is to set up a full-time position, but rotate occupants on a yearly basis. However, too rapid rotation handicaps long-range planning and denies the incumbent a real chance of getting comfortable with the role, acquiring and sharpening skills and accumulating methods and materials. A third method is to fasten staff development responsibilities onto an existing administrative position. This approach can bring the disadvantage of moving staff development over into the realm of line administration, as well as diffusing the energies of a person already committed to other responsibilities.

It is possible that the staff development person could be elected for a given term, like an ombudsman, but the idea strikes me as inadvisable. The political process of election does not mesh well with the kinds of work expected of a staff developer. Another possibility, perhaps for a college with very limited resources, would be to contract for staff development services. Services could also be obtained through consortial arrangements or by sharing within a district. Although intensity of local aid is less possible this way and district politics can hinder effectiveness, the interinstitutional arrangement can be a catalyst and a source of continuing expertise as Lance Buhl points out in Chapter Seven.

Activities

If the staff development program can be likened to an iceberg, we have been talking about the base. We have not yet talked about the tip. The tip is program activities, highly visible and, for many people, pretty much all there is to the program. What has been talked about so far — the setting, needs assessment, structure, staffing, as well as the topics of financing and evaluation to come — are the part of the program that are fundamental and important, but much less visible. Staff development activities might include any or all of the following:

1. New Faculty
   a. Orientation seminars: familiarization to the college, exploration of the role of instructor, history and philosophy of the community college.
   b. Workshops in curriculum design (auto-tutorial, media applications, starting objectives), evaluation of student work, instructional strategies.
   c. Field trips into the community and other colleges.

2. Experienced Faculty
   a. Seminars and workshops on instructional strategies and curricular design.
   b. Assessment of instruction, in-class visits, video-taping, student reports and development of growth plans.
   c. Incentive grants for innovative projects.
   d. "Master Classes" taught by faculty to faculty in areas of special interest or competence.
3. Part-time Faculty
   a. Orientation to college goals, policy, services.
   b. Seminars on techniques of teaching.
   c. Workshops for interaction with full-time faculty.
4. Classified Staff
   a. Orientation to the community college as a place to work, familiarization with policy, personnel, facilities and services.
   b. Seminars on assertiveness, conflict resolution and problem solving, working with students and faculty.
   c. Workshops on safety procedures, equipment maintenance.
5. Management

   Orientation to management for recent arrivals, roles, expectations.

   Workshops on time management, stress management.

   Workshops on management skills, supervising, evaluating, budget development and monitoring.

   Seminars on theory and practice of governance, institutional structures and functions.

   Seminars on personal and organizational management development: analysis of expectations of positions and the fit of individuals into the positions with discrepancy, fitting plans generated.

Planning Program Activities

How do you go about planning a staff development activity? This is a frequently asked question. My strong recommendation is to plan staff development activities very much as you would plan a curriculum. The close parallel between staff development programming and curriculum development is easily overlooked; perhaps it is difficult to see colleagues and peers in the role of learner or a staff development program as a curriculum. At any rate, there are advantages to be gained by planning of activities in the way one would plan for any learning experience. For one thing, curriculum development is a process with which many educators are familiar and often good at. Another is that it can put an emphasis on positive, growth-oriented outcomes. Still more, it enables the planner to pick and use well-established techniques and conventions.

Who is to do the planning? It is desirable to have one person heading up the planning. The staff development specialist is a natural for this, but there may be instances when the task is better "sub-contracted" to someone with a particular expertise. It is a good idea in all cases to have an advisory group or at least a good sounding board. The larger the scale of the enterprise (such as a college-wide retreat) or the more potentially controversial the topic (sensitizing faculty to the needs of minority students), the better it is to have an advisory group.

Before launching into the planning, though, certain preconditions should be explored (by either the staff development person or the person charged with planning responsibility). One necessary step is to verify the need to which the activity is addressed. Another is to scout out potential obstacles. An estimate should be made of the potential participation. Thought should be given to the fit of the proposed activity into the larger design of the overall program. The availability of resources should be assessed, as well as the degree of support the activity might get from management, faculty and other influential parties.

Once the pre-conditions have been studied, the planning process might go something like this (though the steps are numbered, do not conclude that the process is linear . . . indeed, as in planning curriculum, a good deal of the planning is concurrent):

1. Given the needs to which the activity is addressed, formulate specific goals (what the activity intends to do) and begin to state objectives (what the learner should be able to do or have experienced as a result of the activity). Anticipate evaluation of both learner gain and activity effectiveness in stating goals and objectives.
2. Select the content, or substances of the activity; gather materials, equipment, supplies if necessary. Organize the content in relationship to steps 3 and 4.
3. Select an appropriate format for the activity. Anything that is an effective format for learning is a plausible candidate; lecture, discussion, small groups, experiments and demonstrations, auto-tutorials, self-paced, independent reading, field trips or any other workable format should be considered.
4. Determine the teaching/learning strategies. Anything that works is worth considering.

5. Identify and locate required resources.
6. Set a time frame for the activity and plot the logistics.
7. Plan for the evaluation of learner gain and for the evaluation of the effectiveness of the activity.

Consideration needs to be given to the differences in the "realities" as perceived by each of the five potential clientele. For instance consider how the message "the staff development workshop will meet on four successive Fridays from 3:00 to 5:00 p.m." would fall on the ears of a faculty member. "Oh, no," the faculty member might groan, "another meeting to add to my over-burdened load." A classified staff person might say, "Hey, that's fine. I could use a few hours away from my desk on a Friday afternoon."

Faculty members as participants have some interesting, and not always lovable, characteristics. They seem to prefer short-term courses, which suggests that semester-long courses will not be popular. I recall one faculty member who was teaching a course to other faculty on how to develop auto-tutorial materials, commenting, "They come late and leave early and don't do their work on time." Faculty members also frequently carry habits of correction and criticism into the program activity, and not infrequently find a group of colleagues a congenial place to unburden the frustrations of the day. Though generalizations can be made about group characteristics of clientele, you will need to assume heterogeneity within clientele, as in any other group of learners.

This leads to a consideration of the matter of participation in program activities. Unless there is some very potent regulation compelling client participation, the problem of participation is parallel to that of enticing students in an elective course and keeping them there. The staff development person should be prepared to pull out all the stops in applying all she knows and can find out about making a program as attractive as possible.

Finding workable incentives — or "motivating the learner" — is difficult. The problem is made all the more difficult by the prevalence and persistence of dis-incentives working against participation (such as the self-concept of many instructors that they are overworked and have no time or energy to spare, or the belief that development is, after all, an everyday activity consummated in the act of teaching).

Tangible incentives that work are unit credits for participation, monetary compensation, credit toward salary advances, and/or promotion and reassigned time. Less tangible incentives include the promise of the mastery of new skills, knowledge that will succeed in the classroom, the personal rewards of "breaking out of a rut" and the challenge of new knowledge and relationships. Still another incentive is to be found in policies requiring minimum standards of participation. The incentive I seek is the internalized expectation of every professional that development and growth are an expected and normal part of professional life — and that this norm will be supported by the resources of the institution so that development activities are not an "add-on" but an integral part of professional functioning.

Logistics require careful attention. Publicity should go out well in advance and have a follow-up reminder. Personal contracts should be made to ensure an adequate participation for group-based activities. Sign-up coupons to return are a good way to get a participant to signal a commitment. The activity should be held in a comfortable, accessible place, with amenities, such as refreshments, available whenever possible.

Building a Program

Think big, but start small. I strongly recommend an additive, incremental approach to program building. Staff development should start with a long-range view of some future time when a full-scale program might be in operation. But at the outset, it is best to mount small-scale activities carefully selected for the significance of the need addressed, and potential for successful implementation.

As programs across the country build their own histories, there are patterns emerging. One such pattern suggests program "life stages." There appear to be three stages. The first is the starting up stage. The second is the maintaining, or operational stage, when the initial program activities are in place and working. The third stage is regeneration, when the program recycles the needs assessment process and supplements or provides for the succession of the original goals. The third stage is the stage of program maturity.

A mature community college staff development program resembles a mosaic; seemingly disparate and discrete elements will, when viewed from a proper perspective, merge to form a unified picture. The mosaic will depict activities in the process of winding down, those that are in the planning stage, and those that are in full operation.

Financing

The question of financing staff development is the blockbuster question for many colleges; the query, "Where is the money?" will too often bring the doleful response, "There is none." Though finding financing for staff development is difficult, it is not impossible. Staff development does not cost as much as it would seem and, in many cases, much of staff development is already budgeted for. Furthermore, there are ways of paying back program expenses. Little cost is incurred when existing organizational arrangements are realigned to provide for the establishment of a staff development position.

This is not to minimize the difficulties involved in financing staff development. "Costing-out" a program is difficult, finding sources to defray program costs is difficult, justifying the costs in terms of value returns to the institution is difficult. In these times of financial stringency and the steady state, it is difficult to secure funds for staff development. A big part of the problem in getting staff development funds is that staff development is not perceived as a central, essential function of the college and thus entitled to parity in the allocation of "hard" money. The problem lies largely in the consciousness of those who manage the budgeting process; for staff development to get a fair share, it must be perceived as a valued operation whose costs are justifiable.

Wide and Narrow Budgets

There is no standard way to set up a staff development budget. Examples of different ways are to be found in other parts of this sourcebook. It is useful, however, to consider two approaches: the wide budget approach and the narrow budget approach. (See Figure Two.)

In the former approach, all expenditures related to staff development are rounded up and put in a single category. The result can be a sizable sum. As an exercise, plug in the allocations for those items in Zone A — plus Zone B — that are funded at your college. A notable advantage of the wide-budget approach is that it declares that staff development is a serious business. It has disadvantages, however. By being a big budget, it is very visible and, because staff development is usually considered close to the luxury class of expenditure, vulnerable. Furthermore, a big budget requires a budget manager, and to put the allocation of discretionary funds in the hands of the staff development person is to move that person into a line administration function. The big budget approach makes the college look good and up-to-date, but there is still the danger of creating the specious impression that, because there is activity and budget (and look what a whopping percentage it is!), there is a program. In fact, there may be no program at all except in the way the bookkeeping is done.

I recommend the narrow budget approach. In this approach, only items directly related to the operations of the staff development office are included. This approach underscores the designation of the staff development specialist as a *staff* person, not line. The narrow budget is less vulnerable.

Figure Two
Wide-Budget and Narrow-Budget Approaches

Zone A	Zone B
1. Sabbatical leaves.	1. Staff development specialist salary and benefits, $25,000-$35,000
2. Conference and travel	2. Staff development secretarial salary and benefits, $9,000-$10,000
3. Reassigned time for program development	3. Office expenses, $500
4. Reassigned time for in-service training	4. Travel and conference expenses for staff development personnel, $600
5. Guest speakers, lecturers, consultants, and resource persons	6. Materials and supplies related to staff development, $500
6. Incentive grants for innovations and program development	8. Staff development workshops and seminars, participant compensation, resource persons and consultants, $4,000
7. College retreats and conferences	
8. Instructional salaries for staff development teaching	
9. Media preparation and reproduction support services	9. New faculty program, $2,000 per faculty member

Source of Funds

Lest the obvious be left unremarked, it is highly desirable that the staff development program achieve a formal and regular status in the college budget. As Figure Two suggests, a good part of staff development costs may already be in existing budgets. Nevertheless, a serious program is going to require new money. Public community colleges receiving state support through reapportionment have a means of defraying program costs readily at hand, regulations permitting. That is, staff development activities can be set up as classes for whatever unit value is justifiable, participants enrolled and reapportionment claimed.

Program costs for new faculty can be defrayed by salary savings which, over time, add up to an appreciable amount. The new faculty program at Los Medanos College set out to find out if the hiring of young, inexperienced instructors (backed up with a thorough, on-campus, year-long preparation program) would effectively defray costs. Such instructors, by virtue of having little or no experience, would have lower starting salaries than newly-employed faculty with salary credit given for experience. It was found that the long-range savings were, in fact, appreciable and did defray a large portion of program cost. New faculty got the savings, but in terms of formal staff development rather than high initial salary. And they very much applauded the program.

Another source of new money is grants. Grants from foundation and government sources have been essential ingredients in propelling the staff development movement along. For all their obvious advantages, grants do bring problems. For instance, a grant proposal is usually prepared on the basis of expectations of the funding agency — not the realities of the institution. The way things ought to be are stressed, not the way they are. Thus, commitments are made to ways of doing the business of staff development that can turn out to be awkward or unrealistic. Grants also breed a false sense of security. The need to find sources of "hard" money and to integrate the costs of staff development securely into the budget are easily put off so long as the grant is there. Perversely, the grant also has a tendency to make the project seem like a nice add-on, an adornment, but not something essential.

A college that is serious about staff development and wants to find a way of creating a full-time staff development specialist position might look to the reorganization of the management offices as a means of piecing together a position. "Instead-of" choices can be made among management positions and services in order to make room for a new staff development position. If a dean leaves, two divisions are merged, or if a couple of assistant dean slots open, executives may find that it is far more productive to convert those openings into a staff development office than it is to replace the offices. Creating the staff development position at Los Medanos demanded a conscious choice between a deanship and a staff development officer.

Evaluation

Evaluation of staff development is absolutely necessary, highly desirable but very difficult. All the standard problems of program evaluation emerge, complicated further by the nature of staff development in the community college. One complexity derives from the great difficulty in stating worthwhile goals in a manner that is agreeable to measurement. Still another complexity derives from the nature of the information. Some is quite substantial, like the fact of an event, or the installation of a new curriculum. Other information is less tangible; the fleeting nature of people's findings, a new way of seeing things, a changed way of relating to people or the institution.

Among persons interested in staff development, there is a growing interest in the techniques and problems of evaluation. As the early chapters of this sourcebook indicate, there is a very promising interrelationship between evaluation and the theory and practice of planned change and the introduction of innovation. Not the least of the reasons motivating the search for effective evaluative procedures is the need to establish worth and credibility of staff development.

In the meantime, any staff development person is going to have to be alert and vigorous in prosecuting evaluations of program activities, of the program as a whole and of her role and function. Fortunately, this activity is closely related to the necessary, ongoing needs assessments and thus does not call for episodes of heroic effort; evaluation can fit in as a normal part of events.

Some Approaches to Evaluation

The opportunities for informal, formative evaluation are virtually continuous when staff development activities are in progress. In fact, a staff development person might well wish on occasion that there be a respite from the steady precipitation of feedback. Messages of appropriateness and progress during a one-to-one consultation are usually clear and readily forthcoming. If not, you can ask the person, "How are we doing?"

Remarks and comments in passing supply evaluative feedback. The other day, a technician passed me in the hall and said, "Hey, when are we going to have those classes again?" He was referring to last year's seminars on problem solving and conflict resolution in a work setting. "I sure liked those," he said. After the initial twinge, I made a mental note: the time to crank up another round of activities for the classified staff clientele. At a management meeting, the business officer passed me a note, "Any more thinking about a workshop for faculty on budget? Several say they want more." After a management seminar, a dean who was not present says, "Hey, I hear I missed a good session."

For what it is worth, the staff development person is an instrument of evaluation. This is a sensitive function, requiring a great deal of self knowledge and candor on the part of the "instrument," as well as, on occasion, a thick skin. The continual incoming stream of information has to be noted, studied, apprised, put in context and acted upon.

It is very helpful for the staff development person to have both formal and informal sources of feedback and advice. An advisory committee is very helpful. Colleagues in similar work on other campuses constitute a priceless resource for testing ideas, brainstorming, fantasizing scenarios, venting feelings and (perhaps vitally important) for getting bearings on the highly personal question, "How am I as a staff development person doing in relationship to others like myself? How do I look?" Assistance in this process is on the horizon as several national networks of staff development specialists and regional associations are forming. As these mature, normative standards, ethical strictures, upper and lower limits of competencies and "image" will be established and made available as evaluative yardsticks for assessing performance and setting standards.

Patronage Measures and Participant Report

Patronage measures are useful and almost always applicable. Patronage measures are simply a form of head counting. How many came? How many enrolled? Raw data obtained in patronage measures will not be especially informative until there is enough history at a particular college to establish trends and to lay the basis for reasonable expectations. The hard question hidden in this measure is, "How much is enough to justify the time and cost?" It is useful to think the question through in advance and to share the problem with persons who will be the most interested in the information. Once, when the college first opened, Los Medanos tried out an idea for a voluntary evening workshop on teaching strategies for part-time instructors. Early on, I kept the college president informed. Though a preliminary survey of the part-timers (plus an estimate by program directors) had established a need, neither of us had any idea how many would show up. I hazarded that, if no more than twelve actually signed up for a specific workshop, then the project would be scrubbed. For a multitude of reasons, fewer than twelve signed up and the project was indeed scrubbed. Without the background established by the early discussions, the low number could have been taken negatively. As it was, the event added strength to an essential norm behind staff development efforts — that risk is appropriate and that an occasional "no-go" event is to be expected.

Patronage measures include counts of how many persons availed themselves of individual consultations, how many wrote out and completed growth contracts, how many did a self-paced course, and the like.

True, patronage measures do not tell you, except by inference, what the impact of the activity was on the individual participant. Self-reporting measures can provide more qualitative data. Procedures for self reporting are familiar, widely used and require little discussion. An end-of-activity evaluation, which can include self reports on perceived value and impact, is important for several reasons. Such evaluations provide a basis for corrective planning should the activity be repeated. Further, it gives the participant a feeling of closure and a sense of being involved in the staff development effort. It also provides reportable information that can be circulated and publicized throughout the college.

Large-Scale Approaches

Changes in the institution can be used for evaluation. If a program activity has been a series of workshops on the development of auto-tutorial materials, then evidence may be sought on the actual implementation of those materials. However, it would be a mistake to let the criterion of success or failure rest on such a measure unless the actual implementation was a clearly stated and feasible goal of the project. Changes in the environment can indicate overall program impact, such as changes in morale, of interpersonal relations, of loyalty to the institution. Such changes are difficult to measure. Care should be taken not to oversell the potential of staff development as a means of making such global changes.

The new faculty program at Los Medanos College was extensively evaluated and can be offered here as a large-scale evaluation project. It was a longitudinal study, using a variety of techniques. The evaluation was keyed to the goals of the program. For three successive years, each entering group of new faculty was given the Omnibus Personality Inventory, the Institutional Goals Inventory and a questionnaire developed by Leland L. Medsker. Two years later, the same instruments were administered to the same group. In the meantime, the external evaluators interviewed the participants, visited program functions and reviewed documents. Student evaluations were also included in the data base. The findings were positive on all goals and especially affirmative on the value of the program in promoting individual professional growth. The full evaluation study is available in printed form.

Personal Reflections

I am optimistic about the future of staff development, though I am properly sobered by the problems a new program faces and am concerned about the careless way good ideas like staff development become panaceas to be picked up, exploited and cast aside. I remain confident in the ability of persons to grow and change in a learning environment, and I believe institutions have the capacity for renewal and regeneration though some experiences have been discouraging.

I advocate program status for staff development and prefer to think of the content of the program as a curriculum with the participants learners. This should put me on the developmental, humanistic wing of the staff development movement. I think it makes very good sense to integrate staff development into the organizational structure—formal and informal — of the college, and to sink a taproot deep into the source of institutional vitality itself—its mission, goals, philosophy and its commitments. Though there are risks in doing so, I advocate the institutionalization of staff development, which involves "officing" it and staffing it, preferably with a full-time staff development person.

When I am asked, "How do we get a program started?" my response reveals a bias toward thinking big but starting small. I find myself torn between theory and pragmatics. It is essential for a program to have a long-range plan, an informing model and a persuasive set of beliefs inherent in it. Yet, a program is known by what it does and tomorrow's possibilities ride on today's successes. I have seen whole years consumed in conducting needs assessments, designing models, orchestrating political arragements, with nothing to speak of actually happening. Think big — but start small. Build a program step by step, starting with clientele and activities that have a high degree of probability of success; help the ripple effect carry out the good news.

Among staff development people I know, there seem to be two groups: the "grand designers," and the "one-step-at-a-timers." Personally, I think a program needs a grand design, but needs to operate on a step-at-a-time scale. When it comes to actually programming activities, thinking small is a virtue. Think small in terms of the time required, the number of people involved, the outcomes. Let the aggregate of activities add up to the grand design, rather than putting everything into one huge enterprise.

You can't win them all — today. I have come to think of any clientele in a "rule of thirds." That is, one third are ready and willing for almost anything, one third are available but need some convincing, and one third are not interested. Fortunately, the same people are not always in the same third . . . people do change slightly. A not-interested person one year may be available another. So don't burden an activity with the expectation it will appeal to all of the staff. Be satisfied with reasonable turn out. But put on your thinking cap if it is the same people over and over again. Perhaps there is not enough variety in the activities, perhaps communication is flawed, perhaps the program is conveying a negative — though unintended — message. Plan in the long range.

An activity will be helped if you do your homework. This includes a careful scouting out of the needs and interests of a clientele, as well as a lot of preliminary talk with key administrators, faculty influentials, committee persons, association officers and the like.

The staff development person would do well to include as many persons as possible in the act. Mentors, teachers of "master classes," faculty, all become a part of the program when they have significant roles. This heads off the "one-person show" effect and hedges against over-exposure and burn-out.

The more people that have done work for the program, the better. They will most likely gain an elevated awareness of what staff development involves. For the college as a whole, keep up a steady effort to keep the subject alive (but not intrusive). The staff development should get out a newsletter, especially at large institutions; announce activities periodically; do a lot of moving around talking to people; make presentations at committees, unit meetings and gatherings of faculty and administrators.

There are two properties of staff development that require mention. They will become important concerns for the staff development person and the mature program. One is entropy, the property of winding down; the other is self-liquidation. Entropy is endemic and acute in the staff development sector — perhaps because the work of staff development is rarely routine and requires large investments of energy. In my more discouraged moments, I think that staff development would, in fact, just simply wind down and disappear without a constant paying in of new ideas, new approaches, new faces.

The problem of self-liquidation is related to this. As one staff development colleague is fond of quoting, "Needs met are no longer needs." Though it is virtually impossible to exhaust all possible needs, it is possible for a program to "use up" the more easily identified and agreed-upon needs. Left are those hard core needs shrouded in conflict, obdurate and, yes, boringly persistent.

These two concepts do have a dismal aspect to them, but they are also very much part and parcel to the essential spirit of staff development, which is renewal. Entropy must be resisted with energy, and new goals must replace old in that migration of needs. The trick is to keep the staff development effort rolling and recycling along as the needs of the institution and its personnel evolve. That is enough to keep us all busy for a long time to come.

6

The Nontraditional Setting

by Thomas Clark

Tom Clark completed his undergraduate work at Allegheny College, received his M.A. in philosophy at Cornell University, then went on to an Ed.D. in educational psychology at Cornell. Consistently student-centered in his career, Tom has served as a dean of students within the Claremont Colleges, founding director of the higher education program at the University of Massachusetts, as well as the University Without Walls program there, and dean of an Empire State College Regional Learning Center before assuming directorship of the Center for Individualized Education. He is widely respected for his understanding of student-centered teaching and for his sensitivity to the needs and concerns of faculty in nontraditional programs.

This chapter in many ways is a basic document for all the other chapters. It carefully delineates the kinds of individual differences among students which professors need to consider if they hope to be particularly effective. The chapter also describes the stresses placed on professors who try to teach differently than their traditional colleagues, and this predicament is faced by anyone who deviates very much from familiar practices in an effort to serve learners more effectively. Finally, Clark's chapter reminds us that teaching improvement programs often are treading new ground and therefore need to be intentional about documenting and disseminating their learnings to those who may follow.

Introduction

Historically, American higher education has had what might be called "nontraditional" colleges, such places as Goddard and Sarah Lawrence, Black Mountain and Berea. Within "traditional" institutions, there have been nontraditional programs such as the Micklejohn and Hutchins experiments in general education. However, in the last decade, partly as a result of the student movement, which strongly reminds us that much of higher learning held little value for college students, alternative academic programs have multiplied.

Institutional responsiveness of this nature has been positive, since many things which define "traditional" higher education are inappropriate to many of today's students. Traditional higher learning takes place on a college campus, in courses which meet during set hours for approximately sixteen weeks apiece. Many potentially able students cannot get to a campus or cannot meet at regular hours spread over several months. Their jobs, their children, their physical restrictions, their isolated location just will not permit them to conform to the traditional college location and schedule. Traditional undergraduate education takes place between eighteen and twenty-two years of age, with graduate education usually following immediately. Today's student, however, is as likely to be thirty-six as eighteen, and those extra eighteen years just may have resulted in "college-level learning," even if it did not happen on campus. To approach the thirty-six or sixty year old merely as a more wrinkled and stouter version of the typical college freshman is indeed to say that the human intellect is a blank slate until college professors write on it.

Traditional higher education prescribes a series of "courses" in academic "subjects," generally to transmit the knowledge, skills and values of one highly educated generation to the next. The process is typically standardized — taking notes in lectures and discussions, reading texts, taking exams and writing papers. The professor determines what students should study, when and how. The professor also is the sole judge of how well the student learns. Nontraditional college education, in contrast, often puts the student rather than the professor in the center ring, then adjusts the objectives, the content, the teaching style, the learning experiences and even the method of evaluation to fit the unique differences of that individual.

As such nontraditional approaches have developed, professors have had to learn new roles and skills, even new attitudes. They often find themselves in radically new jobs. In many such nontraditional settings, faculty development is becoming a central need. Professors find that they need organized opportunities and skilled assistance in learning how to handle the demands of new academic programs which serve new students. This chapter's purpose is to share early learnings from such faculty development programs, especially from the activities of the Center for Individualized Education, a network of faculty development teams in nontraditional academic programs at a variety of institutions.

Because of the importance of the student in such settings, the introduction of this chapter is devoted to an examination of the individual differences among students and their implications for teaching improvement. I will turn then to new roles in situations to which faculty members must adjust in order to respond to student differences. The faculty development activities of Empire State College and the broader Center for Individualized Education network will be used to illustrate ways to conduct in-service development consistent with nontraditional principles and needs.

Although academic programs called "nontraditional" vary from each other almost as much as they vary from the traditional, most have in common a desire to respond to individual differences among students. What are some of the ways in which students are different? They are different in terms of sex, chronological age or place in the life cycle, stage of ego development, marital status, work and life experience, cognitive development, race, and social class. They come to a college for a variety of reasons and, therefore, have a variety of expectations regarding the teaching-learning process. They learn effectively in different ways or have different learning styles. Some learn quickly while others learn slowly; some need a prescribed structure while others structure learning activities for themselves; some are working at introductory levels while others are working at very sophisitcated levels; some learn effectively by beginning with theory while others learn best through a field experience or application and choose to study theory simultaneously or later; some want discipline-oriented study while others prefer comparative, interdisciplinary, problem-oriented or thematic study.

It is precisely because of all these individual differences that many nontraditional programs were established. They begin with an awareness of and respect for these individual characteristics. When faced with such a heterogeneous group of students, the response is to individualize — not to standardize. Such programs deviate from traditional college teaching in one or more of six dimensions: location, time, content, learning activities, evaluation and authority. In order to grasp the faculty development needs of nontraditional programs, each dimension deserves consideration.

Location

The first factor with which institutions of higher education have experimented is the location of the learning experience. The characteristic that makes many academic programs nontraditional is the fact that learning activities occur through correspondence study, through mediated courses, through a field placement, an internship, a job, or at a storefront satellite center. The recognition that effective learning can occur at home and in a variety of settings other than in a classroom has been demonstrated by many institutions which have organized academic programs in part or entirely nonresidential. Prime examples of this type of nontraditional program are Goddard College's Adult Degree Program, the University of Oklahoma's Liberal Studies, and the University of Nebraska's SUN Program. This change in thinking regarding the place where learning occurs has created access to higher education for many individuals for whom a residential experience was impossible. Students who are hospitalized or homebound, imprisoned or tied to a job, too rural and poor to get to a college, are just a few of those who can obtain college learning only if it comes to them. Change in location has meant, as well, that faculty have learned to work in different ways to make a program successful. Working with a student through correspondence or over the telephone, functioning as an evaluator for instruction that is performed by an on-the-job supervisor/tutor, making video tapes in a television studio or traveling to a series of field placement sites and store front satellites are all activities which faculty have to perform if the extended or nonresidential program is going to work.

Time

The second characteristic which can cause a program to be called nontraditional is the timing or scheduling of learning activities. One of the most widespread innovations in the pacing of learning activities is the Keller Plan or P.S.I. — Personalized System of Instruction. This nontraditional approach recognizes the fact that individuals learn at different speeds. Working from this premise, a faculty member constructs a course in content modules or segments which can be learned at the student's own pace. Self-paced learning using programmed texts and tests provide the student with the opportunity to proceed slowly or rapidly through the course. This alternative of self-pacing or personalized instruction offers great flexibility. Indeed, since the student can engage in ongoing self testing, such programs offer the potential of greater subject mastery. A student can obtain frequent, timely and personal feedback; new material is not introduced until the concept, theory or formula is mastered and understanding demonstrated. P.S.I. has made a significant impact on courses in many institutions, and this alternative meets the needs of many students for flexibility in the pace of their learning.

Another major innovation in regard to the element of time is the new academic calendars which have come into existence as alternatives to the traditional semester. The tri-mester and quarter system were fairly early variations. The 4-1-4 academic calendar, a more recent innovation, provides an opportunity for an institution to use two semester length periods for learning activities and a one-month period for specialized courses, highly focused seminars, travel study courses, individual student projects and a variety of individualized learning opportunities not often possible in the traditional two semester academic calendar. This alternative provides an opportunity for faculty and students to engage in experiences which enliven and enlarge the curriculum. They also provide the occasion for individual projects which have specific purpose for specific individual students.

Beyond 4-1-4 in flexibility is the modular calendar, which designs courses in variable blocks of time from as little as a week to as much as a year. An even more recent extension of this flexibility is contract learning, which varies the time of a learning experience to fit the particular needs of each contract and which regards time spent learning prior to enrollment as legitimate experience to be evaluated for evidence of college level learning.

Each of these time variations places new demands on the professor to arrange learning experiences and evaluation in a much wider range of time frames than the traditional semester or quarter.

Content

A third element which characterizes nontraditional programs is experimentation with course content. The content of most traditional learning activities has been organized to conform with existing disciplines or professions. During the last decade, however, there has been a significant growth of interdisciplinary courses, thematic and problem-oriented courses which are usually multidisciplinary in nature, and professional and vocational courses which intentionally integrate theory and practice.

The spread of interdisciplinary, thematic, problem-oriented and professional-vocational courses as alternatives to the solely discipline-oriented course have challenged faculty to reconsider new connections among academic fields, to work in ways broader than their area of research specialty, and often to engage in team-teaching experiments with colleagues in their own or in other departments. Faculty development can help professors meet each of these challenges while confronting the resistance to such approaches because they challenge the manner in which knowledge has been organized historically and the method in which professional academicians have been socialized. The development of these new content configurations in single courses has led to such new majors as Comparative Literature, Social Psychology, Environmental Studies, Black, Chicano, Puerto Rican, Native American and other ethnic and racial studies, Women's Studies, and other new configurations of knowledge.

Content experimentation has been extended to programs which provide students with the opportunity to design individual majors which have integrity and are defensible because the resulting program both is responsive to the needs of a specific individual and meets institutional goals and standards. Among the growing number of examples of this nontraditional approach are the Bachelor of Liberal Studies Program at State University College at Brockport and the Bachelors Degree with Individual Concentration major at the University of Massachusetts/ Amherst. In these two programs and others, the student, in concert with a self-chosen faculty advisor, articulates a program of study which combines courses and independent studies in ways which make sense to that unique individual. This individual plan is submitted to a faculty panel, which reviews it to be certain that it has consistency and integrity and makes a complete, albeit unique, whole. The committee has the opportunity to approve, deny or recommend revision of the plan to the student and her faculty advisor. For the faculty member, the role of advisor is critical to the process, and becomes a task very different from that normally involved in assisting a departmental major choose among pre-determined specialties, since it requires not only effective advising skills but the ability to conceptualize new arrangements of parts of disciplines into new wholes. Efforts to improve advising quickly becomes an important and popular faculty development activity in nontraditional programs.

Another innovation in the area of experimentation with content is the development of competency-based academic programs. Competency-based courses are those which are carefully intentional about anticipated outcomes of learning activities as well as about the methods, standards and indicators or evidence which will be employed in evaluating whether the expected level of competence or performance has been satisfied. Many institutions have individual courses or entire departments whose course offerings are competency-based. There are, as well, several institutions which have established entire academic programs which are competency-based. Notable among these — each with its own approach — are Alverno College, Community College of Vermont, Mars Hill College, Metropolitan State University, and Sterling College.

In each case, the focus for faculty has been on the articulation of learning outcomes or competencies and the identification of alternative routes a student may pursue in accomplishing them. The advent of this approach has caused faculty, administrators and students to rethink the meaning of the institution's academic program, the organization of the curriculum, the nature of the learning activities, and the methods of teaching and evaluation. In most such instances, how to plan, teach and evaluate for competency have been central components of faculty development.

The innovations implicit in nontraditional approaches to content have required major conceptual shifts for the faculty involved, since in each of these examples, faculty have had to engage in a total process of reconceptualization of knowledge, advising and approaches to teaching and evaluation. It is easy to underestimate the amount of in-service development needed when traditional conceptions of content are challenged.

Learning Activities

Once an individual faculty member of a group of faculty accept the fact that effective learning can occur in a variety of places other than solely in the classroom and that content can be approached from a variety of perspectives, there is normally the growth of options in regard to the learning activities and resources which can be used. Thus a student can gain understanding of a topic by reading books and attending lectures, by using self-directed programmed materials, by using mediated materials such as films, audio-tutorial, or educational television programs, by using a field experience or internship in combination with appropriate readings, or by group discussions and group projects.

This increased diversity of available learning activities provides greater opportunity to match the needs of the learner with the appropriate type of learning activity. The challenge for the student and often for the faculty advisor is to gain insight and awareness regarding student objectives and learning styles so that they can choose activities which are most appropriate and effective. For the student, the important issue becomes "How do I learn best?" For the faculty member working in a nontraditional program which offers a variety of learning activities, there are at least three important issues: 1) Do I have the advising skills necessary to assist the student in assessing his or her objectives and learning style; and, if not, how can I develop them? 2) Do I have the skills and time necessary to create optional learning strategies and resources for students to use in accomplishing their objectives? 3) Do I have the ability and time to guide and evaluate widely diverse learning activites? These three topics comprise a faculty development agenda for programs which use learning activities beyond the traditional lecture-discussion class.

Evaluation

The next characteristic which frequently identifies a nontraditional academic program is the manner in which learning activities are evaluated. Instead of the evaluation process being a mystery, many faculty have been experimenting in courses and independent studies with innovations in the evaluation which work to de-mystify the process. Implicit in most of these innovations are the qualities of clarity and intentionality. The faculty statement, "I know an 'A' paper when I see one" is changed to a narrative statement which is frequently a negotiated agreement regarding performance between student and professor. Particular attention regarding the clarity of the agreement is paid to its component parts. The three essential items in the process of evaluation are the methods or means which will be used in the evaluation process, the criteria or standards which will be employed in assessing the work, and evidence or indicators which will demonstrate that the work has or has not been completed at a particular level of proficiency. This process, normally applied to work which is sponsored or supervised by a faculty member, is currently being used in hundreds of institutions to evaluate or assess learning which has been gained through work and life experience. The work with evaluation as an integral part of the learning process has increased rapidly in the last decade, particularly with the advent of contract learning, the interest in the "learning society," and the interest in the evaluation of experiential learning which has been nurtured by the Council for the Advancement of

Experiential Learning.

The primary issue for faculty involved in this innovation is summed up in this simple statement, "How do I do evaluation which is intentional; that is, how do I write explicit methods, criteria and indicators?" Assisting faculty members as they come up with good answers is another important and popular part of faculty development for nontraditional programs.

Authority

There has never been much question in the traditional teaching-learning relationship about who was in control. The teacher-learner relationship was based on the parent-child, superior-subordinate mode. The teacher was the ultimate authority. Many new academic programs have experimented with modifications of authority. This experimentation has taken many forms and has meant new responsibilities for both the faculty member and the student.

Many of the experiments begin with the assumption that effective learning occurs when authority and responsibility for the learning activity is shared. A second assumption is that motivation will be higher if learning activities are designed — through negotiation — to meet a student's individual needs. A third assumption is that the student has a greater potential for becoming a self-directed and continuing or life-long learner if he is provided with that opportunity when involved in a formal learning activity. It is important to note that in the experiments with authority, authority is *shared* by the faculty member and the student; it is not "do your own thing" for either.

A place where faculty members frequently begin to experiment with the dynamics of shared authority is the negotiated syllabus. This process involves engaging with a student group in negotiating the content areas, learning activities, bibliography and evaluation process which will define a course. The negotiated syllabus has been reported to have a better chance of meeting the needs of both faculty member and student than many traditional, "professor determined" courses. Another variation of this experiment is independent study — wherein student and faculty member negotiate a plan for the student to pursue independently a course of study in a particular area. As in the case of negotiated syllabus, the content area, learning activities, bibliography and process of evaluation are negotiated. Frequently, a learning contract is employed to articulate the outcome of the process of negotiation. Yet another variation is the negotiation of the product or outcome of a course. This involves the negotiation of what the student will do (a paper, performance, examination, etc.) to demonstrate that learning has occurred. Thus, the focus of evaluation is the component of the learning process which is negotiated.

In each of these examples, the experiment involves movement from teacher-centered or teacher-determined learning activities to whose which are more student-centered. In each case, the innovation is dependent upon the faculty member giving up some power so that the student is empowered.

Experimentation with authority is often the area of nontraditional academic programming that faculty approach with the greatest timidity, primarily because most professional academicians have been trained in teaching-learning situations which employed a highly authoritarian model. Until recently, it was simply assumed that when the graduate degrees were achieved, the superior-subordinate model was to be replicated. Because it is so hard for most professors to share authority with students, or even to recognize that they are authoritarian when they mean to be collaborative, faculty development is needed.

Individualized Education

Some new academic programs maintain that all the dimensions I have mentioned should be adjusted to meet the needs of each and every college student. The term used for such ambitious programs is "individualized education," not to be confused with "individualized instruction" which varies only one dimension, time. The philosophic premise underlying individualized education is that because students are unique individuals in learning, they should be approached as unique individuals in teaching. Faculty members who work in such programs do not start with the premise that education starts with academic content or with themselves as teachers; they believe that education should start with the student. Because most individualized education programs are open to an extremely diverse range of students in age, preparation, interests, styles and situation, that starting point can be most anyplace.

Although there are differences in institutionalized policies and procedures, institutions which offer individualized programs share the common characteristic of providing the student with the opportunity to design — in cooperation with faculty members — a unique academic program. The individualized program begins with the student's objectives. The important questions that the student and faculty members must discuss are: Why are you here as a student? What do you want to learn? What do you need to learn? Faculty and students work on a one-to-one basis and in groups to negotiate these objectives; that is the starting point for building an individual set of learning activities for that particular student. The second aspect of the learning process which is individualized is content. What the student will study is based on his objectives. The third aspect which is individualized is the mode of study. Decisions must be made regarding whether the study will be disciplinary in nature or interdisciplinary, multidisciplinary, thematic or problem oriented, professional or vocational. Once the mode of study or the conceptual approach to the content is determined, the faculty member and student can decide how to structure the learning activities.

The fourth, fifth, sixth and seventh aspects of the individualized process involve answering questions related to the structure and nature of the learning activities. To make these decisions, critical questions regarding the student's learning style must be answered. These are questions of appropriate pace, questions of appropriate type of activity, questions of appropriate place and questions of appropriate learning resources. The pace or timing of the learning activity has to be decided and is a key element in individualizing the structure of the activity.

The next structural questions which must be addressed involve the activity and the place — will the learning activity occur in a classroom through a course or through an independent study, a field based experience, a lab experience, a supervised internship, mediated and print based modules, or a unique combination of these? Appropriate learning resources must then be selected.

Most institutions which offer an individualized option use a wide diversity of learning resources in order to assist the student in effectively carrying out the individual degree program. These resources extend or expand the concept of "campus" to include many heretofore untapped facilities and people. Museums, public libraries, industrial plants and laboratories, social service agencies, businesses, churches and performing arts centers all provide vital settings wherein observation, supervised internships, apprenticeships and field placements occur. These settings are frequently used to enliven the student's learning experience or to imaginatively link theory to practice. This extension of the learning experience "off the campus" is a characteristic common to most programs which have implemented individualized programs.

The use of people who are skilled practitioners in a variety of areas but who are not full time academicians is another major learning resource.

Community Faculty at Metropolitan State University and Community College of Vermont, Practitioner-Mentors at Rockland Community College, Adjunct Faculty and tutors at Empire State College are all titles used by various institutions to designate talented individuals who possess expertise in a variety of academic and professional areas in which students have an interest. These individuals, employed for specific periods of time to meet specific student needs, expand the ability of the institution to respond to individualized degree programs. They have the added advantage of being cost-effective. And the student is able to pursue a learning opportunity even though the institution may not have a full-time faculty member in that particular area.

The expansion of resources also includes mediated and print-based modular courses, correspondence courses, television programs and topical annotated bibliographies. The use of this diversity of learning resources expands the idea of the campus, demonstrates that learning can occur in a number of settings, involves individuals from the community who are not full-time faculty but who can teach, and causes the student to realize that learning resources are abundant if sought. Life-long learning can become a reality.

The eighth and final aspect of the individualized process is the innovative uses of the process of evaluation. Evaluation, particularly in the context of contract learning, becomes an integral part of the learning process due to its integration into the description of individualized learning activities. The intentional articulation of the specific methods, criteria and indicators which are to be employed in judging completed learning activities causes evaluation to become more than simply "testing."

Individualized education, then, is an educational experience which starts with the student's objectives and creates an academic program in which content, mode of study, pace, place, learning activities, learning resources and the process of evaluation are individualized. It includes nearly all of the practices used in other nontraditional programs.

New Teaching Roles

Most faculty members in traditional academic settings think of themselves as subject matter experts or disciplinary specialists. Professors are trained in disciplines, hired and rewarded for that competence, and expect the teaching function mainly to entail passing along some of their competence to students. Professors who begin working in a nontraditional program, however, discover that their disciplinary competence is only part of the story. Several roles besides the traditional "knowledge-dispensor" and "judge" were identified by faculty teams of the Center for Individualized Education: (114)

1. *Facilitator-Counselor*

   Because professors in individualized education often shift from teaching subjects to helping learners, they must learn to be learning facilitators and, on occasion, counselors of individuals or small groups. Although this less directive and more personal role seemed awkward at first, faculty members began to discover its merits, as these quotations indicate: "I found that it was difficult, awkward, to lecture when I was working with students one-to-one, or in small groups, so I gradually learned to become a facilitator of the learning process." "It is difficult to escape being a counselor when working in an individualized program because many things which are going on in an individual's life, such as change in marital status, change in value system, a change in perspective, are brought into conversations about the learning process and have to be discussed."

2. *Broker-Negotiator*

   Faculty members indicated that the change in authority relationships engendered by their nontraditional program necessitated their learning how to negotiate with students rather than dictate to them. Also, because a wide range of learning resources besides the teacher are used in individualized education, the faculty member needed to become a broker for the student in obtaining the learning experiences that student needed.

3. *Instructor-Tutor*

   Professors in nontraditional programs do teach, of course, but they often do it in nontraditional ways such as one-to-one; in intensive weekend residences; by computer or programmed instruction; in interdisciplinary thematic, or problem-oriented ways; in short modules. These variations very often are new to the teacher who has been taught by more traditional means.

4. *Evaluator*

   All professors must evaluate, but faculty members in nontraditional programs said that new skills had to be learned to shift from letter grading schemes to approaches which required much greater explicitness regarding the criteria, the indicators and the methods of evaluation. Written evaluations, or learning contracts, evaluations of experiential learning or "portfolios" of prior learning and competency testing are three examples of the nontraditional approaches to evaluation required of these faculty.

5. *Administrator*

Nontraditional teachers often must develop, organize and coordinate a wide range of learning resources such as tutors, field supervisors, peer teachers, student task groups and mediated materials. Because each student may be doing something somewhat different from any others, this becomes quite a chore. The administrative and paperwork demands of nontraditional teaching have little room for the absent-minded professor.

6. *Developer and Coordinator of Learning Resources*

When the teacher in class and the textbook at home are not the only vehicle for learning, the professor must be able to find, develop, and coordinate various other learning resources such as field placements, internships, peer teachers, counselors, community faculty, tutors, museums and libraries. In effect, the professor must create a "stable" or "pool" of people and places which offer a wide range of learning opportunities for diverse students.

7. *Creator and User of Instructional Materials*

All professors use instructional materials, mainly books and articles, but the nontraditional teacher also must learn to use programmed learning guides, computer-assisted instruction, audio-visual materials, PSI modules, educational television. Moreover, because many nontraditional programs do not have instructional materials readily available, professors must learn how to create materials appropriate to their students' learning needs and situations.

8. *Planner of Individualized Programs*

Few faculty members in traditional programs must think through, with a student, an entire degree program which re-

flects that particular student's prior learning and learning objectives. The closest most of us get to that situation is academic
advising, which usually is constricted by prescribed courses and
requirements. In individualized programs, the prescription is in
the hands of the professor and student, within general institutional parameters. Nontraditional professors, therefore,
must learn how to design not just a course but meaningful
degree programs for and with their advisees.

   This complex set of professional roles — which are usually necessary to
the implementation of these new academic programs — are different
(with two exceptions) from those needed to perform a traditional faculty
role. The skills needed to perform these roles are not those included in
most graduate degree programs; they must be developed through experience.
   Although there has been a great deal of learning regarding the new roles
and the skillls needed for those roles, faculty teams of the Center for
Individualized Education articulated a number of questions which were
important, in different institutions, to the improvement of the new programs in which they were involved. Faculty also voiced a number of
questions germane to continuing development of program effectiveness.
Some of these questions included the following: How do we evaluate
learning contracts, courses, field experiences and so forth in terms of
effectiveness in meeting individual objectives? How do we effectively evaluate prior/non-formal learning? How do we assist students in becoming
effective self-directed learners? How do we teach students to find learning
resources for themselves? How do we set up a learning resources "bank"?
How do we train community resource people to be more effective instructors? How do we provide quality services to populations not usually
reached by postsecondary education? How do we develop materials which
meet the educational needs of these populations? How do we combine
high and consistent standards with individual flexibility? How do we make
contract learning, narrative evaluations or individualized "majors" acceptable and useful to students and simultaneously to graduate schools, potential employers, credentialing agencies and accreditation teams? How do
we relate effectively to more traditional academicians? How do we survive
an extremely heavy workload?
   In order to develop effectively the skills required for these new roles and
to answer these questions presented above, faculty members and ad-

minstrators at many institutions which are nontraditional or have nontraditional academic programs have initiated faculty development activities. The types of faculty development activities which are ongoing in nontraditional programs are almost as diverse as the innovative programs themselves. A sample of these activities will be discussed later in this chapter. At this point, it is important to comment that an institution which initiates a nontraditional program without simultaneously initiating a consistent and parallel program of faculty development is making a mistake. Faculty need, want, and frequently organize their own development experiences; however, it is usually a more effective effort if the formal resources of the institution also are involved as collaborator if not partner in the development of highly skilled faculty.

Institutional Types

Before discussing faculty development activities in institutions which have nontraditional academic programs, it may be useful to review the types of institutional environments in which nontraditional programs exist and briefly mention some of the problems involved for faculty in each setting. We are finding that these settings are important factors in determining what needs to be included in faculty development.

Free Standing Institution

The first institutional type is the "free standing" model. This means that the institution provides only nontraditional programs. Empire State College is one such institution, serving individuals through a statewide network of regional centers and units and offering completely individualized degree programs and learning contracts. Another example is Metropolitan State University in Minneapolis-St. Paul, which serves a highly urban population and employs a competency-based degree program organized in learning contracts. A third example is Mars Hill College which serves a more traditional college age student through a competency-based academic program. Several problems seem characteristic of free standing nontraditional institutions:

1. Traditional graduate programs do not offer opportunities to learn the skills necessary to perform the faculty roles as they are described in these institutions.
2. Faculty may not have a colleague group which is defined by the disciplinary department, and this absence may create a condi-

tion of professional isolation.

3. Some faculty have a concern that their involvement in a totally nontraditional institution may preclude their ability to move back into a traditional academic program should they elect to do so.

4. Faculty engaged in building a new institution and a new pedagogic model often do not find the time to "keep up" in their discipline or engage in research in their academic specialty.

The objective of a faculty development program in a free-standing institution may not be simply to organize programs which assist faculty in learning or refining skills for new roles but to assist faculty in working out satisfactory solutions to questions of professional identity and mobility.

Additive Program

The second setting is one I call the "additive" model. Many traditional institutions add on nontraditional academic programs which use the resources of the traditional campus-based programs, including departmental faculty. They also may reach out into the community to serve a different population than is currently served by the traditional academic programs. Most nontraditional programs are additive, and the most widely known is the University Without Walls (U.W.W.) program, which was initiated by member institutions of the Union for Experimenting Colleges and Universities in 1970.

The U.W.W. program model works to implement individualized student degree programs which employ contract learning, use a wide variety of learning resources and engage in the evaluation of learning from work and life experience. The success of the U.W.W. programs have prompted many institutions to develop similar programs. Many such programs serve adult students. These programs are normally staffed by faculty who are also involved in traditional academic programs and who are members of traditional departments. Other examples of additive approaches include interdisciplinary programs, cluster colleges and programs for groups of students with special interests or needs such as women, minorities, prisoners or the handicapped.

The problems confronted by faculty who work in programs using this model seem to be as follows:

1. By having to work in both a traditional and a nontraditional academic program, faculty find they must learn new profes-

sional roles while simultaneously performing traditional ones.
2. The institutional reward system is frequently very specific and filled with precedents in regard to evaluation of professional performance in traditional roles and very ambiguous regarding evaluation of professional performance in new roles.
   This can create a situation which is schizophrenic in nature and is potentially anxiety producing to all but the most secure and/or tenured faculty member.
3. The faculty member who becomes involved in the nontraditional program may be considered somewhat "odd" by colleagues and may find a certain amount of alienation from colleagues, particularly if the reward system is ambiguous about participation in new programs.

The objective of a faculty development program in an additive model may be not only to organize programs which assist faculty in developing skills essential for working in the nontraditional program but to conduct organizational development in order to change the faculty reward system. Another objective may be the organization of a colleague support group for the faculty involved in the nontraditional programs so that there is some sense of ongoing dialogue, advocacy and aid outside the individual's department.

Substitute Program

The third institutional type is the "substitute" model. This means that the institution has made the decision to substitute a nontraditional for a traditional academic program, frequently in cases which there is no longer enough student interest to make the traditional program financially viable. The model also may emerge when a decision is made to re-evaluate the institution's mission and curriculum and substitute an entirely new curriculum, calendar and academic processes for a model which existed before. Examples of this latter approach include Sterling College, Mars Hill College and Alverno College. Some of the problems confronted by faculty who work at an institution which is undergoing changes of this nature are reflected in the following statements:

1. Faculty report that the changes in assumptions about teaching and learning involved when implementing a new curricular model are often frustrating and anxiety producing. There is great desire to return to the old model.

2. The development of the skills and roles necessary to implement the new model are often met with resistance and require risk, patience, persistence and a sense of humor.
3. The new curriculum model frequently involves a change in organizational structure as well as in institutional policies and practices. This often involves not only doing things differently but also working with an entirely different colleague group.

The objectives for a faculty development program in the substitute program might include assistance to faculty in understanding and committing to a new philosophy regarding teaching and learning and in the implementation of the practices which enable the model to work. Faculty may need help in developing the skills necessary to implement the new professional roles which are involved in implementation of the program. Attention may need to be given to maintaining an ongoing dialogue regarding the nature of faculty, student and administrator experience with the new model so that discussion, evaluation and probelm solving are built into the change process.

In the case of each of the three institutional types, the institutional setting of the nontraditional program and the emergent new faculty roles present unique problems and requirements for faculty development activities.

Purposes

We have found in early faculty development work for nontraditional programs that the six dimensions of variation from traditional higher education, the new faculty roles demanded by these variations, and the new program settings themselves all contribute to formulation of in-service objectives. In brief review, here are some of the most important professional development objectives which have emerged among the faculty of these innovative programs:

1. Assistance to faculty in enabling diverse students to learn in a wide variety of locations.
2. Assistance to faculty in varying the pace and timing of teaching to fit student backgrounds, styles and current interests.
3. Assistance to faculty in organizing and teaching subject content in areas other than (though often including) their disciplinary specialty.
4. Assistance to faculty in designing and implementing a wide range of learning activities appropriate to diverse students.

5. Assistance to faculty using nontraditional approaches to evaluation.
6. Aiding faculty in sharing authority regarding learning objectives, activities and evaluation with students.
7. Aiding faculty in learning how to facilitate and counsel learners.
8. Aiding faculty in becoming better learning brokers and negotiators.
9. Aiding faculty in strengthening their range and depth of skills as instructors and tutors.
10. Aiding faculty in becoming learning administrators.
11. Aiding faculty in becoming developers and coordinators of diverse learning resources.
12. Aiding faculty in creating and using nontraditional instructional materials.
13. Aiding faculty in planning with students individualized degree programs.
14. Aiding faculty in developing a colleague support group for nontraditional teaching.
15. Aiding faculty in keeping up with their traditional discipline and research.
16. Aiding faculty in moving back into traditional programs.
17. Influencing the development of institutional incentives and rewards for nontraditional teaching.
18. Counseling faculty who feel somewhat anxious because of the complex new demands of nontraditional teaching, on the one hand, and the complex old demands of traditional professorial careers, on the other.
19. Aiding faculty in finding opportunities for career variation and growth within nontraditional education.
20. Aiding the local organization and administration in becoming more supportive of nontraditional programs and teachers.

These twenty objectives are more than enough to keep a faculty development program active. Each local program, of course, will have its own priorities among these, plus a few special goals of its own. Perhaps the most important thing we have found is that because of the many unique teaching roles required when faculty really do try to respond to individual learning needs, and because of the personal and organizational stresses inevitable in deviation from the *status quo*, faculty development for nontraditional learning programs must attend, as Jack Lindquist emphasized in earlier chapters, to the person, the task and the situation.

Structure

Nontraditional programs use three different faculty development structures, each of which has advantages and problems. These are the formal center such as the Center for Individualized Education, the faculty development team, and the *ad hoc* project.

The Center Approach

Claude Mathis and Chet Case in earlier chapters stressed the advantages of a formal center or program with a continuing, professional director and staff. Most of those arguments hold for nontraditional settings. A solid funding base, a visible focus for developmental activities within the institution, the impartiality of staff rather than line responsibility and identification with institutional mission rather than any particular faction are some of the benefits I see in structures such as the Center for Individualized Education. Disadvantages include the fact that a faculty development center is not a normal line item in institutional budgets and therefore is very vulnerable in periods of fiscal cutbacks. If eliminated, no force for teaching improvement may remain in the institution. Also, having a center permits other people to say, "Let the center do it," so that all in-service functions get piled on a small, already overburdened staff. Everyone else becomes client rather than co-developer.

The Center for Individualized Education has certain features others may find helpful. First, because nontraditional programs must develop so many of their own materials, the center devotes part of its attention to research and development of an understanding of faculty roles and requisite development needs and to the preparation of background materials and exercises appropriate to faculty activities. Other centers should anticipate this need to develop their own understanding and tools of the trade, for the material in Bergquist and Phillips' handbooks or other resources aimed at traditional programs are not going to fit nontraditional circumstances, except by careful adaptation. We assume that part of our staff time will be consumed in research and development for faculty development; in addition, we have instituted a release time program for faculty members so that they can conduct studies and develop materials on their own.

Second, because our faculty are the most knowledgeable people regarding their unique development needs, we have created a faculty-administrative task force to help us develop center programs. This group meets quarterly because of the decentralized nature of our operation but the phone brings us together on a regular basis. Such advisory groups should not only contain persons interested in faculty development themselves but also opinion leaders for other faculty and administration. We believe a good part of the trust and credibility which comes our way does so because of the trust and credibility earned by our task force.

Third, because nontraditional programs constantly are engaged in dissemination and further development within their own staffs, within the broader institution and within higher education, the center reserves part of its structure and function for dissemination, networking and collaborative development. Our assistant director devotes his time almost exclusively to work with faculty development teams and projects in institutions beyond Empire State College that are interested in individualized education. Many of our materials are published for a broad audience. A formal network of seven other institutions shares with us the planning and implementation of faculty development throughout these institutions. One vital consequence is the slow development of a national as well as local support group of educators who value working together and are buoyed in their own, often isolated, work.

Fourth, because it is altogether too easy for a nontraditional program staff to conclude that we have invented the answer, the center has a National Advisory Board of persons distinguished for their contributions to and insights into individualized education. We have not used the strength of this board as we should; but when we need outside perspectives on how we are doing, advice on what needs to happen next and aid in locating grants, this board has been very helpful.

Within the college, the center director reports directly to the vice president for academic affairs and maintains informal liaison with various learning units through task force members and deans. We have taken care to maintain these communication lines and to remain outside line administration and faculty governance as they relate to policy making personnel. Perhaps because of this nonpartisan stance, the center seems to have considerable support from both faculty and administration. Perhaps another reason for this support is that we try to collaborate with interested groups and individuals regarding every important decision. This takes time and can be frustrating, but it also makes the center ours — the faculty's and the administration's and the network teams' — not mine.

The Task Force Approach

The Center for Individualized Education has an advisory task force, but center staff do most of the actual work. In some institutions, the task force itself is the primary work group. A group of persons interested in faculty development and respected by colleagues is appointed, usually by an executive administrator, to develop and carry out faculty development for the nontraditional program. If luck is with this team, some members get released from other duties so that interest can be matched with energy.

Task forces tend not to conduct a full array of research, development and dissemination activities. Rather, they concentrate on a few well-planned activities such as workshops and bag lunches. They use themselves, colleagues and an occasional consultant instead of professional development staff to plan and implement events. If bound together by strong interest and by the personal rewards of participation in a meaningful group, task forces can make a real difference.

The problems I have seen in the task force approach are that its voluntary efforts get too little institutional support to be sustained, that its dependency on voluntarism is a fragile base for ongoing services and that it is dependent on only limited expertise. If, however, the task force receives substantial time and money and moral support from the institution, if its members have or can gain the required expertise and if team membership can be sustained and developed this approach has the decided advantage over the central model of being by and for the participants. Also, task force members develop their own knowledge and skill in the act of helping the development of others.

The Ad Hoc Project

Several faculty development efforts in nontraditional education are financed by government or foundation grants. They run for the duration of the grant and often involve orientation and training for new roles as well as the generation of instructional resources, equipment and materials. Good examples are the programs at Mars Hill, Sterling, and Davis and Elkins colleges. This approach also may evolve when a group of faculty involved in a particular innovation, say a decision to evaluate college level learning from work and life experience, decide to hold a weekend workshop to learn how to implement this process.

Ad hoc projects can meet an immediate need at low cost. They also can be a catalyst for more regular, locally supported, faculty development or for other *ad hoc* projects as the need arises. They can sensitize institutional leaders to the considerable need for faculty development in order for nontraditional programs to work effectively. Several institutions with special projects continue to engage in faculty development, in part because of the boost given by short-term, *ad hoc* activities. On the debit side, they involve little initial commitment by the institution. Their specific project orientation may affect few faculty and make faculty development labeled as only for that project. They rely on temporary staff and volunteers whose knowledge and skill are often lost to further faculty development when the grant or the weekend workshop ends.

My Own View

I work in an *ad hoc* project, the Center for Individualized Education, whose Danforth funding ends this year. I also work in a center and with several faculty development task forces. Frankly, I think the ideal situation is to combine these three structural approaches. We simply could not have done all the workshops, all the publications, all the networking activities we have done in the past three years without a substantially funded center and professional staff. Faculty members, though enormously capable, simply do not have the time nor background to do all we have accomplished and to handle the many administrative and liaison tasks placed upon us. On the other hand the center seems to have become a focal point of pride and promise for many faculty and staff within Empire State College and network institutions, and a main reason, I believe, is that the center in good part is the faculty development task forces in the college and beyond. No center staff could generate the staff involvements and wide-ranging development activities which these task forces have managed.

Were I to develop a structure for faculty development in nontraditional programs, therefore, I would start in whichever of these three ways is feasible: a line item center, or specially funded project, or a low budget task force. But then I would move to include the other two models. More special projects will be needed, if our work is any indiciation, for we only have scratched the surface of what it takes truly to individualize education for diverse students. More faculty volunteers or more task forces are needed if we ever are to tap the expertise within nontraditional faculty and generate the ownership and involvement needed to make our work fully rewarding. And there must be a stable focal point, hard to dislodge and respected widely, if faculty development is to endure through hard political and economic times. In any nontraditional program or institution genuinely committed to continuous improvement and renewal, all three structural elements seem to me essential.

Staffing

Whether the structure of the faculty development project associated with the nontraditional academic program is the center approach, the task force approach, or the *ad hoc* approach, there are a series of roles which must be performed. The seven roles which seem to be essential to this effort are designer/planner, facilitator, teacher, technician, counselor/advisor, administrator and researcher.

The role of designer/planner is essential to the faculty development project. Implicit in this role are not only the skills necessary to plan conceptually the overall objectives of the project and the rational regarding how it will make the nontraditional programs more effective, but also the ability to design (in collaboration with colleagues) each of these components of the project, such as research projects, video-feedback projects, issue oriented workshops and skill development workshops.

The role of the facilitator is necessary since it is normally essential to work with faculty and administrative colleagues in the implementation of activities to meet perceived individual and program needs. Development leaders cannot dictate to the person who in many cases invented the program they are helping to implement. The ability to listen, to question openly, to facilitate groups, to take advice all help to define the facilitative leader.

The role of teacher is perhaps at the center of the faculty development specialist's function. The project coordinator may be the person who instructs colleagues about the philosophy of, need for and strategies involved in the implementation of the nontraditional academic program. She may be a model teacher in the nontraditional program or the individual who implemented the pilot program or headed the group which brought about the new program's development. The director of the faculty development effort, because of her work on the development of the new academic program, may also possess the skills necessary to work with students in new ways and therefore may be a central figure in teaching these skills to colleagues.

The role of technician is necessary given the activities of many faculty development programs. Work with video and other audio-visual equipment necessary in the development of training materials often requires a rather sophisticated level of technical skills. This role, like several others in this list, may have to be learned if the individual who takes on the job of faculty development specialist does not possess the necessary skills prior to accepting the position.

The role of counselor/advisor is one which may be unanticipated by the individual moving to the position of faculty development specialist, task force chairperson or project director. In the nontraditional academic setting, colleagues may seek out the individual who occupies one of these roles because of a frequent perception that such a person is impartial and therefore can be a trusted collegial advisor. This is particularly true when a faculty member is going through the process of learning new skills or is ambivalent about making the career shift which is often involved when deciding to work in a nontraditional academic program. Working to assist colleagues in solving professional (and sometimes personal) problems requires caring, confidentiality and the ability to communicate in an empathic way with colleagues regarding their concerns.

The role of administrator is often necessary, particularly when the faculty development project is funded by a grant. Fiscal management from budgeting to billing to writing quarterly reports is a frequently invisible aspect of operating a faculty development project. The implementation of workshops as a development activity requires not only human relations and group dynamics skills, but design and administrative skills. Successful faculty development projects and effective workshops occur in part because of efficient administration and attention to detail.

The role of researcher or scholar is included primarily because of the fact that many development activities require significant study prior to design and implementation of the activities. For example, there are a large number of articles and books available which deal with the topic of the advising and counseling of undergraduate students; however, it is a laborious task to find the few articles which report research on or describe the process of advising and counseling adult students. Therefore, the preparation involved in designing a workshop in advising skills for faculty who work with nontraditional students may require rather thorough bibliographic scholarship in order to locate materials which are appropriate for such an activity. The role may require original research as well. The topic area concerning new roles for faculty who are involved with nontraditional academic programs is, for instance, one in which research is just beginning. Consequently, the individual responsible for faculty development may discover that he must engage in original research simply to understand what new faculty roles entail.

Since few individuals possess all of the skills requisite to perform all of these roles at the time of their initial involvement in a project, it is usually necessary to adopt one or several approaches to attain adequate staffing for a project:

1. Hire a colleague (either full or part-time) who has skills which are complementary to those of the project director or coordinator. (This is often the case when the budget for the project is substantial enough to afford it.)
2. Hire several colleagues as "in-house" consultants to complete specific projects or to perform specific tasks.
3. Hire "outside" consultants who are known to have expertise in specific areas of research or skill development which are germane to the project's goals.
4. Recruit the voluntary assistance of colleagues and/or outside consultants. (This is difficult to do, unless there is some kind of "pay-off" — such as learning about the way a particular innovation functions or the pledge of reciprocal assistance.)

We have used all these alternatives in the Center for Individualized Education and find that their effectiveness is particularly a function, once again, of the person, the task and the situation. Perhaps the best advice is to begin early to develop a "stable" of colleagues and consultants on whom you can rely for particular tasks.

Activities

A wide range of activities is possible to accomplish the faculty development objectives I listed earlier. A first step, however, is to discover just what are your own institutional and staff needs. I favor an interview process with administrators and faculty, individually and in small groups. In preparing for such interviews, it is helpful to read about or converse with individuals at other institutions with faculty development activities so that you can try out those possibilities on interviewees who may need a little prompting to see what faculty development might mean or do.

A second step, which is complementary to the first, is to construct and circulate a questionnaire. The use of a questionnaire can frequently engage a broader number of faculty and administrators in the needs assessment process than can the interview method. It can also assist in establishing priorities for development activities and help predict the level of interest in any given activities.

These two techniques are useful not only when establishing a faculty development operation, but they also serve as vehicles for ongoing evaluation of program activities. Intentional and ongoing use of a faculty/administrator task force for guidance and criticism as well as the frequent use of questionnaires and interviews can enable the institution's program to be continually responsive to the changing needs of the faculty and the institution.

With this information in hand, my next step has been, and would be, to discuss the findings with appropriate task forces and authorities, then create a program plan for their review. In essence, these interactions begin to define what faculty development really should mean for our program. And as a final step, faculty members and administrators receive another brief questionnaire, this one listing the proposed faculty development activities which emerge from prior interactions. They are asked to rank order their personal priority of activities, activities in which they would participate and any others not listed but vital to them. At each step, the participative task force acts as principal advisor to the program coordinator (or as decision maker if there is no coordinator).

Out of this process at Empire State College has emerged the following priority activities:

1. New "Mentor" Workshop
2. Workshop on Evaluation
3. Workshop in Advising and Advising Skills.
4. Workshop for Associate Deans on New Directions in the Academic Program
5. Workshop for Deans on Personnel Policies and the New Professional
6. Workshop on Individualized Education in the Context of the Learning Group
7. Workshop on Group Process Skills and Organizational Behavior
8. Workshop on Adult Development
9. Workshop on Career and Educational Planning, Degree Planning, and advanced Standing in the Context of Contract Learning
10. Writing Skills Workshop

The emphasis on workshops is partly the function of having such a geo-graphically dispersed faculty that it takes a special event to get them together. But workshops frequently have served as springboards to follow-up activity in local learning centers; that follow-up is encouraged by inviting teams that carry back to their centers a report and a plan for further development.

Workshops in Detail

Two of the center's workshops are described here in some detail to illustrate the nature of the work involved in the planning, design, implementation and evaluation of these activities.

The first example is the New "Mentor" Workshop. This activity was planned in response to a strong statement by faculty at Empire State College that new faculty should have the opportunity to participate in a comprehensive orientation to the new roles they would be required to perform, to receive initial training in the skills necessary to perform these roles and to engage in extensive discussion of the academic policies and procedures which define the process of individualized education at Empire State. Experienced faculty said they wasted much time and encountered much frustration learning on their own how to do mentoring.

The first step in designing this workshop was to consult with a large number of faculty, administrators and students regarding what they thought should be the components of such an activity. Since many of the new faculty were still being appointed, it was not possible to consult with them in regard to their needs.

The second step was to take all the advice gleaned from the consultative interviews and weave that information into an initial design for the workshop. This was a difficult task, since there were many questions regarding individual differences in the participants, the most effective way to present a concept, the group dynamics of the situation and the factor of time.

Once the initial design was agreed upon by the planners, what existed was a list of topics and a schedule with blocks of time allocated to each topic. At this point, we realized that original materials would have to be developed, since training materials for such an activity did not exist. The decision was made to develop a *Contract Learning Casebook*, which would provide an illustrative set of sample student learning contracts to demonstrate the range of learning activities in which students were involved with

Empire State College
New Mentor Workshop
The Institute On Man And Science

Workshop Schedule

Tuesday, September 2

12:00 noon	Check-In
	12:30 p.m.
	Lunch
1:30	Introduction to the Workshop — Tom Clark, Director, Center for Individualized Education
2:00	"Student Perspectives on the ESC Experience"
	Research on Student Characteristics and Experiences — Tim Lehmann, Director of Program Evaluation
	Small Group Interview of Recent ESC Graduates
	General Discussion
5:00	Social Hour
6:15	Dinner
	"Individual Differences & Individualized Education" — Arthur W. Chickering, Vice President for Policy Analysis and Evaluation
8:15	The Degree Program — "The Educational Blueprint"
	Examples and Discussion — Mike Plummer, Associate Dean, Northeast Regional Center at Albany
	Robert Hassenger, Associate Dean, Niagara Frontier Regional Center at Buffalo
10:00	Wrap Up

Wednesday, September 3

8:00 a.m.	Breakfast
9:00	"The Role of the Mentor at Empire State College" — John Jacobson, Vice President for Academic Affairs
9:30	The Mentor Skills
	Video Tape Presentation Demonstrating:
	Sensitivity to Individual Differences
	Asking Evocative Questions
	Listening
	Negotiating
	Advising
	Record Keeping

Wednesday, September 3 continued

10:15   "Fishbowl" — Analysis and Response to Video Tape Presentation

         Experienced Mentors — Perl Mindell, Northeast Regional Center at Albany

         Rhoda Wald, Long Island Regional Center East at Stony Brook

         James Garbarino, Genesee Valley Regional Center at Rochester

         Robert Carey, Center for Statewide Programs

11:00   The Student-Mentor Interaction: A Case Study/Role Play in Triads

         The Mentor Role and Professional development — Paul Bradley, Director of Institutional Research

12:30 p.m.   Lunch

1:30 p.m.   The Assessment/Experiential Learning: Policies/Process/Case Studies — Al Serling, Office of Program Review and Assessment

         Jane Shipton, Long Island Regional Center at Old Westbury

4:30   Case Study I: Assessment Committee Meetings

5:00   Social Hour

6:00   Dinner

8:00   Case Study II: Assessment Committee Meetings

9:00   Committee Reports

9:30   Critique and Discussion Observers

10:00   Wrap Up

Thursday, September 4

8:00 a.m.   Breakfast

         Learning Resources — Robert Pasciullo, Assistant Vice President for Learning Resources

         ESC Modules/ESC Residencies — Albert Schwartz, Director of Residencies

         Internships, SUNY Independent Study Courses, Cross Registration

         Tutors — James Feeney, Associate Dean, Long Island Regional Center at Old Westbury — Jerry Sircus, Mentor, Lower Hudson Regional Center at Suffern

11:00	Contract Learning — Introduction — Tom Clark
	Presentation of the Contract Learning Casebook — Tom Clark and Scott Chisholm
12:00 noon	Lunch
1:30 p.m.	Learning Contracts: Case Study Simulations in Triad Groups
5:00	Social Hour
6:00	Dinner
	"Empire State College: Future Development" James W. Hall, President
8:00	Evening Discussion — Topics to be Posted
10:00	Wrap Up

Friday, September 5

8:00 a.m.	Breakfast
9:00	Contract Case Studies
	Contract Digests and Evaluations
11:15	Workshop Evaluation
12:00 noon	Lunch and Wrap Up
1:00 p.m.	Depart

faculty. A second purpose of the *Casebook* was to provide a broad array of sample contracts for faculty who had never negotiated a learning contract with a student. The second major training aid to be developed was a fifty minute video tape demonstrating the skills requisite for performing the mentor role. The time involved in developing these materials without precedent models was extensive.

The final step in planning was the negotiation with all the individuals who would be involved as presentors — students, experienced faculty and administrators — and attending to the countless details which must be coordinated, such as meals, lodging, travel, equipment, supplies, the participants and the schedule.

The workshop was the first systematically organized orientation for new faculty at the college. The four-day program offered an "in-depth" introduction to individualized education, an opportunity to meet new colleagues and the time possible to engage in comprehensive discussions regarding the college's academic program and the mentor role.

The last major activity on the workshop schedule was evaluating the workshop. This was achieved by sending a questionnaire to all participants several weeks after the workshop and through a telephone interview with a stratified random sample of participants approximately one year following the activity. The information gained from these two procedures proved extremely valuable in the planning of follow-up activities.

The second example is the center's Workshop on Advising and Advising Skills. As in the case of the New Mentor Workshop, this workshop was an activity which was designated by many of the faculty to be of major significance, since advising is a key element in the faculty-student relationship when individualized contract learning is the primary pedagogic mode.

The workshop involved teams of two or three faculty members from each of the college's eight learning centers. The three-day experience addressed the objectives of advising and the ingredients of an effective process. The workshop had several emphases:

1. Analysis of the components of effective advising — sensitivity to individual differences, asking evocative questions, listening, hearing, cooperative planning
2. Skill development exercises in each of the component areas
3. Analysis of audio-video case study presentations
4. Simulation/role playing exercises which integrate "skill refine-

ment" with the analysis of case studies
5. Discussion of career planning, personal counseling and academic advising

The design of this workshop called for sending to the participants a packet of appropriate readings on the topics of academic, career and personal advising and advising skills several weeks prior to the event. This task proved to be extremely difficult, since a search of the literature revealed that most of what was available on advising and counseling of college students focused on individuals who were of traditional college age. Because the participants were from programs and/or institutions which serve adult students (average age 36), most of the extant literature was inappropriate. This aspect of workshop planning (the availability of appropriate materials) in faculty development activities which serve nontraditional students is a characteristic which is important to note.

Participants in this activity included faculty and administrators from Empire State College, faculty members from several of the center's network institutions, and three consultants from other institutions. The schedule displayed below will provide a more complete idea of the workshop activities. Note that activities alternate between a presentation/discussion mode and direct experience in advising or portfolio planning. We have found that presentation of concepts and tips are helpful but that the faculty role in nontraditional learning needs to be tried out by participants in order for it to be understood and appreciated. This direct observation and trial is especially important when presenting nontraditional teaching to traditional faculty members who need to see it for themselves and do it themselves. Also, teaching involves skill as well as knowledge, so practice with observation and feedback is used in order to hone teaching skills.

One aspect of this workshop which is worth particular comment is the fact that several participants from one of the College's regional centers convened a one day "Mini-Workshop" on Advising and Advising Skills for the entire faculty of that division. This workshop used the team of participants in the first workshop as peer-teachers or facilitators for their colleagues in the second workshop.

I have learned a great deal about conducting workshop activities through the experience of doing them. Some of the following statements which articulate these learnings may seem obvious, but they may provide a review for individuals who find themselves responsible for planning and

Empire State College
Center for Individualized Education
Workshop on Advising/Advising Skills

Workshop Schedule

Wednesday, February 18, 1976

5:00 p.m.	Social Hour
6:00	Dinner
7:30	Introduction to Workshop — Tom Clark
8:00	The Goals and Process of Advising — Dr. Dee Appley, Department of Psychology, University of Massachusetts

Thursday, February 19, 1976

8:00 a.m.	Breakfast
9:00	The morning session (9-12 noon) will be devoted to simulations (role-playing exercises) which focus on five skill areas: responding to individual differences, asking evocative questions, listening, hearing, and cooperative planning. The simulations will be conducted in triads.
10:30	Coffee
12:00 noon	Lunch
1:30 p.m.	Three Types of Advising
	This general session will feature three presenters — each will briefly address one of the following topics:
	Academic Advising — Dr. Jack Lindquist, Empire State College
	Personal Counseling — Dr. William Kraus, University of Hartford
	Career Counseling — Dr. Dee Appley, University of Massachusetts
	(The focus of each presentation will be on the development aspects of these functions, i.e., academic/intellectual development, etc.)
2:15	Coffee
2:30	Small Group Discussion
	The general session will break into three small groups; the presenters on each topic will rotate among groups — each spending approximately 30 minutes with each group discussing issues pertinent to the topic.

4:00	Free Time
5:00	Social Hour
6:00	Dinner
7:30	Simulation/Case Study I

The Case Study will involve several problems in regard to a learning contract in which a student is working. It will work to integrate skills analyzed and issues discussed in earlier sessions.

9:00	Adjourn

Friday, February 20, 1976

8:00 a.m.	Breakfast
	Simulation/Case Study II — Introduction: Tom Clark

The Case Study will involve degree program planning and portfolio preparation. The session will combine a focus on skills as well as academic development, personal development and career development.

10:15	Coffee
12:00 noon	Lunch
1:30 p.m.	Small Group Discussion
	What have I learned?
	Questions remaining?
	Future Developmental Activities?
2:30	General Session:
	Reports from Small Groups
	Next Steps
3:30	Adjourn

implementing such activities.

1. Consult broadly regarding the topic(s) for the workshop activity with faculty and administrators who are like to be the participants. This will provide an inventory of the issues, needs, contradictions and concerns which give the activity life.
2. Respect the participants. It is important to recognize that the participants are all unique individuals — that the values, needs and ideas of those who will engage in the activity will have commonalities and differences.
3. Be flexible in the design of an activity and always consider a range of alternative approaches before deciding on a "final" design — keeping in mind that a variety of circumstances may cause a last minute change of plans. In other words, do not become so enamored with a design that you fight any change.
4. Plan activities which provide general information, appropriate research data and the experience of other institutions, but which combine the didactic approach with "hands on" experience. Most people find information more useful if they have a chance to apply it. Case studies, role playing, games and simulations are all experience-based activities which provide an opportunity to accomplish this.
5. Use faculty colleagues who have expertise in consultant roles. This fosters a peer-teaching norm which is extremely gratifying. It recognizes resident expertise, provides an opportunity for workshop participants to be presentors as well and is in itself another form of faculty development.
6. Select materials and consultants with attention to making the greatest impact in the shortest period of time.
7. Listen to what participants say when they evaluate an activity. Be prepared to learn from both flops and successes. Operationalize these data when designing follow-up activities so the same mistakes are not replicated.
8. Be aware of both the personal and professional needs of the participants. In other words, give people an opportunity for some recreation and conversation as well as work.

In summary, planning a workshop with and for faculty who work in programs which individualize should be consistent with principles and practices the faculty seek to use when working with students.

Planning of follow-up activities and the use of a peer-teaching model is one way for greatly increasing the impact of a development activity. In this case, the initial and the follow-up workshops involved over fifty percent of the college's faculty on a voluntary basis.

The workshop has been the primary development activity which the center has sponsored, but it also has used several other approaches to provide development opportunities for faculty, administrators and staff.

The Planning of "Follow-up" Activities

A well planned workshop activity should have follow-up activities built into the design from the time of initial planning. The assistance of inside and visiting consultants should be enlisted in thinking through the follow-up activities so that not just one set of ideas is involved in this process. This is an essential part of workshop planning if the impact on the individuals and the institution is going to be more long-lasting than just the workshop itself. The planning of follow-up activities should involve not only task force members and consultants but workshop participants as well. One of the most effective strategies which the center has used has been the scheduling of planning time for follow-up activities in the workshop schedule. This is normally a small group activity followed by a sharing and comparing of plans with the larger group of workshop participants. Such a device provides for intentional planning of follow-up activities rather than leaving them to chance and good intentions. Follow-up activities are frequently replications of the workshop experience itself with workshop participants acting as teachers or trainers for their colleagues who were not in attendance. This "each one teach one" model also places a different level of responsibility on workshop attendees, since they know they will probably be expected to disseminate information and skills to their colleagues. The center frequently assists in follow-up activities by providing design assistance, materials and frequently a consultant or facilitator.

Center Outreach

A teaching improvement program for nontraditional education is pioneering in the understanding and skill needed to teach this new way. Such programs therefore have the obligation of disseminating what they learn to other institutions. The Center for Individualized Education, for example, has a Faculty Intern Program designed not only to enable faculty members to conduct and publish studies related to individualized education but to share such studies through formal publication. Such works as A. Paul Bradley's "The New Professional: A Report on Faculty in Individualized Education;" Arthur W. Chickering's "A Conceptual Framework for Educational Alternatives;" Thomas Clark's and Scott Chisolm's "Contract Learning Casebook;" and Elizabeth Steltenpohl's and Jane Shipton's "A Guide to Resources for Life/Career/Educational Planning for Adults" all were commissioned and distributed by the center. Particular topic areas were selected through the needs assessment described earlier, and publications either were invited or chose in competition. A much more elaborate publication program is the major outreach strategy used by the Council for the Advancement of Experiential Learning. (137)

Publications, however, are effective mainly for people already interested in their message and capable of using it. Often, there is a caution, skepticism, or lack of know-how which greets nontraditional approaches to teaching. For that reason, I advocate a "hands-on" outreach program in conjunction with publications. Again to use the Center for Individualized Education as an example, we work closely with a network of seven other nontraditional institutions as a first outreach step (and, because these institutions are sophisticated in nontraditional education themselves, as "in reach" to keep Empire State College up on the latest developments elsewhere). We also conduct numerous workshops on traditional college campuses to introduce individualized education to their faculties. Alverno College conducts similar workshops, but on its own campus so that participants in "Visitation Day" can see competency liberal education in action and talk to Alverno staff or students about it. Also, all eight institutions in the CIE network put on a National Workshop on Individualized Education which evaluations said was highly successful. Finally, the center maintains close liaison with other networks which have similar interests such as the Union for Experimenting Colleges and Universities and CAEL. In this way, mutual sharing and cooperation is extended across the country.

The Use of Consultants

The other contributors have stressed various factors to be considered in using consultants. A few points, however, are well worth heeding when using consultants for nontraditional programs. Such persons need to be knowledgeable about nontraditional education. We have had excellent consultants who did not succeed with some Empire State faculty because they had little experience in individualized education. On the other hand, when conducting workshops for traditional faculty, the consultant needs to have traditional credentials and experiences as well as respect for traditional teaching. It seems best to find consultants who are comfortable and effective on both the traditional and nontraditional campus.

A second point is that consultants involved in nontraditional programs need to be able to behave in a manner consistent with the nontraditional approach. A stand-up lecture is one part of individualized education, but individualization of that lecture and of other consultant duties is needed. For a program which emphasized teacher-learner collaboration, a collaborative approach is visibly modeled; the medium is the message.

Third, regard consultation as a way to give nontraditional faculty members opportunities to shine. Too often, administrators appear on conference panels or as workshop leaders when what is needed is a person with first-hand teaching experience. Conference presentations, workshop consultations, or publications on nontraditional learning each can offer faculty members opportunities for greater visibility and status as well as for the enjoyment and learning which can come from consulting experiences.

Financing

Costs of programs vary widely depending on the nature of the program activities, the amount of equipment necessary, the cost of materials used, the number and cost of consultants employed and the amount of transportation required. Potentially the least expensive faculty development operation is the task force model in a campus-based institution. This is possible if individuals serving on the task force are doing so as a volunteer effort or are on released time and if all activities of the workshop variety are held on the campus. Such an arrangement has all the potential disadvantages of this approach cited earlier, but it is potentially the least expensive.

The center model operating in a de-centralized institution, such as Empire State College, is potentially one of the most expensive, since in this model there is a full-time staff (director, assistant director, secretary) and a great deal of travel involved (due to the de-centralized nature of the institution).

The budget is a direct result of cost of staff and program activities; however, there are a variety of ways to save money, since economy is usually the norm in a faculty development operation. Here are a few ideas on economical planning:

1. Plan meetings at sites which require the least travel.
2. Be prepared to negotiate or bargain with innkeepers, caterers and purveyors of other services such as printers, film rental agencies, travel agencies, and so forth.
3. Always ask: What is the most effective activity at the least cost.
4. Be prepared to "barter" services with outside consultants and faculty development colleagues from other institutions to cut down the cost of consultants.

These commonsense ideas have been revelations to many individuals who have approached the center for advice in initiating faculty development activities. It is also important to remember that money is not the only currency. Many individuals — faculty and administrators — will involve themselves in the planning and implementation of faculty development activities because of commitment to the idea underlying a particular activity or for the status that involvement may bring.

Many faculty development projects during the past five years have been funded by grants from foundations or the federal government. Such "soft" money support has several advantages:

1. the funded project frequently has the freedom to experiment with a variety of activities;
2. it can be an impartial operation within the institution;
3. it provides the catalyst necessary to initiate a faculty development program;
4. it can provide the funds required to make faculty development more than a voluntary activity.

The primary disadvantage is the fact that the project may not be able to be continued once the grant money is used, simply because the institution cannot afford such an ongoing function.

"Hard" money support is the most secure position for a faculty development operation, but it has the potential disadvantage of being perceived by faculty as the "tool" of the administration. If this is the case, the operation may have fiscal security and little client interest.

Evaluation

Evaluation, both summative and formative, is an essential ingredient to the implementation of all faculty development activities. Whether the activity be an internship, an action research project, a workshop or the preparation of a publication, evaluation is necessary to keep the activity directed towards its objectives.

For evaluating workshop activities, the center staff have used follow-up questionnaires mailed to participants, engaged in evaluation of the activity individually and in small groups as the last session of a workshop and frequently designed workshops so that there are times built into the design for formative evaluation. All these strategies have proven to be beneficial — even if the data generated are not always positive.

Another strategy which has been useful is to engage consultants from outside the project to attend an activity or to interview a sample of participants. Such an "external" perspective can bring a sense of objectivity not always present in staff or participants. The evaluative data and criticism received by such an individual can be invaluable in keeping the focus of activities on objects and assisting in keeping development activities consistent with changing institutional needs.

Personal Reflections

Faculty development as an institutional activity in postsecondary education is a neophyte. In-service training has been an ongoing activity in primary and secondary education for many years, but for a variety of reasons having to do mainly with a perception that such activity was unnecessary, it is new in postsecondary education. Working to implement a faculty development program has provided that opportunity to learn and, frequently, relearn many things.

First, living with ambiguity and taking risks in planning and implementing programs for and with faculty is a new experience. The faculty development officer is essentially a teacher but relationships are very different when the "students" are your colleagues. This frequently produces a certain amount of loneliness, since you are no longer a line administrator or perceived as a faculty member.

The second learning involves the rediscovery of negotiation skills. Negotiating with faculty, administrators and purveyors of services is an ongoing part of the job. This is particularly true when the considerations are always a new formulation of four concerns: individual development, institutional development, program development and budget.

The third rediscovery is the fact that attention to details in planning faculty development activities is a constant and tiresome fact.

The fourth learning is how to juggle a number of concerns simultaneously and how to wear the hats of designer/planner, facilitator, teacher, technician, counselor/advisor, administrator, and researcher at the same time. This has been tough because it has required personal change and learning new skills.

The fifth skill I've learned is how to synthesize ideas and create new forms. In a nontraditional college, many faculty development activities cannot be traditional program models adapted to another campus setting. This has often meant developing new programs and new activities. This too has been a challenge.

7

Professional Development in the Interinstitutional Setting

by Lance Buhl

Lance Buhl carries the burden and blessing of a Harvard M.A. and Ph.D. in history. He has been a lecturer in history at Harvard and assistant dean of arts and sciences at Cleveland State University. He has been the founding director of the Center for Effective Teaching at Cleveland State, chairperson of the Chancellor's Advisory Committee on Instructional Development (Ohio Board of Regents), director of a consortial faculty development project for northeastern Ohio called Educational Consulting Study. Lance currently is director of Projects for Educational Development, a Cleveland-based educational service. He has published both in history and in professional development and is an active consultant regarding the improvement of teaching and learning.

This chapter is a fitting end piece for this section on teaching improvement programs, because it provides a conceptual framework within which to place much that has been discussed earlier. Also, this chapter places stress upon a part of the teaching improvement process which has been mentioned but not spelled out earlier: creating institutional conditions supportive of teaching improvement. As programs mature, this attention to the organizational situation faced by professors and students understandably increases.

Introduction*

One of the most encouraging aspects of the professional development movement since 1970 has been the emergence of interinstitutional programs. On financial grounds alone, cooperative efforts among colleges and universities to meet the professional development needs of faculty members and administrators commend themselves to our serious attention.

The importance of multi-campus efforts, however, transcends the dollar sign, for such undertakings attest to the commonality of our situation, independent of institutional differences. We soon learn that divisions among two-year, four-year and graduate educators are, fundamentally, artificial and counter-productive. All postsecondary educators face tough fiscal issues, doubts about the effectiveness of our classroom efforts, personal renewal needs, a changing student clientele. Interinstitutional programs allows us to experience our commonality and to learn from one another. These programs often permit a kind of experimentation in format that is difficult to achieve within organizations. Thus, the College Center of the Finger Lakes and the Council for the Advancement of Small Colleges have nurtured a host of innovative ideas that have formed the cutting edge for professional development.

Interinstitutional efforts foster extensive dissemination of experiences and ideas about professional development. The notion of "networking" has taken on new relevance in postsecondary education as a force for renewal largely because of intentional cross-institutional programs. It is clear that the startling expansion of the professional development movement over the past five years has been aided considerably through programmatic connections between and among colleges and universities.

The programs providing information for this chapter are representative of the broad picture. They constitute a varied lot, ranging from the very small (three cooperating institutions) to the very large (members of a national organization). Formal consortial arrangements, of course, predominate as the pattern for interinstitutional programs: Associated Colleges of the Midwest, Cleveland Commission on Higher Education, College Center of the Finger Lakes, Great Lakes College Association, Kansas

*The author wishes to thank Sam H. Lane, Associate Director of the Educational Consulting Study, without whose contribution in ideas and energy to ESC this chapter would hardly have been possible, and Laura A. Wilson, whose research into other interinstitutional programs was diligent and insightful.

City Regional Council for Higher Education, New Hampshire University and College Council, and Society for Values in Higher Education, to name only those described in this volume.

Other forms are practical as well. One program is regional in nature, using an eight member consortium (Cleveland Commission on Higher Education) as fiscal agent, but offering services to fifteen other institutions, regardless of type. At the state policy level, the California State University and Colleges System has spawned a successful program to encourage and coordinate efforts among the member institutions. The Chancellor's Advisory Committee on Instructional Development of the Ohio Board of Regents has been given responsibility to promote efforts among all of the state's postsecondary institutions (public, private, two-year, four-year and graduate) on behalf of improved teaching. One consortium has grown up as the result of an interinstitutional professional development program: The Institute for Teaching and Learning, housed at Spelman College. And two programs — those of the Small College Consortium and the Project for Institutional Renewal through the Improvement of Teaching — are national or regional in scope.

In all, these interinstitutional professional development programs have functioned primarily as catalytic agents for renewal. They stimulate useful "reactions" within and among institutions, reactions that will lead to healthier functioning for the achievement of educational goals. They are not the principal ingredients in the mix. Program directors are not likely to get confused about that. But the catalytic function is and will remain powerful. Many on-campus programs today either would not exist or would be less well advanced were it not for interinstitutional efforts.

Purpose

In an age beset by "systems" language, it is gratuitously, if not disagreeably, said that defining purpose should be a first, central and conscious step taken by anyone interested in building a professional development program. I will say it anyway and argue intentionality has special meaning for directors of interinstitutional programs for teaching improvement.

If there is doubt about the importance of purpose, consider three aspects of the situation. First, the ability of "external" persons to influence on-campus conditions for teaching, learning and other activities amenable to professional growth is very limited. Second, interinstitutional programming must compete (often with on-campus programming) for increasingly scarce resources in at best a "steady state" condition for higher education. Third, professional development, as defined over the past five years, incorporates many of the most emotionally charged issues in higher education: teaching evaluation and improvement, managerial development, personal counseling and growth; not surprisingly, it continues to hold an uncertain place in the hierarchy of faculty and administrative values.

The practical effect of these constraints is experienced in one of two ways. For some interinstitutional program directors—including the majority of those in the programs reviewed here—the constraints mean that they work essentially on a "self-destruct" basis. Their projects are grant generated, expected to "get some things started" and programmed to go out of business in three to five years. For others, those who manage stable consortia and for whom professional development is one of a number of services they provide, the constraints are likely to mean that down the line there will be shift in emphasis, even in definition, of "professional development." In both cases, the realities strongly imply that is is wise to think of professional development programming for the improvement of teaching as cyclical work. At some predictable point in time, a "go/no go" decision will be made about the continued feasibility of the program.

Another consideration comes into play with special force in light of the cyclical nature of interinstitutional professional development programming. It is the personal — the ethical — aspect of development. Professional development work is a force calling on faculty, administrators, staff and students to change one or more of their behaviors or attitudes. Two to five years is not a long time to work toward personal and institutional change. How easy it is to promise too much. And deliver too little. The challenge is to define clear contracts related to expectations, learning and particularly to the ownership of change and of the innumerable problems it raises. There is no greater failing in professional development efforts than inducing people to alter the ways they relate to students and to one another without also attending purposefully to the matter of those institutional conditions which may or, more likely, may not support them.

All these forces boil down to one thing. Each program director ought to be able to make a strong case that the investment made in her program has resulted in improved institutional functioning *at least equal* to results that could reasonably have been expected through investment in other programs or areas. Indeed, that ought to be the ruling premise made at the outset of program development.

Defining a Model for Change

A review of the several programs which are considered in this piece suggests that the problem of intentionality is handled by defining or adopting a model for change. The value of a model is that it increases intentionality and, to the degree that the criteria of excellence are spelled out clearly, it facilitates evaluative efforts. As a group, the directors of these projects identify improved teaching and learning as the ultimate purpose of the efforts. Definitions about achieving that goal tend to group in three ways, each approximating a general model for change. The distinctions are, of course, cleaner than reality acknowledges. None of the programs fit precisely or exclusively under any one model. But goal emphases in these three directions are marked.

One model works on the assumption that any movement toward personal and professional growth, so long as it is valued both by the individuals involved and by the particular institutions served, works toward organizational health and will, ultimately, benefit students. This model has been more or less explicitly adopted in the professional development projects of the California State University and Colleges System, the Project for Institutional Renewal through the Improvement of Teaching, the Great Lakes College Association and the Kansas City Regional Council for Higher Education. The officers of these programs are by no means passive or indifferent to the outcomes of the efforts they facilitate. They have made a conscious choice, however, to discover where the human energy for change is on campuses served and to accept the definition of desirable goals for professional development as the "clients" write them. If the direction taken is consistent with the ultimate purpose of increasing educational effectiveness, the project managers rest comfortably with this client-centered approach.

The second general model is an instructional development one. Its primary assumption is that the surest way to improve conditions for learning is either to systematize course design or to strengthen and extend the teaching skills of faculty. Adherents of this two-edged model—principally the Danforth supported project at Spelman College and that of the New Hampshire College and University Council—offer faculty a variety of services which focus directly on the teaching/learning interaction. Accordingly, the arena for consulting and training with the client population is smaller, though no less elegant, than that used by the adherents of the first model.

The third model operates on the assumption that personal and professional growth in teaching are necessary but not sufficient. The behaviors of members of the institution other than involved faculty and their students also must change if it is intended that most students will learn more, more efficiently and more effectively. Faculty and administrative skills in collaborative decision making must be strengthened and policies altered to ensure that organizational health and teaching/learning effectiveness are maintained over time. The group of interinstitutional programs most closely associated with this organizational development model include those of the Cleveland Commission on Higher Education, the College Center of the Finger Lakes, the Small College Consortium and the Ohio Board of Regents.

I want to pay particular attention to the third model, partly because an author has some privileges (and biases) but essentially because it builds on many of the assumptions of the first model and many of the techniques of the second. But it does go beyond both, particularly with reference to what we might refer to as the dynamics and politics of institutional change.

The Conditions for Teaching Model

All persons responsible for professional development programs resonate to the force of the question: How can we increase the probabilities that these efforts will pay off over the long run, that increased teaching and learning, personal, administrative and interpersonal competencies will be maintained? The terms of the third model, more than those of the first or second ones, begin to get at hopeful answers.

My colleague, Sam Lane, and I have developed and adopted a variation of the third model in our work for the Educational Consulting Study of the Cleveland Commission on Higher Education. Our experience with the model is illustrative of several aspects — some helpful and some less so — of the organization development perspective. That perspective is encoded in an exciting, vigorous and growing literature on the application of behavioral science research to complex human institutions. The strength of the literature lies in its ethical and philosophical commitment to personal as well as institutional health and effectiveness and, equally, in its empiricism. We discovered a congenial outlook. Our comfort has increased as writers and consultants recently have begun to establish the relevance of the research to postsecondary education. (68, 102)

Our model consists of a statement of the conditions we would like to see in any of the institutions to which we offer services. Our overriding concern is that the conditions for learning in each institution will be organized course by course so that most students will achieve the learning objectives set for them at high levels of competence. Our operational purpose, then, is to see that the teaching function is honored at least at par with other forms of professional activity and honored as a form of describable, learnable, modifiable and dynamic problem-solving activity. The model holds that a college or university facilitates effective teaching and learnings when

1. the nature of the instructional process and the kinds of evidence necessary for making tentative judgments about its effectiveness are specified in reasonable conformity to effective teaching practices identified in the literature on learning;
2. significant numbers of faculty are allocating their professional energies systematically and experimentally to adopting effective teaching practices over extended periods of time;
3. institutional policies specify that increasing teaching/ learning effectiveness is an important operational goal;
4. formal administrative decision making processes are consciously and systematically shaped to support and reward documented faculty efforts to increase teaching/learning effectiveness; and
5. the faculty as a whole consciously encourages and supports those faculty who have opted to increase teaching/learning effectiveness systematically.

The second point of the model is central. In expanded form it defines what we mean by "professional development in teaching":

the commitment of individual faculty members to organize, for extended periods (three to five years), personally satisfying career patterns around 1) a search in the literature on learning for teaching/learning formats considered conducive to learning for most students and 2) the systematic application of experimental principles in adapting such formats and assessing their effects on learning.

This formulation gets beyond the limitations of instructional development as it is often practiced, which is to emphasize the creation of teaching services (audio-visual departments, evaluation services, committees on teaching, centers for training and consultation, information dissemination mechanisms). Such teaching services are necessary but in themselves cost-ineffective because they affect relatively few faculty and, consequently, only a limited number of students for a limited span of their academic careers. Our model rests on the assumption that the key to sufficiency and to cost-effectiveness of professional development efforts, defined in terms of impact on student learning, is to encourage a "critical mass" of faculty to get involved in teaching improvement within each regular instructional program of the institution. Faculty, in the final analysis, define, organize, monitor and evaluate learning. Unless they make a commitment in sufficient numbers to affect the learning experiences of most students, the goal of improving the effectiveness of the teaching/learning enterprise in measurable ways remains a pipe dream.

Once focus shifts from support services *per se* to *numbers of faculty* committed to improving the conditions for learning, an equal demand is placed on other variables within the institution — the nature of institutional goals, administrative attitudes and behaviors, colleague attitudes and behaviors, policies and practices that tend to encourage (or discourage) systematic attention to teaching. Over the long run, professional development programs in teaching will not be limited to creating instructional support services. They will be planned, systematic efforts to encourage enough faculty to get seriously involved in altering the conditions for learning so that the learning experience of most students in the institutions will be enhanced. Such programs will work toward changes in the "cultural" — the attitudinal and behavioral norms, values and policies — of the organization. They will have to become as advocacy oriented as they are service-oriented.

The advantages of the model for us are several. We make constant references to it. By doing so, it helps us answer the questions concerning the what's, the how's and the who's of change. It is conceptually satisfying and grounded on some real evidence about human behaviors in complex organizations. It provides some criteria against which we can make decisions about where and at what level of sophistication we ought to be putting our limited resources. It has helped us, thereby, "target" institutions which are receptive and ready for professional development. By the same token, it provides criteria for evaluation of our efforts and the state of professional development in northeast Ohio. In short, it meets our needs for intentionality, for purpose.

Sam and I also know the disadvantages of using an "organizational development model" such as ours. For one thing, it is a high risk model and, because there is so much to do to promote cultural change, it can set us up for failure. Quite easily, we can look at the long-term change objective and fail to perceive the small signs of movement and improvement. Second, it is a difficult model to sell. Indeed, its assumptions and hypotheses about organizational life and about teaching are resisted by many in postsecondary education who sincerely believe that academic organizations are quite different from other complex institutions. Third, the model ultimately demands hard data, and hard data about educational outcomes and about institutional change are hard to come by in academe, which has only just begun to get sophisticated about institutional research. Good instrumentation to assess environments for teaching simply do not exist. One questionnaire which we have developed is only in the field testing stage. The data are preliminary at best and the instrument still in need of careful refinement. Finally, three years — the time frame for our project — was not enough time to affect much change in any of the institutions we served, despite the great readiness of some to get on with serious professional development.

On balance, however, the conditions for learning model is more useful than not. It is arguable that programs which make a comprehensive definition of the problem of improving teaching, which adopt an organization development perspective, and which can measure growth in hard data will operate in an environment in which professional development in teaching ultimately will be the norm.

Even if interinstitutional program officers decide against adapting the general model for their own use, the perspective it establishes might be useful to them as they think through the essential first step: defining purpose. Table One graphically displays the central dimensions found to at least some degree in any professional development program for teaching improvement. Readers are invited to study the table and to use it both to assess the present status of professional development within the institutions they serve and to decide on the configuration of a model for professional development with which each feels comfortable. The anchor points — what constitutes "relatively little impact" and "significant impact" — together with other specifics will vary from one assessor and planner to another. The utility of the exercise can be increased by inviting colleagues to answer the leading question posed for each dimension and to assess the programs of, or determine the goals for their own professional development program.

Table One:
Measurable Dimensions of Programs
For Professional Development in Teaching

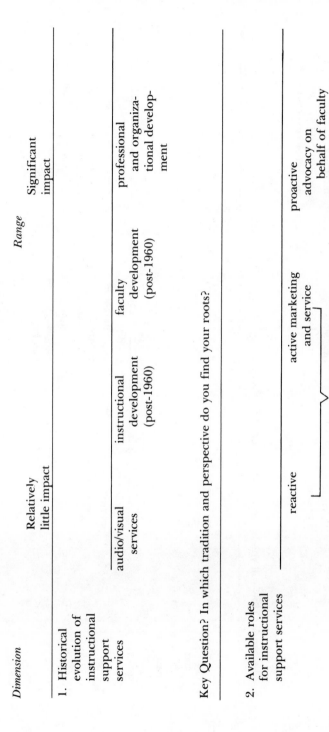

Dimension	Relatively little impact	Range	Significant impact

1. Historical evolution of instructional support services

audio/visual services — instructional development (post-1960) — faculty development (post-1960) — professional and organizational development

Key Question? In which tradition and perspective do you find your roots?

2. Available roles for instructional support services

reactive — active marketing and service — proactive advocacy on behalf of faculty committed to improvement

acceptance of institutional culture "as it is"

Key Question: How will you or do you relate to faculty, staff and administration (message, tone)?

3. Cost-effectiveness of services	impossible to assess in terms of learning outcomes	evidence of increased morale of clients served	measurable change in terms of increased morale *and* learning outcomes reported

Key Question: How will you or do you track cost-effectiveness?

4. Extent of faculty involvement in teaching improvement services	- "receivers" of services - scattered few	- active use of and interest in nature of services - still a distinct and uninfluential minority within faculty	- they determine nature of services and use them extensively - "developing" faculty constitute a "critical mass" in all academic units

Key Question: What are or what do you want to be the patterns of use of your services?

5. Nature of dominant
   instructional
   orientation of
   faculty

faculty-centered instruction:	learner-centered:
unidimensional	multi-dimensional
unsystematic	systematic
unexperimental	experimental

Key Question: To what extent do course descriptions, syllabi, and faculty attitudes and behaviors stress the needs of the learner?

6. Institutional goal
   and policy statements
   relative to teaching
   and learning

- statements are vague, general and behaviorally irrelevant	- statements are clear, specific and criteria-oriented
- teaching is not highlighted as the critical factor in personnel decisions	- teaching is weighted at least at par with or more heavily than other professional activities

Key Question: Is "effective teaching" considered a "given" of professional competence or is it something to strive for?

7. Extent of administrative support for efforts to improve teaching

- inconsistent, unsystematic with little call for, or attention to, documentation - "development" is for the faculty	- consistent, systematic with high demand for, and dependence on, documentable professional growth - "development" is for everyone, including administrators

Key Question? How often do administrators talk about development, in what contexts, with what kind of budgetary commitment and with what connotations?

8. Extent of peer support for efforts to improve teaching

very little, seldom public and often negative or indifferent	frequent, public, interested and policy-relevant

Key Question: Do most of the influential faculty exhibit flight/fight or approach/nurture behaviors in relation to teaching experimentation and innovation?

9. Impact of teaching on learning

undetectable or, at best, random with meager data base	discernible patterns described in terms of solid baseline data about learning experiences and achievements of students

Key Question: Can your institution come up with convincing evidence that it has helped the majority of its students to achieve learning objectives at respectable levels?

Structure

Program directors are properly concerned with structural issues for three reasons. They want to know

1. How much influence the responsible officer(s) of the sponsoring agency will expect to exert on program management.
2. How the formal relationship with the institution receiving or providing funds for the program will affect the program's initial and continuing credibility with the client population.
3. What, if any, formal links should be established with client institutions and how such links are most usefully established.

The sponsoring agency's influence in program policy and direction is an important issue. Most of the directors of programs reported in this chapter, however, do not experience formal structure as a critical problem. Some essentially are their own bosses, they and their programs existing fairly autonomously within the legal and fiscal definitions of the sponsoring institutions. Some work as officers of the agency; their programs are practically organic functions of the larger organizations. Only one or two have found relations with the sponsor to be problematic. The key to good working arrangements — ones that allow a maximum of autonomy within the context of accountability — seems to be developing explicit understandings about the what, who and how of policy making and reporting. Successful professional development programming requires flexibility, especially in responding to client needs. Tight control of the program by the sponsoring agency may inhibit responsiveness. As much as possible, program directors should strive for explicitness about the rules which govern the relationship at the outset and, as time goes on, should review those rules periodically in the light of new directions and needs.

The second issue has largely to do with deciding whether the fiscal or sponsoring agency should handle funds only or whether its role should be to "validate" or promote the program. Programs with official ties to policy making agencies, such as the Office of the Chancellor of the California State University and Colleges System or the Ohio Board of Regents, face this issue most squarely. Timing is at issue. Initially, endorsement of the idea of professional development by a chancellor may be helpful for establishing validity of the program. Later the realities of academic politics in a state may be such that it is more useful to establish at least the illusion of program autonomy. The "validating" function of an official state agency may be less valuable, if not counter-productive, as time wears on.

For most programs, this issue may be important at the outset but neutral thereafter. The perceived legitimacy of the sponsoring institution may help establish the program's credibility. Doors are opened, an audience created. As a program gains its own reputation, it may be purely conjectural as to which — sponsoring agency or program — more positively enhances the image of the other. In any event, it pays for program directors to milk what credibility they can out of the fiscal agent's status.

Building Relations with Client Institutions

The most important structural issue concerns building relations with client institutions and populations. A typical pattern is to make contacts with the presidents, other senior academic administrators and key faculty members of the target institutions. Few perhaps have gone about the task so carefully and systematically as did Claude Mathis and Robert Menges of Northwestern's Center for the Teaching Professions as they established the Danforth Faculty Development program for the Associated Colleges of the Midwest. Over a six month period, Mathis and Menges held meetings with the ACM deans, council; the presidents of each member institution; several researchers who knew the characteristics of each institution very well; and groups of faculty, students and administrators on each ACM campus. By the time they were ready to inaugurate the first joint program, Mathis and Menges had established credibility and had created an openness to their ideas. In the case of the California State University and Colleges programs, on the other hand, a critical problem was tardy development of good relations with the system's faculty senate.

Another typical pattern, especially for maintaining credibility in and access to client institutions over the long run, is to create an advisory committee or council of representatives of each institution involved. There are choices to be made.

1. How should the membership be chosen (by administrative appointment, by faculty election or even through program suggestion)?
2. Is access better assured by faculty or administrative membership?
3. Should the committee be purely "advisory" or be a true "steering" group or even constitute an informal staff body?

The decisions among these choices should be made with reference to the political realities of the situation and with clear regard for the degrees of support and/or freedom of action that are desired.

In the case of the Educational Consulting Study, presidential appointment of someone (administrator or faculty) with a clear interest in or responsibility for professional development in teaching was the quickest way to establish access. The board became ECS's first "sales market," as it were. On several occasions, its members met to consider ideas and suggest strategies for implementation. More important, however, has been the role board members have taken as ECS liaison agents within the twenty-three institutions to which services were offered.

Staffing

The quality of any program has to bear some relationship to the abilities of its staff. So much is obvious. One would think, however, that the available range and depth of abilities, in turn, should bear some relationship to size of staff. Directors or coordinators of interinstitutional programs must be profoundly talented because, with but a single exception, the central professional staff of each program considered here ranges from a single half-time member to two full-time equivalent members. This is independent of number of institutions served, of the goals and objectives of the program, and of the type and range of activities and services provided. On the face of it, we seem to make our lives more difficult by insisting on minimal staffing.

The decision to keep small staffs is deliberate. It seems the better part of wisdom is to maintain a neat, compact organization, particularly when so many of the institutions served face severe economic crises. Where political considerations play a role — at the state policy level, for example — creation of another "bureaucracy" is unseemly and courts trenchant and loud criticism. Intentional also is the strategy of creating competent staffing within client institutions to carry on the work. The trick here is to manage training and consulting through which cadres of campus-based trainers and consultants develop. Finally, most programs were initiated "on the come" — conceived through proposals written when we could not be sure just how great the demand for our services would be.

A common tactic — one worth adopting — is to build into the budget a relatively healthy consulting line. This is especially important for programs which adopt an explicit commitment to train, or to provide other direct services to, clients. This allows building a staffing capability as needs emerge.

Even with the use of external consultants, the disadvantages of a small central staff problem — too many balls in the air — remains and may be complicated by a new set of demands to identify, screen and select, monitor, and evaluate occasional consultants. There is the danger of farming out too much of the work and losing visibility within the institutions served. Ensuring quality of service is more difficult in working with *per diem* staff than supervising *per annum* staff.

Establishing a Consultant Pool

Another issue to confront directly is to decide how to build the pool of consultants from which to draw. Some directors favor relying heavily on skilled consultant/trainers from within the interinstitutional setting. Both the Cleveland commission on Higher Education and the Kansas City Regional Council programs have relied on this strategy on the grounds that there are long term payoffs in recognizing local talent and encouraging its use in the region. Some, by the very nature of the program, work through larger, sometimes national networks of trainers and consultants. Most programs resort to both options for recruiting consultants. Other considerations aside, the critical factors in deciding which type of consultant — local or national — are the extent to which broad reputation seems warranted, how much one is willing to pay in *per diem* fees and travel, and the extent to which it is desirable to promote the use of local resources.

A valuable practice is to use external consultants to the program itself. Typically, they are hired as program evaluators. By the careful selection of experts, program directors can both satisfy the necessity to get sound evaluative data and develop a training relationship with an external consultant. In essence, consultant/evaluators become adjunct staff. This description is bound to make some uneasy. Shouldn't the relationship between evaluator and program officer be clinical and "clean," unsullied by normal social intercourse? If the sole purpose of the evaluation is to generate a summative report — either at the end of the program or at the stage where a go/no go decision about continued funding is at hand — a positive answer is sound enough. But in most cases the intent of evaluation is to improve an ongoing program. This "formative" approach and relationship is both appropriate and powerful. The data generated can be sound and usefully inform the decision making process, especially when the evaluator views her role as problem solver as well as problem-poser.

The Project Manager Approach

The ideal approach to the entire problem of creating an effective and expendable program staff might be labeled the "project manager" approach. This, at least, is what I would use more deliberately next time around.

1. Define the program in terms of discrete packages of effort, individual projects that have a beginning and an end, and a set of desired outcomes.
2. Farm out the management of each project, either to internal staff (including yourself) or to individual consultants.
3. Do it on an explicit contract basis. Each contract would constitute an agreement to perform and/or manage the project according to carefully negotiated and detailed specifications about objectives, nature of program components, target dates, resources and evaluative strategy.
4. Pay special attention to how training and consulting events, where they are to be used, will model the principles the program espouses.
5. Be intentional, too, about how managing the project meets the professional development goals of the staff member or consultant who signs on.

Establishing contracts with external consultants can be an essential part of a successful project manager approach. In one instance received funds to conduct a training program for faculty and administrators responsible for professional development on their respective campuses. We needed consultant/trainers with a variety of skills to make the program successful. We selected six, negotiated for their time and sent them, as the basis for negotiation around their responsibilities, a letter of agreement, which read in part:

Our expectations are that each day's session will

1. be about 6-8 hours long;
2. result in new/refined products and skills in the subject matter described by [your] topic;
3. model sound instructional design;
   a. minimal learning objectives . . . will be specified and communicated to (even negotiated with) participants;
   b. learning activities participants will be asked to engage in will be described;
   c. sessions will place heavy emphasis on participant involvement; these are workshops, therefore lecturettes (rather than lectures), discussions, projects, case study analyses,

simulations, role-playing, games and other activities . . . should be relied on; especially desirable are work
materials that encourage participants to problem-solve and
to chart and assess their learning;

   d. sessions will be individualized as much as practicable . . .;

   e. evaluation of sessions will be built in . . .

4. proceed on a "giveaway" basis; we should open up and share
from our bags of tricks . . .;

5. be linked to printed resources [assigned reading, handouts,
short lists of critical readings];

6. encourage the development of a group of people who are able
to and will interact with one another supportively.

The ECS staff and the consultant/trainers met as a group a month prior
to the beginning of the program to test these expectations, share ideas and
develop a common thematic identity for the program.

Attend to Personal Needs

There is another "should" I would urge on program directors. Pay
attention to your own and to your individual staff members' needs — for
career nurturing, for training and for support. This triad of needs is
interrelated by virtue of a single fact: Our work is not mainstream
academia. We can seem pretty odd folk to academics for whom "legitimate" education takes place primarily in classrooms in institutions with
walls and attendant trappings. It is true that we can argue plausibly that we
are educators, working primarily with adults (faculty, administrators and
staff). But that is not enough. We need to attend consciously to making our
efforts credible on paper and in practice.

Assuming that professional development programs have cyclical histories and that many are of the "self-destruct" variety, program managers
legitimately can consider how their own career interests are served
through their programs. Questions to address include:

1. How does the project cycle approximate and facilitate my own
developmental needs and predictable life "crises"?

2. What can I learn — what new or refined knowledge and
skills — can I acquire along the way?

3. How can my *vitae* best reflect that growth?

4. How will I know — what "traces" will exist as evidence — that
my work has been good?

   a. Will people I have worked with report that they feel better

    about themselves and their students, colleagues, institutions? How many?
  b. Will administrators work more consciously on behalf of supporting faculty who are going about the business of improvement?
  c. Will students demonstrate increased proficiency in learning or increased satisfaction with the quality of instruction?
  d. Will the institutions I worked in or provided services for operate more like communities — with higher incidence of collaborative problem solving?

A particular instance of the need to grow professionally is the training it takes to work to maximum effect as trainer/consultants to others. Skills for assessing and responding both sensitively and adequately to client needs are several and special. While it is true that common sense and on-the-job learning are necessary components of good professional development work, neither is sufficient. We need to expand our theoretical and practical bases of operations intentionally.

My recommendation is for an entire staff collaboratively and periodically to develop a matrix of "needed skills" based on career goals and on experienced or perceived demands emanating from clients. Out of that matrix, the staff would decide which skills are comfortably within its repertoire, which are so specialized or strange or expensive to acquire as to warrant outside consultants, and which reasonably can be acquired by special training. Each staff member could then begin to work on those skills that correspond to her personal needs and preferences. Each, finally, would devise a skill development strategy, some combination of training, travel and applied research that should lead to increased effectiveness and long-term career enhancement.

The trick is to avoid 1) theoretical promiscuity while striving for solid interconnected eclecticism and 2) shoddy training experiences. Fortunately, there is a strong and increasingly congruent disciplinary base in applied psychology and competent training sources for professional and organizational development work. My own list of recommended training sources would include the Gestalt Institute of Cleveland, the NTL Institute for Applied Behavioral Sciences, University Associates, the special training programs of the Professional and Organizational Development Network, course work or special programs in industrial psychology, management or organizational behavior offered by regular academic departments, and programs offered through the various divisions or professional associations of psychology and/or business administration.

One last word on staffing. Program directors should pay special attention to their own needs for support. Support means creating a truly collegial interstaff relationship, a professional community where asking for and offering support is the norm. In my experience it is altogether too easy, even with (or perhaps as a result of having only) a small staff, to get overwhelmed in the process of responding to program demands. Personal needs for sustenance and renewal are neglected. One rule I would adopt, were I to do this all over again, is to include regular and adequate staff conference time, not just to plan program but to trade ideas, share problems and think about future projects.

Activities

There is a hypothesis about interinstitutional programs for professional development that is worth testing. To one degree or another, each of the programs mentioned in this chapter adheres to its tenets. The hypothesis is this: the usefulness and effectiveness of the interinstitutional program for serving the professional development needs of both the persons "developing" and their institutions is a function of its capacity to act as "consultant" rather than as another, occasionally competing, authority and resource consumer. The message in the proposition is that we should become skilled consultants of a particular sort: "facilitators" of change.

There is bound to be dispute about whether change is or ought to be our concern. There seems to me no way to avoid it. Change lies at the very heart of professional development. Our programs have a dual aim: to facilitate the enrichment of the professional lives and effectiveness of academics within their institutional setting (or to better prepare them for leaving those settings) and to enhance the productivity/effectiveness/ efficiency (circle one or more) of those institutions. By our very existence, we call for and engender a series of attitudes and behaviors that were not discernible before. We are adult educators. Ideally, we work toward the integration of personal and institutional moves toward greater effectiveness. However well we do, we pose a series of real problems in the management of change.

The facilitative consultant, while she has some pretty clear ideas about what healthy change means and looks like, also is firmly committed to respecting the needs for change *as clients define them*. The most useful way to express this idea is that the ownership of the definitions and processes of change (development) must remain with those seeking and using the services. The facilitative consultant learns quickly that, however similar professional development problems are across institutions, *each* institution has a unique culture that determines the rate, direction and permanence of change. We ignore these differences to our own and our clients' detriment.

Program Contracts

The facilitative consultant accounts for these differences by establishing tailored "contracts" with clients. In any learning relationship, some sort of understanding implicit and/or explicit exists in the minds of each party concerned. It involves assumptions and expectations about what you will do, what I will do, what he will do, the manner of doing those things, the expected pay-off schedule and the time frame. Consultants most effectively respect clients' ownership of problems and their solution (and their own integrity) when they make each of these aspects of the contracts explicit. The result could be a fairly limited relationship that approximates the classic management consulting relationship — a consultant comes in for a discrete job around professional development, does it according to specifications, and takes her leave. It is as likely, however, that she will get commited to some longer, continuing relationship that involves collaborative efforts to define and resolve problems related to professional development.

Experience suggests that there are some useful guidelines for organizing programs around client needs. The following three rules are offered in the hope that observing them will keep away the devils called frustration and disillusionment.

1. *Find your friends and work with them.* Resist the urge to complain that you are not affecting those "who really need" development. You are not likely to "save" them anyway. Begin instead to build a base of support among those already interested in their own development; then, heeding the advice of Chet Case that we should avoid only talking to our friends, work out strategies for expanding incrementally beyond that base. But never take it for granted. Friends, new and old, need continuing support and encouragement. Another way to think of this is to *Discover the interest and make capital of it.*

2. *Respect the importance of "reinventing wheels."* Resist the nonsense that everything that is worth doing has been done by someone

and that all we need to do is find the model and adopt it instead of recreating it. Where models are appropriate, the processes of problem-solving involved in change are at most processes of *adaptation*. Examples and models, even those matured elsewhere, are heuristic devices. People establish ownership by creating their own wheels of change and learning about themselves while doing it.

3. *Establish incremental strategies.* Resist the urge to grab for the moon the first shot off the pad. You are bound to feel frustrated. Worse, so will your clients. What you define as the moon is a legitimate objective, but to get there you need to think and act instead in terms of achieving successive approximations to the flight pattern that will reach the target. The abilities to forebear, to recognize small changes in the approximate direction and to appreciate them are required. Practice can make perfect (or a reasonable facsimile thereof). In the meantime, read and assimilate the very wise analysis of "Educational Decision Making" in Daniel L. Stufflebeam *et. al., Educational Evaluation and Decision Making.* (106A)

In terms of practical program management, interinstitutional professional developers rely on a variety of specific activities to facilitate change. Training and consulting are the bread and butter (in that order) of development. Workshops and conferences are characteristic but not exclusive devices in which the bread is baked and the butter churned. One-on-one consulting, "Fellowship" programs, information dissemination, grant-making — indeed all the mechanisms found in campus-based programs are used extensively. The critical point is that each activity is highly malleable and should be shaped to serve the goals of the program. A workshop can be used as a one-shot "consciousness-raiser" or programmed to effect more permanent change through instructional skill building or institutional planning. It is the packaging and intended products that differ from program to program and objective to objective.

Circuit-Riding

In this connection it is useful to think in terms of four functional categories of professional development activities. First, there is "circuit-riding." It comes with the territory, as it were. Interinstitutional programs can hardly avoid working to establish a channel of regular communication with each institution involved. The program must be visible; its intent and message available. Fortunately, Ma Bell and the U.S. Postal Service exempt us from having to slap leather each time we need to make contact. Still, most interinstitutional program directors consider it necessary to conduct periodic site visits. The efforts of Claude Mathis and Robert Menges to build credibility within the Associated Colleges of the Midwest form a particularly fine example of circuit-riding. For Joseph Durzo of the New Hampshire College and University Council, circuit-riding from institution to institution to work with individual faculty on specific teaching improvement projects was the central mode of operation.

The contracts made through the circuit-riding process constitute what we might call "second order consulting," those interactions which aim at assessing institutional needs in professional development and the degree to which the interinstitutional program seems appropriate and sufficient to meeting them. The decision involved concerns whether to establish and/or continue a service relationship.

Discrete Programming

What I call "discrete programming" includes 1) introductory workshops, seminars or conferences on facets of professional development and 2) information dissemination activities. The goal is to raise consciousness about and, to some extent, increase skill levels in one or another phase of professional life. In the three years of its existence, Educational Consulting Study staff have conducted about fifty different workshops and conferences of the "discrete" programming type. Topics have included, among others, "Professional Development in Teaching — What Is It?" "Auto-Tutorial Instruction," "Individualized Instruction," "Organizing a Syllabus for Learning," "Evaluating Teaching," "Peer Evaluation," "Administrative Skill Development," "Student Evaluations of Teaching," "Student Motivation," "Alternative Teaching Methods," "Teaching Tips" (a day-long regional conference), "Curricular Revision," "Stating Behavioral Objectives," and "Organizing Systems for Professional Evaluation."

The outstanding characteristic of discrete programming is the "one shot" nature of the activity. That is, there is relatively little, if any, follow-up with participants to reinforce learning that may have occurred. Discrete programs tend, thus, to be low-risk and low-payoff. There is practically no evidence, for example, that another form of discrete programming, newsletters, are widely read within the client population, much less used by many as a resource for changing some personal behavior.

This is not to demean the importance or necessity of organizing discrete program activities and doing so with meticulous care. Activities of this type reinforce credibility and raise consciousness for teaching and for learning. Workshops, conferences, seminars, newsletters and brochures, therefore, ought to exemplify the educational and professional principles our programs proclaim. They ought to be models of the problem solving and experimental approaches in action.

Discrete programming is an inescapable stage of professional development programming. Each project reviewed in this chapter uses one or another of these activities intentionally. They are entrees to more ambitious efforts.

Continuous Programming

Those training and consulting activities which are directed to more permanent behavioral change on the part of faculty members, administrators and even other staff, are long-range, continuous programming activities. While such change may profoundly affect the culture of an institution, cultural change is not the immediate purpose of the effort. Training and consulting in this mode tend to be both extensive (over time) and intensive (systematically geared to the nature and processes of the desired change).

Some sort of follow-up contract with the client or clients is implied or made very explicit in continuous programming. For example, one of the principal activities of the Center for Professional Development of the California State system has been to administer a grants program for institutionally sanctioned proposals for campus-based professional development programs. The director of the center, then, is engaged in proposal solicitations, proposal review, grant awarding, program monitoring and program evaluation. In Ohio, the Chancellor's Advisory Committee on Instructional Development annually conducts a training conference for teams of institutional representatives to assist each team to develop (or recycle) plans for programs in professional development in teaching. Each team agrees to conduct an end-of-year evaluation of the program and report results back to the committee. This program is modeled after the strategy devised several years ago by the Council for the Advancement of Small Colleges in offering continuous programming. At another level, Joe Durzo assisted individuals or groups of faculty in planning and experimenting with instructional change projects considered to be high priority within the institutions. Alternatively, my colleagues and I have organized week-long ECS Summer Institutes on College Teaching, the goal of which has been that each participant will redesign part or all of at least one course according to the principle of systematic instructional design. Fred Gaige, former director of the Center for Professional Development at KRCHE, relied principally on one-to-one consulting with faculty and administrators who faced critical career decisions. What ties these and other examples together is intentionality regarding specific types of individual change.

Systematic Organization Interventions

Activities which aim specifically to increase the abilities of members of a department, college or university to improve the interpersonal and decision making processes of their culture may be called systematic organizational interventions. They involve a set of high risk training and "first-order" consulting activities — survey-guided change planning, training of "internal" change agents and consultants, team-building, role negotiation, whole unit problem solving projects, among others. The length and amount of time required to manage such activities successfully usually are beyond what programs can afford. Seldom do interinstitutional development projects define cultural change as an immediate program objective, or if they do, work at such levels with more than a few clients.

Because personal and professional change makes demands on the culture of an institution, it is important to consider the possibilities for activities at the organizational level. Bonnie Larson of the College Center of the Finger Lakes (CCFL) describes her program in terms of stages of development roughly approximating a progression from circuit-riding to organizational intervention. Ultimately, the CCFL program concentrated on training several skilled internal consultants for change in one of the three institutions in the consortium. The staff of the Educational Consulting Study in Cleveland has only begun, through assisting a small college in defining a comprehensive workload and evaluation system, to approach significant organizational change. It is certainly clear that careful work in each of the three other categories of program activity were and remain essential for successful work in the intervention category.

Networking

There is a fifth category of activity, which, properly speaking, falls in the "continuous programming" domain. It requires special treatment because of the cyclical nature of interinstitutional programs. It tends to involve two sorts of mechanisms; both are complementary and people-oriented. The first stimulates conscious networking among members of the interinstitutional set. People who work in different institutions but who share common concerns and values usually also have different skills and talents and can teach, and learn from, one another. This can be an especially valuable strategy when working with people responsible for on-campus professional development programs. They tend to be somewhat new at the game; often they are isolated by their connection with faculty development from normal bases of professional support. They need a reference group which networking can provide. One of the benefits that could accrue from networking is a system of service exchanges among the members of the network. They become adjunct staff to one another.

The second mechanism provides for learning in collaboration. Networking does not just happen. For all its theoretical attractiveness, it is honored more in the breach than in the practice. Academicians tend to be loners. Collaboration has to be learned. So, if networking seems worth promoting, it is a matter of credibility-building and circuit-riding, for consciousness-raising and discrete programming and especially for behavioral change and continuous programming. Networkers will have to establish agreements among themselves and work to maintain them

Training of Facilitators

Another promising strategy is training trainers and consultants. Think of it as "giving away all the secrets" of training and consulting to people within the institutions who are ready and want to use them. Readiness is as important as desire. Faculty and administrators who are ready often are the ones flexible enough to withstand career change. Serious commitment to professional development programming places heavy demands on individual time and energy. Readiness also implies a commitment to the values that professional development underlie. Very often people self-direct themselves after having gone through activities at the consciousness-raising or behavioral change levels. For others, their own professional training makes them ideal candidates.

However the selection process works, the preparation process should be carefully planned and, like all other activities, be patterned on the models and values of the program.

If training trainers is successful, some fallout is likely to occur. Predictably, the factor of "rising expectations" and concomitant dissatisfaction with career or situations will affect some of those trained. Already risk-takers, a few will come to view themselves and their opportunities in a different light. They will want some different things in life and career and come to find that the institutions in which they work cannot foot this new bill. Overall, the loss is an acceptable, perhaps even hopeful, risk to assume on behalf of building a cadre of skilled professional development resources.

Financing

I am not optimistic about the economic future of interinstitutional professional development programs. Funding in the past has been minimal, measured against the scope of the task. Primarily, the funds have come from foundations and government agencies for specified objectives and limited periods of time. The bulk of the funds are earmarked for staff salaries, consulting, travel, seed-money grants for experimentation and materials. A typical annual budget ranges from $50,000 to $150,000, a variance that indicates little in the way of anticipated effect on significant numbers of faculty or administrators.

Several alternative fund-raising strategies are worth exploring.

1. *User Fees*

    More likely than not, a "user" will be defined as the institution served (not an individual faculty member), although some prorating might be built in to account either for size of faculty or for number of faculty actually served. Very probably, poor institutions will be unable to spare any cash. The better situated ones, consequently, will bear a disproportionate share of the costs. Users' fees may take the form of matching dollar contributions — for every dollar the program raises or contributes to a particular activity, a participating institution will agree to contribute dollars. This approach, of course, depends on raising front money. Overall, the best chance for the users' fee approach to work may lie among two-year institutions.

2. *Consortial Subscriptions*

    A close relative of the users' fee approach is the subscription mechanisms consortia traditionally have used to support themselves. This may not be a very available option because consortia already operate on a shoestring. Supporting professional development out of available consortial treasuries will mean cutting out other programs. Increasing subscription fees seems a dubious proposition. Still the idea is worth exploring. It may be, for example, that a consortium might develop *around* a professional development program. Consider too the possibilities of "in-kind" contributions by institutions. Such might include, among various options, release-time (*not* overtime) assignments of staff for special interinstitutional projects, materials duplication, and space and/or equipment use. This kind of contribution would do equally well as a form for users' fee.

3. *Institutional Center*

Another clever move would be to identify a large, relatively wealthy and probably public community college or university which needs a professional development program *and* has a fairly large and elastic commitment to and definition of community service. The program might be offered to that institution through an arrangement by which it becomes the "principal client/host institution"for services offered both within and outside. Probably, some users' fee set-up for off-campus clients will have to be devised, but at the least, the major portion of line item costs will be assured.

4. *State Funding*

For interinstitutional programs which include public institutions, there may be hope in working for state funding. The game will be political, requiring in all likelihood that the state legislature enact enabling laws and subsequent appropriations for the encouragement of professional development. It is clearly a long shot. There are sure to be compromises to be made along the way, probably with academic groups for whom professional development means only sabbaticals. And there are enemies to be made, including some university and college spokesmen for whom dollars for professional development seem to augur fewer to institutional general budgets. It is not surprising that, while the Chancellor of the California State University has committed hard dollars to the Center for Professional Development, the expectation is that the program will be phased out after a few more years. The Chancellor's Advisory Committee on Instructional Development in Ohio has considered the possibility of permanent state aid from several angles. Realistically,the prospects are not bright. Perhaps, however, there are some states in which conditions are still favorable — a relatively young system, an openness to expanded definitions of profesional development, a still growing fiscal commitment to postsecondary education.

5. *Find an Angel*

The tried and true strategy is to find an angel. Oracles say that the large national foundations are gradually moving away from underwriting professional development. And, as proof of the assertion, foundation officials tend to argue (quite reasonably) that they have acquitted their responsibility by providing seed money to initiate model programs. If national sources are becoming less accessible, there still may be local foundations worth cultivating. Interinstitutional program directors would do well to devise a search and capture strategy. Find out as much as possible about local or regional foundations (or individual benefactors), develop contacts (with staff if there are any) and test out the idea of professional development on them. If there is interest, develop a working proposal, try it out on them, get hold of guidelines from a local college or university development office. Shooting from the hip in proposal writing is risky business; the more professional your proposal, the better the chances of being taken seriously. In any event, permanent funding is unlikely; but sufficient temporary funding may be forthcoming to get a running start or, in the case of established programs, developing a new project state extends the life of the program.

Program Budget

Can the life cycles of programs be sweet? That depends in part on the skills of the program director as a proposal writer. The trick, relative to financing, is to secure comfortable funding over a long enough period of time (three to five years) to make measurable progress toward the goals set. What is "comfortable" funding? In part it depends on the extent of the goals. More basically it means sufficient money to:

	Per year Budget Range
1. assure your own salary plus benefits (do not sell the value of your services short);	17,500 to 30,000
2. hire, if not another full-time professional, a regular part-time expert;	10,000 to 25,000

3. hire a good, well-paid adminis-   9,000 to 12,000
   trative asistant, to help in public
   relations and dissemination activities and in the nitty-gritty of program maintenance (who is making sure that the workshops, in
   fine detail, are staffed, sub-
   scribed, housed, publicized,
   followed-up);

4. hire an efficient secretary who will   7,500 to 9,500
   type 4000 words a minute,
   courteously handle phone calls,
   file in an orderly and consistent
   fashion;

5. hire a sufficient number of skilled   5,000 to 15,000
   consultants to meet growing   at $200-250/day
   and/or unusual needs of clients
   and to meet your own need for
   external evaluators; remember
   that such consultants command
   $400 to $700 per day for similar
   services to private industry;

6. support your own professional   2,000 to 5,000
   and consultant travel needs and a
   large dose of conference costs;

7. provide adequate office materials   750 to 1,500
   and equipment to run an efficient
   consulting and training operation
   (desks, typewriters, "consumable"
   supplies and the like);

8. underwrite the increasing costs of   1,000 to 3,000
   purchasing, printing and dup-
   licating and producing (audio/
   visuals) materials necessary for effective training, dissemination
   and other consciousness-raising
   activities;

9. pay Ma Bell and the Postal Service   1,000 to 3,000
   their just (or unjust) desserts;
10. optional, if using "indirect costs"
    line at 20% of "direct" cost lines:
    purchase such services (do not
    underestimate this one); ac-
    counting, space, management
    and legal that your situation calls
    for; many foundations do not
    pay indirect costs so develop   _____
    realistic direct cost-of-doing-
    business categories.   65,500 to 136,800

These should be familiar categories to all who manage budgets. How
often many of these items are underestimated! It is a mistake to get
caught up in the depression mentality. Almost certainly, even to the
most modest of interinstitutional programs (one full-time professional and one secretary) will cost a minimum of $50,000 per year
(plus a built-in inflation factor, thereafter), *unless* the operation is run
largely on voluntarily contributed time.

Minimally financed programs must, for maximum effect, rely heavily
on volunteerism and/or some other kind of user support, networking,
duplicated "seminal" materials, and heavy and quick resort to continuous programming activities (especially of the "training and trainers" sort).
The human energy (and its by-products) available to do the job always
costs something to someone (or several someones).

The job of program manager is to ensure that the job definition and
the energy we command are compatible. When the latter is in short
supply, she needs to define a modest job description. She should work
hard, at the outset of thinking through her program, at discovering
the energy multipliers, so that minimum funding produces maximum
effect. Providing training, consulting and appropriate materials to
entire academic departments, for example, is bound to be more cost-
effective than providing them to groups of individuals who have no
structured, long-term professional relationships. This is one direction
some on-campus programs are taking out of a similar concern for
maximum impact.

Evaluation

Directors of interinstitutional professional development programs are trustees of scarce resources; their accountability extends both to the manner in which funds were expended and to the results their use seems by all the best evidence to have produced. There are several pertinent guidelines for evaluating program effectiveness.

First, sound evaluation is made possible by clearly defined purpose and, more operationally, the statement of measurable, time-framed, behaviorally meaningful program objectives. Program managers should ground themselves firmly in the theory, language and application of one or more behaviorally oriented management and/or learning-by-objectives systems. Each ought to be able, for example, to distinguish between goals and objectives, program and client objectives, objectives criteria and types of measurements

Second, objectives should reflect realistic predictions of what is possible to achieve, given a careful assessment of resources and constraints. This is particularly important in the management of interinstitutional programs, where on-campus influence is indirect and intermittent. There is a personal phenomenology of goal-setting that should be considered here.

Achievement motivation theorists note that among the most important behaviors that distinguish between those who achieve significant results and those who habitually fail to do so is moderate risk-taking, that is, setting objectives which involve a fifty-fifty chance for success. Attaining the goals will mean stretching and running hard, but the exertion is likely to produce success. High risk-taking describes the behavior of the amateur and the perpetually losing gambler. Seldom does the bet pay off. Taking low-risks produces lots of goal attainment but little of significance.

Third, the *strategy* of evaluation should be built on the distinction between formative and summative types of evaluations. This jargon is worth knowing. Formative evaluation is the sort of operation undertaken periodically during the course of the program's life. Its outstanding characteristic is that the data are used primarily by *program staff* to help them make decisions for program improvement. Summative evaluation is the sort used primarily by *someone outside the program* to decide whether the program was worth (or continues to be worth) funding. In a very real way, staff have lost control over the use of that information. Both forms of evaluation are (or should be) undertaken within the framework of the program's goals and objectives. A full measure of allowance, however, should be made for intended outcome. All programs have them; formative evaluation, in particular, should respect them and lead to ways in which desirable ones can be optimized and undesirable counteracted. The real trick of organizing evaluation is to integrate the two purposes of data-gathering so that the need to know and the demand for decision making are satisfied for all parties all along the way. Openly sharing the results of formative evaluations with those to whom program managers report *and* inviting their collaboration in resolving particularly thorny issues which arise might well constitute a valuable and powerful mechanism for integration of evaluative modes.

Fourth, data should be collected about *inputs, outputs,* and *outcomes.* Input data concern the allocation of resources and should include an accounting of the total professional time bought by project funds, as well as numbers of client contracts and numbers and types of participants involved in each type of service offered. Output information relates to the immediate effect of services on clients: sense of the value of the activity (determined by participant reactions to paper and pencil evaluations), documents and other materials produced during or in conjunction with the activity. Most important is outcome information — the long-term behavioral or attitudinal changes that indicate reasonably strongly some movement toward the ultimate goals and objectives of the program. Most hopefully, the changes discerned will be *in* students' increased efficiency and effectivess in achieving significant instructional and curricular objectives.

A "product" orientation is probably the most useful approach — concrete examples of "things" that happened as a result of program activities. These include protocol materials, working papers, new or revised course descriptions, curricular materials, statements of revised institutional policies, case studies, articles, other research products and student "artifacts". The data base should be established quickly and systematically and strategy devised for noting changes in the client population and systems as new data develop.

Fifth, it is important to specify the kind of measures that will be taken to demonstrate changes in desired directions. This is a demanding task. Without a solid checklist, evaluations tend to become an afterthought without much meaning. For each level of change sought, the following question needs to be answered in some detail: "How will I know it when I see it?" The problem then is to decide *how* the data will be collected, summarized and reported. It may be useful to give these guidelines some concrete reality, to tie together earlier discussions of models and activities.

I made specific reference here to the model Sam Lane and I developed in connection with our management of the Educational Consulting Study. A chief advantage of the model is that each of its five dimensions or "keys," can be anchored to some meaningful criteria for assessment. Table One sets up a general assessment graph for each dimension of our model (lines 4 through 8). Within the terms of those dimensions we developed specific program objectives which, if achieved, should assist several institutions in approximating the model itself. We also wrote an instrument for assessing an institutions's environment for teaching which provides useful data about professional development needs. The instrument is in the field-testing stage and the data preliminary. Still its use at several institutions suggests that the categories are critical ones. Our hypothesis is that they are significantly related to learning outcomes (Table One, line 9) as well. Arthur Chickering's study of "Student Experience of College," for example, suggests that the hypothesis is valid. (21, 21a) At the very least there seems to be a parallel or congruent relationship.

It is possible, as well, to extend the model to outline a planning and assessment strategy for professional development programs in teaching, including interinstitutional projects. Lines 1, 2, and 3 of Table I define what we believe to be significant attitudinal, behavioral and hard dollar indices of program impact. Again, at least hypothetically, these dimensions bear a congruent relationship to indices of faculty and administrative attitudes and behaviors and to that of student learning.

Finally, to guide our planning and assessment, we took one further step. We developed an "expectancy table" (see Table II) which, if it did not always inform our decisions, at least helped us to put them in context. We wanted to avoid the trap, filled by many a busy "developer," of thinking that running "dog and pony" shows has more than an entertaining effect on the audience. As one of our colleagues put it, "Workshops *do not* equal professional development!" Table II represents our attempt to shape Table I into a decision and assessment matrix that renders our model more helpful to us. Essentially the vertical axis represents steps on the way toward achieving the terms of the model within any institution (Table I, lines 4-8); the horizontal axis represents kinds of activities that approximate the historical, attitudinal and operational progression we think effective professional development programs take (Table I, lines 1-3).

Table II: Expectancy Table

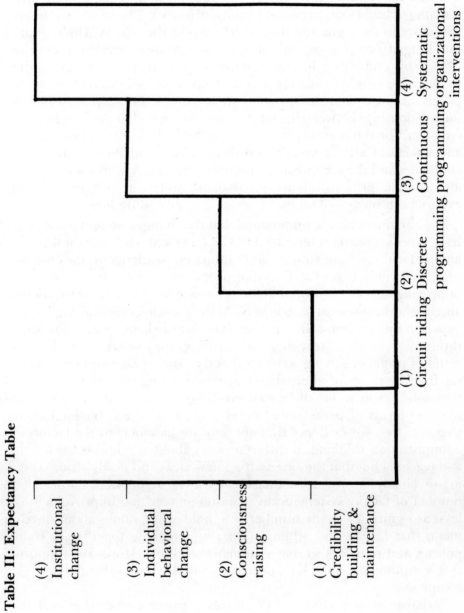

The graph is based on the conjecture that the *nature of desired change* is a function of the kind of services we can provide. Circuit-riding, in person or by phone, accomplishes little more than establishing the service's credibility. Without credibility, however, it is difficult to move to other kinds of activities or build toward more meaningful impact. The same logic holds as you move to the right and towards the top of the matrix. Discrete programming efforts produce raised consciousness or awareness of new ways of thinking and acting, but rarely if ever do they result in overt behavioral change. It is highly unlikely that you can jump directly from discrete programming to significant system interventions. Two explanatory notes: the relationships between the kinds of services and changes sought are not only functional but cyclical as well. Feedback about the appropriateness and quality of service greatly and directly bears on the maintenance of credibility and the receptivity of more professionals in the system to new ideas. These relationships are also dynamic and ideal: progress seldom is experienced or described by an unbroken, ascending line.

It is also important to understand that the changes we seek at each level have specific criteria referents. At ECS, we talk about behavioral changes among faculty, administrators and untimately, students. At the credibility stage, we would expect to find that people in a college concerned about improving instruction would make reference to ECS as a useful resource and might recommend us to others. At the consciousness-raising level, we expect to find evidence that, as a result of our work, people are thinking in different ways about teaching and learning: they speak of teaching as a series of problem-solving activities that they can master and modify; they say that the range of alternative teaching/learning transactions is broad; they talk less in terms of "instructional" or "faculty" development and more in terms of professional development. At the behavioral change stage, we look for evidence that not only are members of the faculty and administration thinking in different ways about conditions for learning and teaching but that they are putting new ideas and newly acquired skills to use. Finally, at the institutional change level, we might discover that the number of faculty systematically working on teaching improvement is at least as significant as the number who hold other values about development, that faculty and administrators are working together to change policies and practices so that systematic teaching efforts are supported, that institutional monies have been committed to such efforts. The cycle is complete.

Perhaps the best advice after all this is to remember that evaluative statements are tentative judgments at best. Not everyone will agree that they are validly stated. But, working in a probabilistic world, the most we can do as conscientious professionals is to develop arguments about effects within the terms of intended outcomes, noting unintended ones as well, and marshall sufficient evidence to render the arguments plausible and reasonable. And, the most we can expect from others is respectful attention to our judgments, the evidence on which they are based, and, where disagreement occurs, equally tentative statements of alternative interpretations.

Personal Reflections

People who begin professional development programs face the roaring need to do something (at our worst moments "something" translates as "ANYTHING!" as in "just don't stand there. . . "). Now this is what is known as an "outreach" need, that is, providing the services promised to the group you said was anxious to have them.

They may, indeed, really want your wares. If the funding agency's program officer, or the person to whom you report within the organization, is looking over your shoulder, you may experience this impulse to act as an "upreach" need — satisfying the money-giver that you are doing something valuable and need her support. It is also possible that you feel the impulse out of your own need to take care of yourself, and if you have one, your staff. That is an "inreach" need. The "something" in each case is different. If you are really unlucky, you may experience these demands on your energy and time all at once. We tend to be unlucky a lot.

Responding to "outreach," "upreach," and "inreach" demands is quite necessary for responsible program management. At ECS, we found it important to be more practical than theoretical in applying our model to the real world. This is made more insistent because we juggle these demands and our responses to them within seemingly iron laws of the management cycle. Table Three spells out the cycle and describes our dilemma.

Table III
The Program Management Cycle

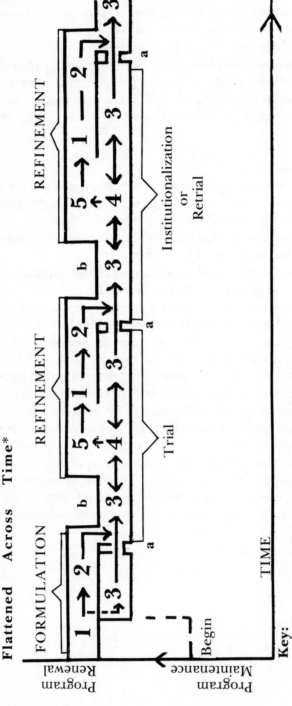

Flattened Across Time*

FORMULATION   REFINEMENT   REFINEMENT

Trial

Institutionalization
or
Retrial

TIME

Program Renewal

Program Maintenance

Begin

Key:

1. Defining (or redefining) program goals and/or objectives
2. Defining strategies and projects
3. Running the program and its projects: organizing and allocating resources
4. Monitoring and feeding back program effects
5. Identifying problems and areas for renewal
a. Periods of program adjustment — disruption, relearning and settling in
b. Periods of uninterrupted program functioning (neither well nor badly, but without active problem, goal or program redefinition)

*The "formulation," "trial," "refinement," "retrial" and "institutionalization" categories are suggested in S.V. Martorana and Eileen Kuhns, *Managing Academic Change*, Jossey-Bass, 1975.

Most descriptions of problem solving (a generic term nicely applicable as a description of program management) assume a neat cycle consisting of *one* track over which we move from stage to stage as we will. Unfortunately, experience suggests that we are constantly shifting between program renewal and program maintenance functions without ever (save at the very beginning of the enterprise) fully leaving either. Programs go on in the midst of our re-examination of them.

Let me put a cap on all of this talk about models and such. Hopefully, our experience offers some clues about decision points that you will face or have faced. Confront reality: chances for effecting permanent change are not very high, given the constraints of time, resources, managerial demands and fixed cultures. Therefore:

1. establish some model (consult your statement of objectives and explore their assumptions);
2. decide the risk factors concerning failure and success; they are very personal factors;
3. explore the likely advantages and disadvantages that working out of your model entails; there will be both;
4. define your own "expectancy table" regarding the relationship between chosen strategies and desired outcomes; and
5. work consciously within the terms of the model.

In short, be intentional not only because your own professional career is involved but also because you are asking other people to change some part of theirs.

Directors and staff of mature interinstitutional programs may find these observations and suggestions old hat. More relevant are responses to the question "Where do we go from here?" My answer contains four distinct but interrelated components. I think we should be about the business of 1) training academic administrators as sensitive, effective managers of the academic enterprise; 2) training faculty and administrators for building comprehensive, but sensible strategies for the evaluation and reward of professional growth in teaching; 3) training ourselves and those we work with to recognize, value and promote the rejuvenating and adaptive potential of the educational process; and 4) training academics for creating real communities of colleagues within existing colleges and universities.

Academic administrators do not much appreciate thinking of themselves as managers. They are not trained as managers, the academic culture eschews the notion that it can be "managed" and institutions do not provide many opportunities for chairpersons, deans, vice presidents and presidents to develop managerial competencies. These facts, in my judgment, explain much about why professional development, especially in teaching, is a haphazard and tenuous thing. But to manage is not to violate systematically all that is good about academia; it is to work for the better integration of institutional and personal needs and goals. These attitudes and behaviors of administrators, particularly those in the critical mid-level positions (chairpersons and deans), must affirm and support professional development if it is to have significant impact in postsecondary education. This means that administrators must develop competencies in a host of management functions, including goal-setting, professional development contracting, budgeting and resource allocation, project development, differential staff planning, personnel evaluation and teamwork. Professional development directors should address the issue of administrative development and devise programs that will meet the need and, by doing so, contribute to the health of instructional improvement.

The most serious intellectual block to professional development in teaching is the belief that teaching and learning cannot be evaluated. Indeed, there are precious few sound models anywhere in postsecondary education for the assessment of teaching. Seldom do strategies integrate sensibly the formative and summative components of professional evaluation — except when it comes to research productivity. With that, academia has organized a fairly reliable system for assisting professional development by answering only the following question: "Has Professor X presented evidence which demonstrates that she continues to define meaningful problems within the discipline and to address them in rigorous and methodologically sound ways?" If academicians will pose an analogous question about Professor X's efforts to define and resolve problems related to teaching and learning in her own courses, they can cut through the intellectual bog about the evaluation of teaching. Our task as professional development programmers is to assist faculty and administrators in formulating the appropriate questions, defining what constitutes meaningful teaching/learning problems, identifying sources for methodologically sound problem solving activities in teaching and devising documentation strategies which rely on a variety of sources of evidence.

Education which stresses competencies in problem solving has tremendous potential as a force for personal and institutional rejuvenation and adaptiveness. I fear that academicians do not see the potential. My experience with faculty and administrators in countless institutions suggests to me that they have pursued their penchant for seriousness about themselves and their work to a fault. Pessimism, rigidity, defensiveness and grimness seem dominant attitudes when the subject of teaching and learning comes up. Yet, the attitudes that are needed in responding effectively to the challenges of new clientele, accountability, increased student/faculty ratios (to name a few of the conditions that beset us) are optimism, flexibility, openness and even joy. Directors and staff should think about ways to model these characteristics in the programs we present. Teaching and learning should be fun as well as work. We have a great deal to do to integrate our enthusiasm for and our seriousness about learning, adult development and experimentalism.

Academicians pay a high price for their rugged intellectual individualism. Its name is isolation. Except in the most superficial sense, the idea of a "community of scholars" is a myth in most postsecondary institutions. Men and women typically do not discover in colleagues sources of support for their own personal growth. I think that the academic enterprise — the environment for teaching, learning and research — suffers in consequence. By focusing on learning, by helping faculty share frustrations and approaches and by fostering collaboration in resolving teaching/learning problems, programs for teaching improvement are natural forces for community building. There are some who feel that institutional barriers to developing synergistic relations are so strong that it is senseless to try to build community inside academe's walls. I do not agree. We have not begun to exhaust the potential for community. Were ECS to continue, I would work much more consciously on stressing how academicians need one another and how they can build mutually productive relations between and among themselves. That, I submit, is finally what professional development in teaching is all about.

8

Summary Recommendations

by Jack Lindquist

Preceding chapters are full of particular ideas and recommendations. But can generalizations be made? The six authors put their collective head together and concluded that twenty propositions about effective teaching improvement programs are worth considering anywhere. The first part of Chapter Eight presents our fearless hypotheses.

The second part of this chapter deals with quite another matter. Even if we knew just what should be done by our teaching improvement program, how can we get it accepted and implemented on our campus? A conceptual framework and a set of practical tips is offered in answer to this question.

The last part of Chapter Eight turns our attention to the future. What challenges and obstacles does the teaching improvement or faculty development field face? How might these issues be approached?

This chapter was written by Jack Lindquist but is based on earlier chapters and discussion among all six contributors. Jack, therefore, assumes credit for all the things you like in this chapter while directing your complaints to Messrs. Bergquist, Buhl, Case, Clark and Mathis. They made me say it.

Introduction

There is nothing like a fledgling field to frustrate one's craving for neatness and order. Professional development to improve college teaching is not a simple, polished subject. The theory is wide-ranging, occasionally contradictory, and still emerging. Practice is going through the stages of trial and error. Systematic research on the subject is sadly lacking.

It would be presumptuous to claim that we have the answer to the question, "How should postsecondary institutions go about the improvement of their teaching?" There remains much to learn. And the answer will vary with each institution, each leader, each professor. But the literature reviewed in earlier chapters and the personal learnings of teaching improvement leaders are beginning to move us in discernable, promising directions. Regard these summary recommendations, then, as hypotheses we think are well worth considering and testing as you search for your own best way to make college teaching one of the most valuable experiences in the lives of diverse college students.

This chapter is written as a series of propositions. The first section concerns the purposes, structure, staffing, activities, financing and evaluation of teaching improvement programs. Fuller explication of these propositions can be found in Chapters Three-Seven under the same headings. The second section concerns the process of initiating and implementing such programs, the change strategies we find most helpful.

In the final section of this chapter, we speculate on the future of professional development to improve college teaching. What are the challenges ahead of us? We recognize only too well (our own job insecurity reminds us) that professional development is a mere babe in colleges and universities. It will need care and feeding, much education, and a tenacious constitution in the years to come if it is to realize its tremendous potential.

The Purposes of Teaching Improvement

Teaching improvement programs, like college teaching, too often seem a bunch of unrelated means in search of meaningful ends. We run workshops on just about everything and consult with anyone who says he has a problem; but to what purpose? We think three general purposes are emerging as the central reasons for in-service programs to improve college teaching.

Proposition 1: A central purpose of teaching improvement programs should be effectively to meet the learning needs of each student.

Discussion: Colleges and universities enroll an increasingly diverse array of students. Many of these students are poorly served or neglected . Yet, promising ways are emerging to understand and to teach various students. Teaching improvement programs can help professors discover, try, master, and evaluate alternative ways to help each student learn. The focus of such services should be not only classroom instruction but faculty-student relations out of class, academic advising, nontraditional approaches to higher learning, the content of what is taught and direct assistance to students to help them learn how to derive meaningful education from their college experience.

Proposition 2: A central purpose of teaching improvement programs should be assistance in the personal and professional development of each staff member.

Discussion: By far the greatest resource and expense of colleges and universities are their staffs, the human beings who are trying to teach, research, govern, administrate, counsel and consult. We no more should neglect the personal and career concerns of college staffs than we should neglect those dimensions in students. Many teaching improvement programs focus only on the teaching task, and that is an underestimation of what it takes to build the kind of committed and skilled staff needed to improve learning. In-service programs need to provide able facilitation and real opportunities for each staff member to clarify his personal and career goals and to identify and resolve problems in the way of achieving those goals.

Proposition 3: A central purpose of teaching improvement programs should be the continuous development of institutional conditions which encourage and reward teaching improvement.

Discussion: Extensive and ongoing teaching improvement is unlikely if the institution does not support it. Incentive and reward policies and practices must place the improvement of teaching squarely in the center of their objectives. Administrators and governing groups must increase their commitment and ability to encourage and reward teaching improvement. Colleagues must strengthen their support for peers who take a chance on new ways to reach and aid diverse learners. A general climate of open self-examination and collaborative problem solving must be created, and substantial professional time and expertise must be given to this educational development and renewal. Teaching improvement program leaders

Figure One

The Relation of Teaching Improvement Purposes to Student Learning

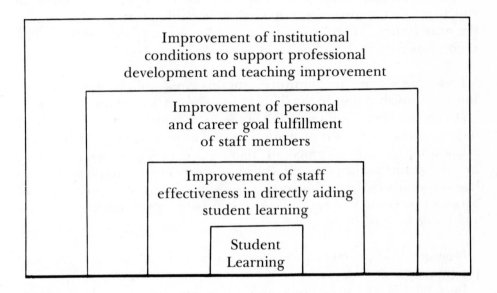

will need to be catalysts, facilitators, and persistent advocates of institutional conditions for teaching improvement.

There is an essential relationship among these three purposes. The rope tying them together is the learning needs of individual students. The question which needs to be asked of each teaching improvement service is, "How can that help particular students better achieve their and our learning objectives?" Figure One expresses the central teaching improvement purposes in relation to student learning. We do not mean that figure to recommend that a program devote most of its effort to purposes closest to student learning. In many colleges, the major problem does not lie there but in major institutional resistances to change or in a staff extremely worried about its future. Each program will need to set its own priorities among the three central areas of purpose depending on current needs. Over time, however, we believe an effective program will need to operate well in all three arenas. And the program which keeps student and institutional learning goals clearly in mind in all arenas will be most likely to improve that learning in the long run.

Structure

Most teaching improvement services are small addendums to collegiate structures, and we do not anticipate their becoming very sizeable units in the near future. There is much that can be accomplished with a small office, however, if the following propositions are honored.

Proposition 4: Teaching improvement services should be staff, not line, functions which report to the highest academic officer of the institution.

Discussion: High location in the academic organization gives teaching improvement services the formal leverage, the visible status, and the direct relationship to academic units and other services needed to obtain support for, and attract participation in, teaching improvement. Staff rather than line responsibility frees this service from the threat of supervision and personnel decision making while giving the service flexibility in defining and implementing its functions.

Proposition 5: Teaching improvement services should be awarded formal program or center status.

Discussion: Much can be done to aid a few professors for a short period, or to aid the initial implementation of a new program, by *ad hoc* faculty development projects. But in-depth assistance capable of serving diverse staff and students over the long haul requires establishment of a permanent teaching improvement of staff development office. Only with such stability can relationships with staff be built, facilitative skills refined, and wide-ranging services be developed and maintained long enough that most staff and students who need such aid benefit from it.

Proposition 6: Teaching improvement services should establish formal and informal ties to academic program units such as departments, to faculty governance units such as educational policies councils, and to faculty opinion leaders so that faculty share in advising and learning these services.

Discussion: The principal change targets in teaching improvement services are faculty members. If they do not feel that such services are closely connected to them, responsive to their concerns and guided by respected colleagues, professors are not likely to support and use such services. Joint ownership of the program by the faculty and the program staff, with influence by administration and students appropriate to their responsibilities and needs, is the delicate balance of power we recommend.

Staffing

Teaching improvement coordinators or professional development facilitators are persons without formal training programs and professional associations to teach them their jobs. They learn on the job, as college teachers and administrators do. We recommend the following means for making this demanding work possible as well as rewarding.

Proposition 7: Teaching improvement staffs should include a small nucleus of professionals plus a network of other institutional staff members on temporary reassignment, of student assistants, of paraprofessionals and of consultants.

Discussion: A stable core staff is necessary to establish program credibility, visibility, expertise and continuous energy. Teaching improvement is not a job one can pick up and do in spare time. Keeping the core staff small, however, enables it to be economical and to develop close working relationships. The network of temporary staff, student assistants, paraprofessionals and consultants in turn permits flexible responsiveness to particular needs for assistance while it broadens ownership of program leadership. And if the old adage is true that nobody learns more than the teacher, these resource persons will be principal beneficiaries of the program.

Proposition 8: The criteria for selecting and/or developing teaching improvement staff should include: 1) knowledge of teaching/learning theory and practice related to diverse student needs; 2) knowledge of teaching improvement and professional/organization development theory and practice; 3) skill in interpersonal relations, group dynamics and communication; 4) ability to serve in expert, facilitating, brokering, leading and counseling roles toward college professors and administrators; 5) respect and empathy for diverse staff and students as well as interest in aiding their growth; 6) administrative, research and teaching technology skills; 7) openness to various disciplines and various approaches to teaching and learning; 8) understanding of collegiate organization and the process of academic change; and 9) a sense of humor, unquenchable optimism and tolerance for uncertainty.

Discussion: If the three central purposes of teaching improvement are taken seriously, program staff members will have to combine the knowledge and skill of instructional, professional and organization development facilitators. No candidate is likely to have this wide range of abilities; but openness, interest, credibility among and respect for faculty and students, plus a background in teaching, research and administration should do for starters. We advocate the above nine criteria, however, as the continuing development objectives for teaching improvement staff members. Soon enough, they will find need of each ability.

Proposition 9: Teaching improvement staffs should devote part of their time to their own self-study, planning and development; and appropriate training and renewal opportunities should be established for professionals in this field.

Discussion: Efforts to improve college teaching inevitably are complex, demanding and frustrating. It is an awesome task and there exists little support for it. Unless time and money are built into teaching programs for the continuing development and renewal of their staffs, these persons will burn out before reaching the level of skill needed to be highly effective. Also, without time to re-examine services and develop new ones, teaching improvement programs will fall quickly into ruts of limited usefulness.

In order to enjoy continuing development, however, some university centers as well as associations such as the POD Network will have to develop doctoral, postdoctoral, and short-term training programs for teaching improvement or professional development facilitators.

Program Activities

What is done in the name of teaching improvement or staff development covers a host of activities. If there is local interest and a chance that the activity can lead to more effective teaching, it probably is worth doing. This is not time to get overly prescriptive regarding ways to improve college teaching. We do believe, however, that there are general categories of teaching improvement activities which most programs should consider seriously.

Proposition 10: Teaching improvement activities should flow from the three central purposes and should include depth and breadth experiences.

Discussion: Staff efforts to aid student learning, personal and career development for staff members themselves and work to create institutional conditions supportive of effective teaching each deserves attention in an intentional but flexible "curriculum" for teaching improvement. Emphases among these areas of activity should vary with shifts in local need or demand. Consciousness-raising activities such as short workshops, colloquia, circulation of teaching-learning literature or local studies and travel to conference or innovative institutions should be used to increase awareness of improvement needs and possibilities. But real improvement for most staff will need in-depth assistance over time. Small grants for developmental projects and expert facilitation of problem solving are two strong means for supporting in-depth follow-through. An effective teaching improvement program, therefore, will need to strike two kinds of balances: one balance among central purposes, the other between depth and breadth services.

Proposition 11: Teaching improvement activities should include aid at the individual, program and institutional level.

Discussion: The most common teaching improvement or staff development services relate directly to individual "clients." That focus is vital, for it permits the most tailoring of services to widely varying individual needs. It has the strength of a one-to-one assisting relationship, it can focus on those individuals motivated to seek help, and it concerns the organizational unit most influential regarding teaching effectivness: the professor herself. But formal organizational units such as departments can exert influence over individual professors who otherwise might be reluctant to seek assistance. Such units have their own improvement concerns and objectives. And if a whole department or school undergoes improvement, far more students can be aided than often can be reached by working with professors one-by-one. At the institutional level, joining forces with institutional research, academic planning, program development and formal governance can enable teaching improvement efforts to reach wide numbers of staff and to affect institution-wide policy and program change.

Proposition 12: Teaching improvement services should focus on five general areas of problem solving: 1) identifying a gap between current and desired teaching effectiveness; 2) searching and developing promising solutions to problems perceived through step one; 3) gaining acceptance and material support for solutions formulated through step two; 4) learning the skill and knowledge needed to carry out solutions decided through step three; and 5) evaluating (both for improvement and for formal judgment) the effectiveness of implemented changes.

Discussion: These five problem solving steps are helpful regarding improvement in any of the three area of purpose and at any of the three levels of service. Without help to individuals or program units in clarifying the need for improvement, there would be neither focus nor motivation for improvement. Without linkage to existing alternatives plus time, money and expertise in developing solutions which fit those local needs and situations, a need may never be matched with a workable solution. Without facilitation in gaining human and material support as well as expertise, the wherewithall to carryout promising improvements would be absent. And without evaluation, a change would lack information needed to correct initial problems and to convince all those whose support is still needed.

These are our general hypotheses regarding program activities. They should concern each of the three areas of purpose. They should include breadth or "consciousness-raising" activities and depth or "problem solving" assistance. They should serve individual staff members but also work with program units and the institution as a whole. And they should provide aid in assessing teaching improvement needs, designing solutions, gaining support, training for implementation and evaluating the whole effort.

Finances

We have noted that teaching improvement budgets range from $2,000 to $2,000,000 without much clarity about what one gets for the money. That range leaves the impression that cost is not a crucial issue in teaching improvement. We disagree. Whether the cost is exacted in overwork or "burn-out" or in the financing of normal workload, the improvement of college teaching does not come cheap. It is slow, complex, demanding work frought with obstacles. The particular budgets we have recommended in earlier chapters seem to us bare bones. In arranging such financial support, we hold the following propositions.

Proposition 13: Teaching improvement budgets should support a small core staff (coordinator and secretary, minimally), travel, supplies, special events and consultation.

Discussion: Core financing for teaching improvement services may run from $30,000 for small, private colleges to $250,000 or more for sizeable universities. However much the amount, the principle is that institutional funders will need to support a basic, enduring core staff and services if there are to be visible, skillfull, credible and effective services rendered over enough time to make an institutional difference.

Proposition 14: A wide range of additional financial supports must augment the basic core.

Discussion: Such budget items as sabbaticals, travel funds, colloquia funds, small grants, work-study, workshop expenses, instructional resources, consultation monies, workload assignments to one's own development and so forth will be needed to broaden teaching improvement services and involve many staff and departments in leading or backing such services. These budget items may reside with individual academic units rather than with the improvement service but teaching improvement leaders should have formal as well as informal opportunities to influence their use.

Proposition 15: Funding for teaching improvement services must come primarily from "hard" money, with grants supporting special projects or start-up costs.

Discussion: John Centra found that seventy percent of the average instructional/faculty developmemt budgets around the country came out of regular institutional funds. That occasionally is "new" money, but as often it will have to be a reallocation of staff positions, of the functions within such offices as instructional resources and institutional research or of work-study monies.

A program of the magnitude we recommend is a miniscule expense in comparison with the contribution it can make to the continued vitality of the institution. Hundreds of colleges and universities are demonstrating in these times of great financial constraint that where there is sufficient dedication to the improvement of college teaching, funds can be found to support improvement services. Preceding chapters contain many practical suggestions on how to find and use such monies.

Evaluation

In-service programs to improve college teaching are the devil to evaluate, for the job is to study learning in one group (faculty, administration, staff) which *may* lead to improvements of learning within another group (students). As if the problem were not difficult enough, rarely is program evaluation given enough money and expertise to allow for a fair chance at success. Yet, without systematic study of these efforts, problems in their effectiveness will not be identified so that they can be rectified, and evidence of effectiveness will not be available to persuade skeptics.

We believe that program evaluation should be a high priority from the beginning of teaching improvement programs and should abide by the following propositions:

Proposition 16: Data gathering and feedback to program leaders regarding program effectiveness, or "formative evaluation," should be built into teaching improvement programs.

Discussion: Like teaching, teaching improvement can proceed merrily along on the unexamined assumption that things are working, when they are not. Already, there are certain assumptions being made about how to aid teaching improvement, few, if any, of which have been put to rigorous test. In order to learn from program experience, therefore, one part of that program needs to be regular evidence-gathering and reflection by program leaders and advisors.

Proposition 17: Evaluation of teaching programs should employ a variety of methods.

Discussion: Surveys, interviews, observations, document analysis and tests all can help illuminate what is happening in, and because of a teaching improvement program. Objectives-based evaluation is useful, so too are "illuminative" approaches or detailed case studies. Human learning and change is just too complex to be studied only by one instrument or one approach. A "triangulation" of strategies can check and augment the insights of any one method.

Proposition 18: Criteria for the effectiveness of teaching improvement programs should be clearly understood and move from the immediate sense of the experience to resulting changes in staff behavior or attitudes to resulting change in student learning.

Discussion: Evaluation often fails because its users are vague about what they mean by effectiveness or because too much (or too little) is asked of a program. Program leaders should endeavor before, during and after evaluation to clarify what particular activities should be accomplished. Early in a program, that impact is most likely to be some degree of staff participation, satisfaction with the experience, and perhaps increased recognition of certain teaching problems or potential solutions. Later, after depth experiences, it is fair to ask if participants exhibit changes in attitudes or behaviors related to program purposes. Eventually, when evidence of staff change is sufficient to expect carryover to students, evaluators must ask whether learning opportunities, satisfactions and changes in behaviors or attitudes are visible in students.

Proposition 19: Evaluation of teaching improvement programs should be collaboratively managed among program staff, formal authorities, faculty and student leaders and evaluation experts.

Discussion: There are many audiences for evaluation of teaching improvement programs. The more each important group is represented in the evaluation process, the more the concerns of that group can be included and the more eventual results can be trusted by that group. A small evaluation team or an expert working with a teaching improvement advisory board might meet this need for involvement.

Proposition 20: Systematic, cross-institutional research on the effectiveness of teaching improvement programs should be initiated.

Discussion: No one institution has enough money, time or access to diverse programs to mount the kind of comparative research needed to assess the effectiveness of various strategies for faculty development or teaching improvement. What is needed is large-scale and in-depth research funded by foundation or federal agencies and conducted by researchers sensitive to the problems of tracking the subtle effects of professional development programs. Without such research, a very promising movement to strenghten higher education may fade, not through ineffectiveness but through inability to discern and extol its effects.

Strategies for Program Implementation

It is a wonder, with so many obstacles confronting college teaching improvement programs, that they get off the ground at all. Such programs suggest to highly trained and experienced Ph.Ds that they could stand improvement. They suggest that college staffs, always vulnerable to public criticism anyway, are less than sensational in one of their central functions, teaching. These programs cost money when no spare cash is available. Their impacts are poorly documented. They appear to intrude into what heretofore was the private domain of the professor, the classroom or advising office. They threaten to infringe on the dean's or chairperson's authority in personnel matters. They carry the comparatively low status of educational or humanistic psychology. They take time no one has free to give. They challenge staff to risk new behaviors which may not be re- warded. They ask staff to expose weaknesses often safer to hide. They are run by persons who often have little background or training for a terribly difficult job.

We could go on. The obstacles to college teaching improvement are many and mountainous. Yet here we are, with over half of the nation's colleges trying to do something in this area. The need is undeniable. But how can such programs get off the ground and maintain momentum?

There are no systematic studies of how teaching improvement programs got accepted, although the Sikes and Barrett case portraits of several fledgling programs in small colleges are well worth reading. (101) Rather, we have as a guide the personal reflections of programs leaders against a background of change theory. This section isolates several propositions drawn from that background. More conceptual and case study depth is available in Lindquist's *Strategies for Change: Academic Innovation as Adaptive Development*. (68) Many practical strategies and tips for program im- plementation can be found in *Developing the Curriculum: A Handbook for Faculty and Administration*. (22)

Resistances to Teaching Improvement Programs

An early and continuing activity of program leaders must be to deter- mine what we're up against. What is keeping us from establishing a teach- ing improvement service everyone supports and uses? The rush of an- swers often fits into the following categories:

Academic Values and Beliefs

Many academic people do not value teaching as highly as they do research, or consulting, or committee work, or family and church. Al- though they feel it is important, the extra effort needed to improve teaching takes second or third place to producing another article or draft- ing another project proposal. And among those academicians who do value teaching as highly as, or above, other things are people who believe teaching cannot be improved through education and training. It is an art or craft, not a science, and one becomes good at it by combining natural talent with experience. Also, there is some evidence that college professors who do place very high emphasis on teaching tend to care most about such teaching goals as mastering their speciality and becoming disciplined thinkers. Teaching improvement programs concerned with interdisciplinary subjects or with the personal development of students rub against their preferences.

Academic Norms

Among the cardinal rules of academe is professional autonomy. Many faculty members maintain that their classroom is their castle and that no one knows more about how to carry out their functions than themselves. Teaching improvement practices which infringe on their private domain, say by student ratings or classroom observation, or which set up certain professionals as "teachers" or other professionals, confront this norm. New programs which get initiated by administrators instead of faculty also raise the ire of professors who feel teaching and its improvement is their business. Among common academic norm is that teaching and learing occur in several four-month courses taken simultaneously and designed by the professor, which are conducted as a series of lecture/discussions in college classrooms, then evaluated by grading papers and examinations. To suggest that college level learning occurs any other way violates this rule of the academic game.

Perhaps the key normative obstacle to teaching improvement is, ironically, "standards." A professor who allows students some say in course objectives and process is threatening academic standards, even though she may be strengthening students' ability to take charge of their of life-long learning. A professor who fails to "cover" all the course material because he has taken extra time to make what he does cover meaningful to diverse students is threatening academic standards, even though retention of material may be higher than it would be if everything were covered.

Social Interaction

Professors are socialized in graduate school and on the job to think of themselves as "sociologists" or "physicists," not "college teachers." They interact mainly with colleagues or apprentices in their own specialties. Administrators and students have their own enclaves. Organizatioal structure and campus geography further isolate subgroups. And there are very few mechanisms available to get people interacting across these barriers despite the need for professors to talk with one another, with persons who might provide technical assistance to them, and with students in order to improve teaching.

Vested Interests

Interdisciplinary teaching may be perceived to threaten disciplinary teaching, and some department leaders will become anxious. A strong faculty development team or facilitator may make the dean think she is losing her authority and influence. Money to finance teaching improvement is money which others believe might have been spent on their vested interest. All this attention to teaching may threaten my investment in research. Any new program is sure to arouse initial concern that it will drain attention, talent and money from other programs.

Personal Anxiety

Teaching improvement services do carry with them the notion that teaching can be improved, and some around here may find out that I'm one of the people whose teaching needs improvement. Dare I expose the problems I have in teaching? Perhaps those problems are worse than I think. Won't I get penalized by being regarded as incompetent by colleagues and supervisors? What if I try a new approach and can't do it. I'm comfortable as I am. I don't want to change.

Skepticism About Teaching Innovations

Many professors initially believe that teaching improvement programs are peddling a bag of worthless gimmicks. However can a computer or "listening skills" improve the teaching of Yeats and Eliot? However can "competency-based education" improve the teaching of late nineteenth century European history, and how can a clear, sequential field such as chemistry be individualized? Show me the method which can get those blockheads to learn? And, the ultimate put-down, "What's really innovative anyway?"

Ignorance of Teaching Problems

Yet another obstacle to improvement is that many professors have very poor information about the effects of their teaching. They do not know what is going on in student heads during class. They do not know how much of the information, concepts and attitudes taught in the course are retained beyond the final examination. They do not know what they do which helps students learn and what they do which gets in the way. They do not know the learning theory which might illuminate problems in their own approachs. Sometimes this ignorance is intentional. Some deans don't want to know they have little rapport with faculty, and some professors don't care to discover that their students cannot understand them.

Lack of Time and Money

The most common obstacle to the establishment and use of teaching improvement programs is lack of time and money. We would like to finance such a center but all our funds are committed elsewhere. I would like to solve a teaching problem I'm having, but after my teaching and research and committee and family responsibilities, I just don't have time to work on that problem. And if I do that instead of getting this article out, I won't get tenure.

There are other obstacles to implementing a teaching improvement program, but these eight give us plenty to worry about. Our strategory for change will need to counteract, circumvent or reduce these barriers if we are to succeed.

Strategies for Change

Our central thesis is that teaching improvement, in order to succeed, is a problem solving process controlled by the professor (or department or college as a collective) but with stimulus and aid by external resources, for example, information, expertise, peer support, political or economic pressure. Teaching excellence is too much a function of the professor's own conviction and voluntary effort, and too much protected by professional autonomy, to be forced upon professors. You can't make professors establish effective teaching relationships with students. The job of a teaching improvement program is to help professors conduct their own development.

At least five important ingredients in the program implementation process can combat obstacles while establishing an adaptive development process. These factors are represented on Figure Two. Each factor is stated below in terms of a proposition regarding what it takes to get teaching improvement services established and used.

Factor 1: The more *initiative* taken to improve teaching, the more persistent and facilitative of problem solving is that initiative, and the more trusted and respected it is by staff, the more likely is teaching improvement.

Discussion: There must be strong initiative for teaching improvement to counter all the forces against it. Such force may be a faculty team, an

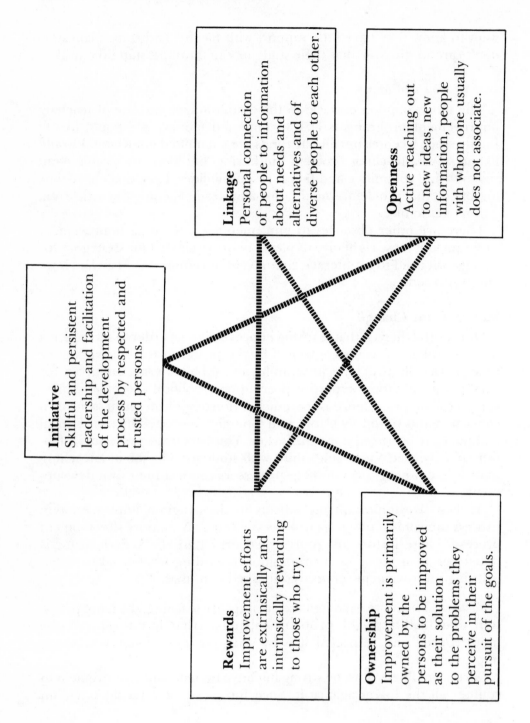

Linkage
Personal connection of people to information about needs and alternatives and of diverse people to each other.

Openness
Active reaching out to new ideas, new information, people with whom one usually does not associate.

Initiative
Skillful and persistent leadership and facilitation of the development process by respected and trusted persons.

Rewards
Improvement efforts are extrinsically and intrinsically rewarding to those who try.

Ownership
Improvement is primarily owned by the persons to be improved as their solution to the problems they perceive in their pursuit of the goals.

energetic facilitator, a determined faculty senate executive committee or dean, and hopefully all of these. Whatever the force, it should be skillful at adaptive development—the stimulation and facilitation of problem solving—and it should be personally and professionally respected and trusted by staff. Building, maintaining, renewing and expanding this force should be a major strategy for implementing teaching improvement. Only by such a force can inertia—the investment of most time, money and attention to maintaining or expanding things as they are—be combatted.

Factor 2: The stronger the *linkage* of staff to information related to teaching improvement; and the stronger the linkage about teaching and learning of staff to one another, to students, and to external resources, the more likely is teaching improvement.

Discussion: Most college staff members have little connection to information on their students, on alternative teaching-learning approaches, on particular problem areas in teaching, on learning theory. In order for information and ideas to flow, staff need to talk with one another, with students, with outsiders about teaching. A central strategy for change, therefore, should be this "social learning," learning together the things we need to know to diagnose and solve teaching improvement problems.

Factor 3: The more *openness* that is exhibited by college staff in searching out new information, new ideas, and new skills related to teaching improvement, the more likely is teaching improvement.

Discussion: People often have their minds set on particular views and particular ways of doing things. When confronted with an alternative, they can think immediately of a dozen things wrong with it. But unless they open themselves to views and behavior other than their own, they are unlikely to attempt improvement. Teaching improvement leaders can begin to create greater openness by modeling it in their own behavior, for instance, by audibly reconsidering a viewpoint when presented with new information, constantly seeking to "keep up" with pertinent theory and practice, organizing trips to innovative programs and small group discussios among diverse staff and students. If done well, efforts to increase openness should decrease unnecessary protection of vested interests as well as decrease ignorance and skepticism.

Factor 4: The more *ownership* staff members, especially faculty, feel for the purposes and activities of teaching improvement programs, the greater are the chances for success of the program.

Discussion: Unless the staff members undergoing teaching improvement activities feel that these services aid them in developing solutions to their problems, not much cooperation can be expected. Thus, earlier chapters have stressed formulating teaching improvement programs with faculty and other staff, basing activities on diagnoses done with staff, having staff advisory boards and structuring teaching improvement events to aid staff in solving problems they perceive. By continually striving to broaden and deepen this sense of program ownership by its clients as well as its financial supporters and its staff, conerns about vested interests, worry over the program's sensitivity to important academic norms and values and personal anxiety about the uses of such services should be reduced.

Factor 5: The more intrinsically and extrinsically *rewarding* is participation in teaching improvement, the more teaching will improve.

Discussion: Early in a program, most rewards for participation may be intrinsic: learning something interesting, honing a valued skill, enjoying a group of colleagues, relishing the challenge of change, feeling more successful with students. Eventually, extrinsic rewards such as professional recognition, career advancement, and opportunities to devote regular workload time to improvements, will be needed to sustain personal commitment. Program leaders will need to attend to both kinds of rewards if teaching improvement programs are to enlist very wide and enduring use.

Tips of the Trade

Contributors have suggested in past chapters many particular ways to fulfill these five implementation propositions. Among the most redundantly mentioned are the thirteen tips which follow:

1. *Find Your Friends and Enlist Their Help*

Early in any program, persons will surface who have a strong interest in teaching improvement, either to improve themselves or to stimulate improvement in others. Help them increase their professional skills as professors or administrators, but then seek their involvement in stimulating or assisting others and train them in that "change agent" role. A sizeable team of skillful volunteers (given release time and professional reward by the institution for their efforts) will be needed to make a dent in the *status quo.*

2. *Build on Institutional and Individual Concerns*

An essential meshing should occur between the mission and the problems of the institution on one hand and the objectives and concerns of individual staff members on the other. Facilitators will find themselves orienting institutional leaders to individual needs and individuals to institutional needs.

3. *Balance Attention to Person, Task and Situation.*

The "real problem" in any given instance may lie within persons, in the way teaching or administering is done, or in the degree to which the institution (and broader sources of influence such as disciplines) supports teaching improvement. But the problem often lies in all three domains, and over time all three areas must be aided toward improvement. Seek a balance of programmatic attention, therefore, among personal and career development, teaching improvement and increasing institutional support for teaching.

4. *Be Various But Persistent*

Many different kinds of consciousness-raising and follow-up activities will be needed to reach various groups and individuals; but a sprinkler does not soak water in unless it is left on the same spot long enough. Stay with those who need or desire aid until they have succeeded, in their mind and your estimation, in accomplishing important improvements.

5. *Mix Tradition With Innovation*

Even in nontraditional programs, professionals find that their concern often is to improve what they already are doing, such as lecturing or mastering a discipline, before considering changes in basic practices. Such concerns are entirely appropriate if they will lead to more effective teaching for that professor's students. If improvement in teaching and learning, rather than innovation, is held as the program's central purpose, a fair mix of new approaches and fine-tuning of existing ones probably will occur. At the same time, as new student needs and new advances in teaching practice occur, teaching improvement facilitators will need to become active disseminators of teaching innovations.

6. *Seek a "Critical Mass"*

Both Chet Chase and Lance Buhl point out that teaching improvement which significantly improves the institution and which encourages the reluctant or skeptical to participate is not going to occur until many staff members, particularly leaders, join the effort. Strategies such as aiding curriculum reform, orienting all new staff members, combining forces with institutional research and planning, working with whole departments and engaging in institutional or leader development have the advantage of affecting more members of the institution than do workshops or individual consultations on the periphery of the main action on campus.

7. *Seek Critical Events*

Often a major eye-catcher or matter of great concern can make a larger splash than numerous small, invisible activities. An institutional self-study, the kickoff of a new program, a highly-publicized development institute, an intervention into a whole department or school or a sizeable demonstration project may obtain greater leverage and spinoff effects than normal programming. Of course, a program composed only of splashy events can lose the effectivness of sustained, often very unglamourous, but effective, services. We recommend a balance of critical events and sustained, low-key services.

8. *Emphasize Collaboration*

Teaching improvement specialists do not have The Answer. Neither do individual faculty members, administrators or students. We must inquire, problem-solve and create teaching improvements *with* the humanities or natural science professors, the engineering and sociology students, the deans and chairpersons, Professional development facilitators should bring knowledge of learning and teaching and administrative and change theory, along with development process skills, to collaboration in which faculty members bring disciplinary expertise and faculty, students and adminstrators bring relevant experience.

9. *Have a Flexible Model But Get Busy*

Facilitators themselves should take time to develop their own conceptual model of how to improve college teaching, for they will need a framework to guide their decisions. But the field is too various for rigid paradigms, and it is wise to begin some activities even before a model is clearly in mind, for actions demonstrate a program is alive while theory is built.

10. *Attend to Yourself*

Lance Buhl and Tom Clark rightly point out that professional development can be lonely work which few colleagues will understand or appreciate. It is not a "career" in the sense of work which leads to higher organizational rewards, for facilitators are neither faculty nor administration. In-service staff would do well to build networks among fellow facilitators, take time to keep a hand in the scholarship and research which might lead to other jobs, and make the work they have as enjoyable and personally rewarding as they can. Be explicit in making the program meet your needs as well as others.

11. *Start Small But Think Big*

Rare is the in-service program which starts with adequate human and financial resources. We agree with Bill Bergquist's suggestion of getting started anyway and doing what a few volunteers and perhaps one staff person can do. But such starts are not going to provide enough energy and skill to improve very much. We submit that no professional development program we know has enough time and expertise to manage the awesome task of aiding improvement in academic institutions. Because of the considerable autonomy of individual staff members in colleges and universities, professional development may be the most powerful strategy for change available; but it will take major efforts to make such a strategy work. As Chet Chase advises, start small, but think big.

12. *Involve Students*

Teaching improvement has to do with the learning of students. They are our ultimate "clients." They should be involved in data-gathering to assess teaching improvement needs, in workshops to analyze such data and to decide what improvements are needed, in orientation to new teaching and organizational approaches and in the formative evaluation of new ways of teaching and learning. They can become excellent consultants to teachers or administrators and to each other. Just having students involved helps to remind us whom we are trying to serve.

13. *Ride the Circuit*

There are at least three good reasons to spend time visiting with faculty and administrative leaders from time to time. One is to keep them abreast and involved. Another is to seek their good advice on needs and solutions, progress and problems. A third is to use such opportunities to educate, to increase awareness of needs and interest in solutions among persons of influence.

In general we find Lance Buhl's delineation of activities into circuit-riding, discrete programming, continuous programming, systematic organizational intervention, networking, and training of facilitators a useful one. We encourage those creating teaching improvement programs to consider developing an integrative curriculum of activities across those six program areas.

The Emerging Challenge

Services to improve college teaching have made tremendous strides in this decade, especially in the past five years. The number of programs has multiplied rapidly. In variety of services, in leader competence and in conceptual understanding, the field has matured remarkably. The program approaches discussed and synthesized in this volume represent very promising ways to improve the learning experiences of college students and the professional lives of college teachers. In many ways, the emerging challenge is to implement, more skillfully and throughly, the kind of program represented by the propositions in this chapter.

The job, however, has just begun. No program mentioned in this volume has reached all the professors who need teaching. No program herein has so changed the face and substance of teaching and learning that the institution is fully renewing. We only are beginning to learn how to join forces with curriculum development or institutional research and planning.

Too many innovations, like staff development, become promises unfulfilled. If teaching improvement is to fulfill its potential, we assert the following challenges will need to be met by action.

Challenge 1: Model programs testing the propositions of this chapter should be developed, studied and disseminated.

Discussion: We believe from theory and experience that our recommendations are sound. But we are struggling ourselves to find ways to follow our own advice, and no program we know has the kind of research component needed to put these propositions to the test. Funders have supported many efforts to get teaching improvement programs started. That support has given us the learnings from experience which we have tried to share in this book. It is time, we believe, to support attempts by well-established teaching improvement programs rigorously to test the propositions we raise regarding a comprehensive approach to teaching improvement.

Challenge 2: Research is needed in each of the three areas of teaching improvement purpose: college teaching and learning, personal and career development of staff and organizational conditions to support effective teaching and learning.

Discussion: Our knowledge base for teaching improvement has been growing over recent years, but there is still much to learn. Careful examination of the differing effects upon diverse students of various teaching approaches and curricular structures are needed. So are studies of how college teachers develop as professionals, how they learn to teach, what difficulties they face and how they cope with those problems. And although we have good reason to believe that the environment within which college teachers and students function can be important, we have few studies of just what those situational variables are and how they can be manipulated. A major agenda item for local researchers and for agencies such as the National Institute for Education should be such inquiry.

Challenge 3: Formal educational and training programs are needed to prepare persons to manage the complex roles of the teaching improvement or professional development facilitator, and professional networks are needed to sustain them.

Discussion: Currently, no higher education program offers systematic education and training for college staff development leaders. Nor is there a planned sequence of training workshops, institutes and conference to which prospective or veteran facilitators can go, although the POD Network *has* begun to meet that need. And although the Faculty Development and Evaluation Newsletter provides some information linkage among staff in the field, its circulation and support need to increase if it is to be effective.

Challenge 4: Teaching improvement leaders need to create mutually supportive alliances with institutional research and planning, with disciplinary associations, with governance bodies, with administration and with student leaders if a concerted and systematic effort to improve university teaching is to occur.

Discussion: The improvement of college teaching is too large a task involving too many aspects of academic life to be done in isolated nooks and crannies of the institution. All the groups concerned with this task will need to find ways to work together. Institutional development projects such as the one at Wichita State University, which unite various approaches to professional development with program review and planning, are much needed.

Challenge 5: Teaching improvement programs will need to address three kinds of problems in the three areas of purpose: serving nontraditional learners, aiding the personal and career development of staff caught in a shrinking academic market and enabling the institutions to improve through development and reallocation of existing resources rather than through expansion.

Discussion: Colleges and universities face hard economic times. The pool of traditional students is decreasing while college costs rise and the competition grows fierce. In response, colleges need to turn to new student clienteles. They need to help their staffs cope with hard times. And they need to improve but will have no more cash to buy new staff or new programs. Teaching improvement leaders will have to be particularly adept at meeting these pressing needs.

Challenge 6: Teaching improvement programs must reach beyond their present faculty clientele.

Discussion: Most program leaders characterize their current clientele as persons committed to teaching, concerned to help students, fairly open to change in their own behaviors, and fairly capable teachers already. Their programs mainly help the good college teacher get better, a worthy service to be sure. But we must reach the inexperienced teacher, the senior professor in an ineffective rut, the faculty members who feel threatened if they expose their teaching difficulties, and those who are not very interested in teaching or in students but who teach nonetheless. Among promising tactics are the following: Work with program units such as departments so that all members get involved. Establish professional development contracts as formal institutional policy. Work with faculty members who do volunteer to enable them to act as "change agents" with their colleagues. Tie faculty development to institutional development activities. Be various so that many individual interests are met. Document and publicize teaching improvements related to your program. And be persistent.

This is small list of challenges but mind-boggling to attempt. All around us, we hear skeptics saying the faculty development "movement" is over the hill, a nice idea which did not capture sufficient popularity or obtain demonstrable improvements fast enough to be sustained. Yet, new teaching improvement programs are being established weekly and very few are being discontinued. The need, and the promise, clearly are present. There may be no more effective way to meet the higher education challenge of the next decade than by aiding staff members as they solve the problems they will face. In the end, we believe the leaders of colleges and universities owe it to the next generation of students to maintain the momentum toward a quality of college teaching which truly enables life-long learning for each.

Appendix A

Selected Teaching Improvement Programs

The Liberal Arts College

Azusa Pacific
Azusa, California

Contact Person: James Holsclaw

Goals of Program

1. To increase the interpersonal contact and the sense of community among the faculty and administration
2. To improve the interpersonal skills of faculty and administration
3. To increase faculty competencies in responding to the individual learning styles and growth needs of students
4. To provide increased opportunities for individual faculty and pursue professional interests and professional activities
5. To encourage faculty to closely examine and confront their central values and beliefs
6. To develop a greater sense of excellence among faculty relative to individual and institutional functioning
7. To increase the awareness of and opportunities for faculty to have meaningful involvement in the decision making processes of the college

Program Ownership and Governance

From the very beginning, this faculty development program was designed "by the faculty, for the faculty." The faculty have assumed sole responsibility for the implementation of this program. The faculty, however, have not had to pay for the program — it has been financed primarily by foundation support. When the foundation dollars are gone, the funding of the program will not be primarily a faculty decision. Therefore, even though the faculty have the opportunity to "run" the program, they do not have the opportunity to make the major decisions regarding the funding of the program.

Because this program is run entirely by faculty, it is imperative that the director of the program maintain close communication with the dean of the college. It is possible that a faculty-run faculty development program could be moving in one direction and the dean of the college in another.

Program Staffing

The director of the faculty development program holds a full-time, twelve month appointment in this position and is responsible for general leadership of the entire program, development and administration of the budget, and general coordination of program activities. He also has several faculty committee assignments and teaches a graduate course during the summer. Each of seven program areas has a program coordinator, who is released one quarter time or credited for campus service at the equivalent level of a major faculty committee or council chairmanship. A twenty-five hour per week student secretary, part-time student graphics artist and newsletter editor are also provided.

External consultants were used extensively in the initial design of the program, and as special resource people for selected workshop experiences. They are how used sparingly, however, for many of the Azusa Pacific faculty feel they could make a similar contribution if only asked. The external consultants have enabled the program staff to gain access to unknown resources, to establish contacts with other projects around the country, to set program directions and to bring prestige to the project.

Program Activities

The seven program areas are: 1) enhancement of subject matter expertise, 2) instructional skills, 3) instructional development, 4) self and social awareness, 5) spiritual awareness, 6) physical awareness, and 7) organizational development. In addition, there is a professional forum, newsletter, resource collection and program evaluation unit, all of which are supervised by the director and coordinating council.

The "Enhancement of Subject Matter Expertise" module enables faculty with grants of up to $500 to develop and implement a growth contract related to their discipline. During the 1976-77 academic year, thirty-three grants were given out, usually for attendance at conferences or implementation of research projects. The Instructional Skills module consists of "Talk about Teaching" coffee hours, assistance in the interpretation of formative evaluation data on an instructor's course, provision of videotape analysis and work with faculty on the development of specific teaching skills.

The Instructional Development module consists of grants of $1,000 given to faculty for the development of a new course or redesigning of an existing course. A faculty member can also receive up to $750 for the purchase and/or production of course materials. Three of these grants were given out during the 1976-77 academic year. Dr. Holsclaw provides consultative assistance to the faculty in their design process.

The three "awareness" modules encompass a variety of activities, including planning for implementing of Faculty Worship Hours, an annual Faculty Retreat (topic for 1976-77 was "How to be a Christian in a Christian College"), Stress Tests, and physical fitness activities. The organizational development module is just starting up.

The Professional Forum at Azusa Pacific includes a formal presentation by a noted professor or author about "significant and current professional issues, practices and methodologies in higher education," refreshments, and a question and answer session. The Resource Collection Corrdinator develops and promotes a comprehensive print and nonprint library to support all of the other activities of the Faculty Development Program. A newsletter, entitled "Focus," describes program activities and features faculty who are participating in the activities.

Program Evaluation

The evaluative process began at Azusa Pacific with a discussion by the Coordinating Council of the question: "Faculty Development, so what?" It became quite clear that the faculty development program outlined in the funded proposal was activities-based rather than goal based. As a result, the council identified the seven program goals listed above. A second step was the identification of different publics who would ultimately be included in the decision about program continuation after two years (end of funding period). Program activities have been designed to meet the needs and expectations of these publics.

A third step involved the specification of outcome indicators relative to each of the seven goals: how will the staff and critical publics know if the program has been successful? Structured interviews and other data collection procedures are being developed around these outcome indicators. The evaluation is being conducted by the Azusa Pacific program staff and faculty, with some external consultative assistance in the design of the procedure. By doing their own evaluation, the staff and faculty believe that they will not only feel more ownership for the results, but will learn a great deal about both evaluative processes and the program.

Program Funding:

Azusa Pacific College received a grant for $97,775 from the Lilly Endowment, of which about one third goes for staff salaries and benefits, and one fourth for grants to individual faculty members. The grant was given as "seed money" to begin a program that probably could not have been started without external assistance. The significant evaluative component of this program makes it an important experiment in faculty development at a liberal arts college. The program is certainly among the most comprehensive and thoughtfully conceived faculty development programs in a liberal arts college.

Gordon College
Wenham, Massachusetts

Contact Person: Richard Gross (President)
Samuel R. Schutz
Judson Carlberg (Dean)

Principles of Program

1. Each faculty member brings particular strengths and weaknesses to his academic community. This diversity of human experiences and characteristics is an appropriate basis from which to plan individual growth and on which to define the educational responsibilities of individual faculty members.

2. Within the context of common responsibilities shared by all faculty there is opportunity for individualized role definition. These roles, often multiple, should correspond to individual strengths and interests, as well as weaknesses and dislikes, with the ultimate objective being the development of a strong faculty in which diverse gifts complement each other.

3. The success of these individual efforts to achieve growth will be best realized when plans are self-designed and self-imposed.

4. Self-imposed plans of action are further enhanced by a specificity of goals and evaluation and by a development process which is both continuous and systematic.

5. An individualized development program has as a fundamental purpose the opportunity for participants to define and to pursue those activities which contribute to professional advancement, and to generate additional evidence in support of promotion, tenure, salary increments and other personnel considerations.

6. Although plans ought to proceed from the individual's self-defined strengths, weaknesses, interests, and dislikes, a faculty member's growth should not take place separate from the shaping force of colleagues and others. Rather the program should

encourage the individual to develop himself as comprehensively as possible, and should provide specific means for dialogue with and assessment by peers and institutional leadership.

Program Ownership and Governance

The faculty development program at Gordon College was initiated through a pilot project involving five faculty members under the leadership of the dean (now president), Richard Gross. Gordon had previously made use of sabbaticals, a research and development fund, workshops and institutes and awards for excellence in teaching to meet the developmental needs of faculty at the college. Gross, however, suggested that something new be added in the form of individualized development plans or "growth contracts." This method draws upon the management-by-objectives approach to administration, but applies it to faculty in an individualized and personal manner. While the program and concepts which underlie the program originated with an administrator, the ownership for specific growth plans — the heart of the program — clearly resides with the individual faculty member.

Program Staffing

The growth contract program is supervised by a faculty development committee, composed of five faculty members and the dean of the faculty. The dean is the formal administrator for the program, but works closely with both the president and faculty in the implementation of program activities.

Program Activities

The professional growth contract process consists of nine steps. First, each voluntary participant draws up an individual profile which includes a self-assessment of strengths, weaknesses, interests and dislikes, a description of current roles and statement of long-range goals and an assessment of current responsibilities and probable responsibilities during the contract period. The second step involves a review of this profile by a committee that has been selected by the faculty member. This committee helps the faculty member accomplish his professional growth plans as well as coordinate these plans with current job responsibilities.

During the third step, the participant formulates his growth plans, indicating what goals he hopes to achieve and relating these goals to his previous assessment of strengths, weaknesses and roles. The means by which these goals are to be achieved are then identified along with a statement of the criteria by which achievement is evaluated.

The growth plan is then reviewed by the committee, modified if needed and submitted in final draft to a college-wide professional development committee. The growth plan is carried out over the specified period (usually one year). Typically, the growth contract involves a range of activities and interests, some of which are specifically job-related (improving one's skills as a committee chairperson), others being of a more personal nature (finding more time for family life). Through the process of developing growth contracts, many faculty are able to effectively integrate their personal and professional concerns, and take action on these concerns with the support and resources of both colleagues and the institution within which they work.

The final two steps of the growth contract process require that a faculty member complete an evaluation of his plan with the assistance of his committee. A final report is submitted to the college-wide faculty development committee. The participant may then choose to begin a new contracting cycle or to wait for one or two years before formulating a new plan.

Program Evaluation

The success of the Gordon College program is in part reflected in the successes of each individual growth contract. The final evaluation which concludes each contract process, therefore, is an ingredient of the total program evaluation. In addition, an external evaluation team from Syracuse University provides an outside perspective on the program. Finally, the program will be evaluated at least indirectly by many faculty and administrators from other colleges and universisites who are now or soon will make use of the Gordon College growth contract process.

Program Funding

The W.K. Kellogg Foundation has funded the program for three years at $111,000. Gordon College has, in turn, agreed to sustain the program for a minimum of three additional years at the level of funding generated by the Kellogg Foundation. The funds provide for the support of individual development plans, sabbatical leves and the costs of administering the program.

Hartwick College
Oneonta, New York
Contact Person: Gerald Perkus

Goal of Program

Enhancement of the professional growth of faculty and other members of the campus community through providing a diverse array of services to meet instructional, organizational and personal needs within a supportive teaching-learning environment.

History of Program

Faculty development at Hartwick College has evolved through several stages since it was first initiated in 1973 (making it among the first programs of this type in the United States). Initially, intensive, week-long off-campus workshops for faculty, sponsored by Hartwick's consortium, the College Center of the Finger Lakes (CCFL), were conducted. External consultants designed and led these workshops, with the assistance of several faculty from the consortium colleges. An expanding corps of workshop-trained faculty (now numbering about one-third of the total faculty), staff and students provided leadership through an informal support network for innovative teaching and learning. This process was greatly aided by the activities of the Strategies for Change staff (Hartwick College was one of the focus campuses for this project). A three-year foundation grant to CCFL in the summer of 1974 accelerated the movement from a consortium-wide workshop-base to a campus-base with a broad range of activities. CCFL has continued to serve an important consultative function.

Program Ownership and Governance

From its beginnings, the Hartwick College program has had strong administrative support. Faculty development was made a subprogram of the Institutional Research Office and Committee in 1974; the faculty development staff is thus accountable to the coordinator of Institutional Research, a full-time administrator, and through her, directly to president (rather than, as usually the case, to the academic vice president or dean). In the early stages, several administrators played key roles in planning faculty development activities. From the start, however, the activities have been conducted either by faculty with release time or by external consultants.

Program Staff

In 1977, the faculty development program was fully integrated with the Institutional Research Office. The new unit is called the Office of Research and Development Services. Several of the faculty who have been most active in implementing faculty development activities will serve as consultants to this office, with two or three course release time.

Program Activities

Faculty development at Hartwick is multi-faceted. Many different activities are initiated in any one year. Interested faculty have been able to observe each other's classrooms and give each other helpful information and support, get together with students in a workshop setting to experiment with different teaching and learning stypes, or take part in a practicum on the improvement of classroom discussion, the use of overhead projector or becoming a better advisor. Faculty can browse through the Higher Education Resources Center (reading the *Chronicle of Higher Education, Change* magazine, or many books of current interest); they can talk with one another about experiential learning at an on-campus workshop; they can also consult with a member of the Faculty Development staff about the best ways to use the data from student evaluation forms, about an idea for a new course design, or about a way to motivate non-majors. In either a workshop or one-on-one setting, faculty can examine the relationship between their personal goals and values and their professional activities.

Faculty at Hartwick also participate in video-tape/classroom diagnosis sessions or attend luncheon meetings during which faculty share problems (for example, using student learning contracts) as well as successes (for example, using student learning contracts) as well as successes (for example, a class in which students show they can share the responsibility for helping each other learn). Faculty attend workshops on personal institutional decision making or receive mini-grants to attend weeklong seminars or national conferences.

In summary, Hartwick College offers four types of services to its faculty: 1) workshops, 2) consultation, 3) seminars and courses, and 4) resources. This college probably provides a greater diversity and number of services to its faculty than any other program of comparable size at a liberal arts college.

Table One

Since 1973, the CCFL and Hartwick Faculty Development program has included four types of activities.

1. *Workshops*

    Workshops in the assessment of experiential learning — part of a two year program "Cooperative Assessment of Experiential Learning" sponsored by the Educational Testing Service.

    A Three-day thematic workshop, "What is Faculty Development?"

    A workshop for the nursing department on simulations.

    A secretaries workshop focused on professional, personal, and interpersonal concerns of the secretarial staff.

    A student workshop on learning skills and learning styles.

    New faculty orientation: a day-long introduction to the college, with emphasis on active participation.

    Four basic instructional workshops focusing for seven days on personal, instructional and organizational components of effective teaching.

    One seven-day advanced workshop where faculty and administrators jointly explored teaching and institutional effectiveness.

    Two three-day instructional development workshops for faculty devoted to specific teaching methodology and course design.

    One three-day advanced instructional development workshop for the entire campus community centered on "Increasing Student Participation in the Classroom."

    One personal development workshop for students and faculty exploring basic values and life goals as they affect improved teaching and learning.

2. *Consultation*

    Individual consultation with faculty, students and staff on: problems in the classroom or department; requests for materials and resources; requests for classroom observations and diagnosis; and personal problems which impinged on classroom performance.

    Year-long consultations with the mathematics, sociology, anthropology, and art departments to help them define their goals and devise strategies for meeting them.

3. *Seminars and Courses*

    Eleven practicums on classroom techniques and on advising skills.

    Forty-two informal colloquia covering many topics, including contract learning, different teaching styles, student dissatisfaction, use of the library, and concerns of the new faculty.

    A December Term course "Encountering College" on teaching and learning provided students with a chance to examine their own goals and values, their learning styles, the classroom dynamic, and ways in which the college functions as an organization.

4. *Resources*

The use of a Higher Education Resource Center where members of the campus community can use printed and taped materials related to improvements and innovation in higher education.

Linking members of the community with others who could serve as resources or collaborators in problem solving.

In addition to the aforementioned activities the following services are planned in the future:

Aiding faculty members in constructive use of information obtained through student evaluation of faculty;

Assistance to faculty members who would like diagnosis of their classroom activity through the use of video tape or other means.

Aiding pairs or trios of faculty who would like to assist one another in the classroom diagnosis:

Consultation for improvement in faculty advising of students;

Consultation in the assessment of nonclassroom and nontraditional learning;

Process observation of committee meetings to help increase efficiency and effectiveness;

Consultations and workshops on career and life transitions;

Support for professional disciplinary and interdisciplinary growth among individual faculty members which relate to improved teaching effectiveness.

Program Evaluation

The Hartwick College program is being evaluated by means of a questionnaire which was developed by an internal evaluation consultant. The CCFL program director will also independently evaluate the program. In addition, through its linkage with institutional research and the Strategies for Change Project, the faculty development program at Hartwick can be assessed in terms of broad institutional impacts over time.

Program Funding

At this point in the program, Hartwick College receives $10,500 per year from the Lilly Endowment as part of this foundation's grant to the College Center of the Finger lakes. Additional financial support (primarily in the nature of release time) is provided by the college. Many costs for the program are also absorbed through the Institutional Research and Development Office.

Regis College
Denver, Colorado
Contact Person: Ronald Brockway

Goals of Program
　　1. To create a climate in which the progressive attainment of effective teaching is an on-going concern of the faculty.
　　2. To build a competent faculty development team, the members of which will be willing and able to assist their colleagues with their instructional concerns and efforts.
　　3. To earn the respect and support of the college community.

Program Ownership and Governance
　　The faculty have a major role in shaping and directing the faculty development program at Regis College. A faculty development team conducted extensive interviews with every full-time faculty member to determine what people were already doing, what kinds of program and services they want, and which faculty members could be resources. These data were collated and used to design current activities.

　　The community of faculty development and research is a regular standing committee of the college. It is made up of six faculty members elected to rotating three year terms, plus the dean of the college and the faculty development coordinator (FDC) as ex officio members. The committee is responsible for the broad parameters of faculty development, including policy and priorities, and allocates the college's specific budgets for professional travel and research. Although the committee presently is made up of the same members as the faculty development team (described below), it is anticipated that future elections will gradually change this. Such a change will broaden faculty input and ownership of the faculty development program. It will also precipitate a necessary and desirable effort to more clearly delineate the committee and team as separate, yet related, entities.

Program Staffing
　　The faculty development coordinator (FDC) holds a quasi-administrative position on a one-half release time basis. He is appointed by and reports to the dean of the college. The FDC is responsible for the faculty development program in its entirety, including planning, budgeting and training. The present FDC has been named as a faculty develop-

ment consultant, classroom diagnostician and program evalator through the CASC Advanced In-Service Faculty Development program. As a faculty member of Regis College, the FDC is able to retain contact with faculty, as a colleague in charge of a faculty-controlled program.

The faculty development team is made up of the FDC and six regular faculty members selected and trained by the FDC. These six faculty development consultants are on one-fourth release time to work with faculty members and faculty groups as facilitators, trainers, and classroom diagnosticians. The team has made only very sparing use of external consultants in either planning for or implementing the program. External consultants conducted a team building retreat on establishing goals and objectives, a training program on classroom diagnosis and a course design workshop.

Program Activities

A faculty development center has been established at Regis College as a place where faculty members can meet and compare notes and experiences with other faculty who are concerned about good teaching practices. Faculty members can also browse through current literature for useful ideas that will help them in the classroom. A comfortable lounge has been provided along with free coffee and a library of instructional materials. A member of the faculty development team is usually present to answer questions, offer suggestions about helpful literature, or serve as a "soft shoulder" for any faculty member who wants to talk. A private consulting room adjoins the lounge.

The committee on faculty development and research allocates the college budget for faculty travel to professional meetings and conventions, as well as for small grants and summer research grants. The faculty development team provides services to the Regis College faculty through group sessions and on an individual basis. Group activities include conferences on instructional issues and methodologies, book discussion seminars and workshops on such issues as student grading and evaluation, and the values and uses of team teaching and interdisciplinary studies. Through a series of in-service training sessions conducted over a three semester period, the six team members have received skills training in various instructional, personal and organizational development techniques (for example, observation, evaluation, diagnosis, interviewing, conflict management and team building).

A primary goal of the Regis College program is to provide students with well-designed courses incorporating the latest research in discipline and the best techniques of instruction. The faculty development staff helps faculty members develop skills in course design and implementation. Twelve faculty members, selected on the basis of competing proposals, are receiving training and consultant assistance in the design, implementation and evaluation of lower division courses. A week-long course design workshop was conducted during May, 1977 for the first six of these faculty. The FDC publishes a monthly newsletter which describes ongoing activities of the center, while also featuring articles by faculty at Regis about educational issues and instructional procedures.

Program Evaluation

The program will be evaluated by means of "Illuminative Evaluation" (Malcolm Parlett and Gary Dearden, eds., *An Introduction to Illuminative Evaluation*, Berkeley, CA: Pacific Sounding Press, 1977). A set of behavioral objectives were set down in 1976. The evaluation will include an analysis of how well these objectives were met. In addition, the faculty development team has established a set of goals with definite behavioral objectives for each semester; an analysis of how well these have been met will be included in the evaluation.

The Illuminative Evaluation should demonstrate the extent to which the faculty development program has fulfilled its goals and objectives. Additionally, it should cast light upon unanticipated results, thus showing any secondary impact on the institution, its faculty and its students. Finally, it should provide information which will be helpful in determining the shape and scope of the program for the future. Making use of a trained evaluator on campus (the FDC) as well as other illuminative evaluators (through the CASC National Consulting Network), this evaluaiton will be within the means and resources of the institution and the faculty development program.

Program Funding

The Regis College faculty development program operates under a $94,381 grant from the Lilly Endowment. Approximately forty percent of the budget is allocated to staff salaries and benefits, another thirty seven percent being allocated for program activities. The grant was undoubtedly given to Regis in part because of its previous activity in the field without external funding, and because of the training obtained by its director, Ronald Brockway, through the CASC program. The ability of the proposal writers to clearly specify the goals of the program, and to translate these into a workable set of objectives and activities probably also contributed to its successful funding.

University of the Pacific
Stockton, California
Contact person: Gene Rice

Goals of Program:
1. To enable faculty members to assess their developing academic strengths and interests; to identify and utilize resources for the nurturance of those strengths and interests; and to merge the growth of talents and competencies of the faculty with changing needs in university programs.
2. To develop a system for coordinating and approving university leaves according to a coherent plan for faculty and institutional development over a five year period.
3. To generate well defined teaching/research projects or special programs conducted through the office of program coordination for the reorientation and preparation required to meet program and staffing needs emerging within the university.
5. To produce significant new contributions to the understanding of faculty development which can be continuously utilized in the various divisions of the university and can become models for replication in other institutions.
5. To produce significant new contributions to the understanding of faculty development which can be continuously utilized in the various divisions of the university and can become models for replication in other institutions.
6. To encourage the growth of the faculty members as individuals, an important goal to an institution which has stressed the positive value of close student-faculty relationships.

Program Ownership and Governance
The program was originally initiated by an administrator and several faculty members without significant involvement by formal faculty governance groups. Faculty are being increasingly drawn into the program and regard it as a genuine resource for their professional development. The

faculty committee for the coordination of academic planning and professional development oversees the program and has a major influence on new program directions.

Program Staff

A half-time director coordinates the program; he has responsibility for faculty development leaves, plans and implements workshops, and provides leadership for various team activities. A full-time associate director manages the office, has responsibility for Teaching Incentive Awards, plans and implements workshops, and works with various teams. A full-time secretary and a computer specialist are also assigned to the program. The director and associate director report to the academic vice president. External consultants have been used in curriculum development, professional life planning workshops, seminars on funding, institutional research projects and the initial planning of the program.

Program Activities

This program is committed to the reallocation and development of the academic resources at the university — personal and programmatic. Hence, there is an emphasis on the coordination of academic planning and professional development. (See Figure One.) The coordinated program makes it possible for faculty members across the university to fully use the abundant opportunities for professional development that already exist at the university.

A major resource that the university is committing to the program is its substantial leave program. Leaves are used not only for traditional forms of renewal and teaching/research activities, but also for reorientation and preparation for meeting program and staffing needs that emerge within the university as a whole. Thirty faculty members each year participate in the leave program. Over a five year period every faculty member at the university will have had the opportunity to obtain a leave in order to examine his own capabilities and interests, assess changing institutional needs and opportunities for professional growth and integrate these into the planning of his own professional development.

FIGURE ONE
A PROGRAM FOR COORDINATION OF
ACADEMIC PLANNING AND PROFESSIONAL DEVELOPMENT

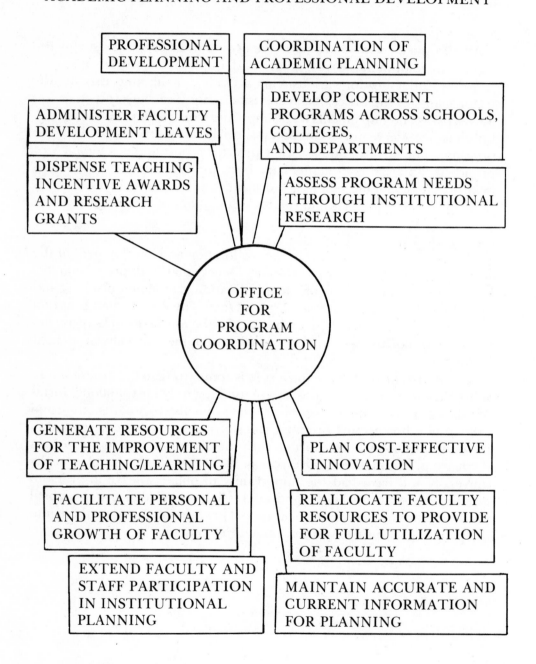

At a time when faculty are often discouraged and generally concerned with their own future and that of the institution, a "Faculty Incentive Awards" program has been established to encourage personal and institutional renewal. Small grants (total amount of $12,000 per year) are given for projects on curricular development (for example, team taught courses or interdisciplinary courses), the examination or application of both traditional and innovative instructional methodologies (for example, research designed to test the effectiveness of teaching) or theoretical papers concerned with central issues in teaching and learning, implementation of faculty exchanges within the institution and development of proposals for outside funding of teaching-learning projects.

Professional development at the University of the Pacific also encompasses a variety of workshops on professional life planning, self-assessment of teaching, funding opportunities, testing procedures and improvement of student writing skills. The program staff makes information available to faculty about outside funding opportunities and publishes a quarterly newsletter. The office also coordinates the institutional research and planning operations of the campus, thereby closely linking professional development activities to the identified needs and goals of the institution.

Program Evaluation

Interviews will be conducted with members of the faculty advisory committee and with faculty who have taken part in the program. Degree and durability of change will be appropriate criteria to assess areas such as the Teaching Incentive Awards and many instructional methodology workshops.

Program Funding

The University of the Pacific has received a grant of $68,000 per year for two years from the W.K. Kellogg Foundation for implementation of the professional development and academic planning program. Approximately fifty percent of the funds are allocated for staff salaries and benefits, with another thirty percent being allocated for program activities.

University of Puget Sound
Tacoma, Washington

Contact person: Steven Phillips

Goals of Program
1. Establishment of a program for departmental consultation on curriculum revision, teaching methodology and departmental organization.
2. Implementation of a series of university-wide workshops and seminars which deal with specific issues of teaching and learning.
3. Initiation of a program of faculty exchange between the University of Puget Sound and other colleges, junior colleges and universities in the Pacific Northwest.

Program Ownership and Governance

The original program, as defined in the funded grant proposal, was designed by administrators; the current coordinator of faculty development at the University of Puget Sound, however, has been given considerable freedom in conducting the program, and has greatly increased faculty ownership for the program through an advisory board and extensive interviewing of faculty at the university. The on-campus and off-campus workshop program has been particularly responsive to faculty needs and interests, both in the identification of topics for the workshops and in the receptivity of the workshop staff to emergent concerns of the participants in the workshops.

Program Staffing

The faculty development program is coordinated by one full-time staff member, Steven Phillips, who came to the university with extensive experience in conducting faculty development programs. Dr. Phillips is assisted by a half-time secretary who is also skilled as a workshop trainer and consultant, and is used in this capacity. The program coordinator reports directly to the academic dean and advisory board. External consultants have been used extensively in the workshop program and as program evaluators.

Program Activities

The departmental consultation program began with a request for each department to identify a particular contact person or group within its department to work directly with the coordinator of faculty development. Each contact person or group then wrote up a plan for use of an external consultant to assist the department in some area of teaching and learning. The consultant then has been brought in to assist the department in such areas as curricular reform, redesign of an introductory course, use of a new instructional method or identification of a new intellectual trend in the discipline.

The second component of the faculty development program is a series of workshops and seminars that vary in length from less than two hours to as much as a full week. These workshops allow faculty to explore in an organized manner their crucial and complex roles as teachers, persons and members of an organization. This program is particularly noted for its intensive, long term, off-campus workshops. In this setting faculty have the time and resources to examine their present performance and plan for the future. Working with external consultants who are experts in the area of professional development, faculty explore in depth their own assumptions about teaching and learning, the relationship between their teaching and the rest of their professional lives, and the way they function within their institution. Two weeklong workshops have been offered each year for the past two years, one in January and one in June. Enrollment in each workshop is limited to between fifteen and twenty faculty. Usually about one third to one half of the faculty participants come from other Northwest colleges and universities.

Since some faculty are unable or unwilling to spend a week away from their home, families and other commitments, several on-campus workshops are held each semester at UPS. These workshops also provide valuable follow-up for the faculty returning from the weeklong, off-campus workshops. These workshops have addressed such issues as decision making, the use of instructional simulations, student evaluation of instructions and teaching-learning styles.

The third component of the UPS faculty development program is faculty exchange. Several faculty each year are given an opportunity to spend an extended period of time at another college or university in the Pacific Northwest. Several of these exchanges are now being established through the Association for Innovation in Higher Education's program for faculty exchange. The coordinator of faculty development is also actively involved in institutional research programs, provision of instructional diagnostic services and training other members of the UPS staff in faculty development consultation and training.

Program Evaluation

An external evaluator has been used at UPS: Edward Kelley from Syracuse University. Kelley conducts interviews and observations and reviews documents from the program in order to make a program assessment. In addition, each workshop is evaluated through use of a post-event questionnaire.

Program Funding

This program is funded by a grant from the Lilly Endowment. The University has made a commitment to continue supporting the program after the foundation grant ends.

Appendix B
Selected Teaching Improvement Programs

The University Center

Program Descriptions

The following sources contain excellent summaries of the activities of university centers and agencies for the improvement of teaching. The report of the Educational Development Program at Michigan State University presents evidence of the university-wide impact of its efforts. Most centers have descriptive materials about their activities which will be sent to anyone requesting them.

Committee on Institutional Cooperation, Panel on Research and Development of Instructional Resources, *Development and Experiment in College Teaching* (Ann Arbor, Michigan, University of Michigan, Center for Research on Learning and Teaching, Reports #1-12, 1966-1976.

Lawrence T. Alexander and Stephen L. Yelon (eds), *Instructional Development in Higher Education* (East Lansing, Michigan: Michigan State University, The Learning Service, 1972).

Mary Lynn Crow, Ohmer Milton, W. Edmund Moomaw, and William R. O'Connell, Jr., (eds) *Faculty Development Centers in Southern Universities* (Atlanta: Southern Regional Education Board, 1976).

Robert H. Davis, Allan J. Abedor, and Paul W.F. Witt, *Commitment to Excellence* (East Lansing, Michigan: Michigan State University, Educational Development Probram, 1976).

Robert M. Diamond, Paul Eickman, Robert Halloway, Eleanor Taylor, and Timothy Wilson, *Syracuse University's Center for Instructional Development* (Syracuse, N.Y.: Syracuse University, 1973).

Albert B. Smith, *Faculty Development and Evaluation in Higher Education* (Washington, D.C.: The American Association for Higher Education, ERIC/Higher Education Research Report #8, 1976).

The activities of a number of university centers and agencies are worthy of note because of the varying emphases which have emerged at each institution. One center, the Center for the Improvement of Undergraduate Education at Cornell University, directed by James Mass, has fallen victim to lack of faculty support for university funding. The Center had a brief but creative tenure as the result of foundation support. The Faculty Resource Center at the University of Cincinnati, directed by Tony Grasha and described below, will be terminated at the conclusion of the 1977-78 academic year because of financial problems associated with the university becoming a state supported institution. Both of these centers leave a legacy of excellence which continues to be of benefit to surviving centers. In addition, the University of Massachusetts Clinic has been terminated, though many of their services have been incorporated into the Center for Instructional Resources and Improvement directed by Sher Reichmann.

Brief descriptions of selected centers appear below, followed by a more detailed explanation of the center which I have directed since 1969. This is given to provide some insight into the values of the staff as well as to describe programs:

Harvard University
Office of Instructional Research and Evaluation
Dean K. Whitla, Director

Activities at Harvard have focused on opportunities for teaching assistants and faculty to engage in discussions about teaching which are organized around courses in which some video-taping of teaching has been done. Much of this activity is supported by the Danforty Foundation, which underwrites the activities of a Harvard-Danforth Center for Teaching and Learning. The Harvard program stresses the personal examination of teaching and the preparation of graduate teaching assistants for their instructional assignments. Course development also is stressed as is some assistance for the evaluation of teaching. Support comes from a mix of inside and outside funding, with the Danforth Foundation providing the major portion of outside monies.

University of Massachusetts
Center for Instructional Resources and Improvement
Sheryl Riechman, Director

The Clinic for the Improvement of University Teaching is a model of teaching improvement strategy developed under W.K. Kellogg funding at the University of Massachusetts, Amherst. It is noteworthy because of the well developed strategy which is used by staff to diagnose and remediate problems which individual faculty have with their teaching. The emphasis is on the process of teaching rather than on course design or technological interventions in instruction. The technique involves a one-to-one relationship with a staff member who works with the faculty member to help identify problems and correct them in a manner which will be reinforcing to the teacher. Kellogg funds have aided the development of the procedure and a national dissemination strategy for training persons in the method who can then apply it at their own institutions.

University of Cincinnati
Faculty Resource Center
Tony Grasha, Director

In 1975, the Institute for Research and Training in Higher Education merged with the University Media Services Center. The new organization, a Faculty Resource Center, has undertaken a general faculty development mission at the university on the improvement of teaching. The center has available a monograph series which provides some practical designs for program elements in a faculty development approach. Tony Grasha has developed a system for analyzing instructional needs, and this is available in published form. The University of Cincinnati represents a practical wedding of both instructional and faculty development strategies.

University of Tennessee-Knoxville
Learning Research Center
Ohmer Milton, Director

This center represents a low-cost operation which has maintained high visibility nationally and on-campus. Two elements are the major parts of the efforts of the center; small grants to faculty for innovations in teaching, and distribution of a publication, *Teaching-Learning Issues*. The publication contains concise and well written summaries of issues which have a general impact on instruction. The center also disseminates relevant selections from the literature of higher education to the University of Tennessee faculty. The mini-grant program, which was in operation until last year, has been displaced by a seminar program for special presentations about teaching. The seminar program has been used quite effectively with graduate students.

University of Texas-Austin
Center for Teaching Effectiveness
James Stice, Director

This center was established in 1972 to provide assistance to teaching faculty in one of the largest public universities in the South. It offers courses and consultation for teaching assistants and faculty which emphasize course planning, evaluation and general problems in university teaching. The center is one of the major resources in the United States for information about Personalized Systems of Instruction. The director of the center is a chemical engineer who introduced the Keller Plan to the College of Engineering for its undergraduate instruction while he was director of the Bureau of Engineering Teaching. Funding is provided by the university.

University of Michigan
Center for Research on Learning and Teaching
Wilbert McKeachie, Director

CRLT was established in 1962 with Stanford Erickson as its first director. The university funds the center and the staff is charged with providing services to faculty and maintaining a research program on instruction. Services provided are of an eclectic nature, usually in the form of individual consultation with faculty. The publications program of the center has emphasized a newsletter, *Memo to the Faculty*, which is a model for communicating with a research-oriented faculty in a manner which both informs the faculty and provides the evidence to support the content. This publication has been used nationally by a number of centers in workshops and seminars with faculty and teaching students.

Kansas State University
Center for Faculty Evaluation and Development in Higher Education
Steven Brock, Director

This center is responsible for the development and dissemination of a national evaluation and planning effort known as the IDEA (Instructional Development and Effectiveness Assessment) system. The IDEA system defines instructional effectiveness as reports by students of their progress on those teaching objectives which the faculty member specifies as important for a particular course. The IDEA system also identifies strong and weak teaching methods or procedures which are related to student progress on the specified objectives. The IDEA system was developed by funds from the W.K. Kellogg Foundation, which is also supporting a national dissemination effort for the system. Many institutions of higher education are using IDEA as the major institutional assessment system.

Syracuse University
Center for Instructional Development
Robert Diamond, Director

The Syracuse center has evolved into a national model for instructional development. Established in 1971, the center is supported principally by university funding. Three operational units — support services, research and evaluation, and development — administer the efforts of the center. Traditional audio-visual services are located in the library. The center is funded to avoid charge-back systems for obtaining support from departments for services provided. The director is an assistant vice chancellor for academic affairs and thus has access to the budgetary decision process. A wide range of services helps faculty develop instructional projects. A graduate student internship program provides opportunities for the center to fill a direct educational function. A major developmental strategy emphasized by the staff is a planning and implementational process aimed at the design of sequential curricula as opposed to individual courses.

Michigan State University
Educational Development Program
Robert Davis, Director

The EDP at MSU is a successful case history for instructional development in one of the largest state university systems in the nation. Educational development at Michigan State resulted from a conscious faculty and administrative decision about the function of teaching in the many programs of the university. To describe the programs would take more space than is available here, for they range from instructional media production, including television and film, to individual consulting services for faculty. The program can be described as centralized, service oriented, emphasizing faculty consultation and improving education through faculty initiative, the application of a consistent theoretical framework and the granting and administration of funds for instructional development. The Educational Development Program has become a necessary part of instructional improvement at Michigan State and has done so by the application of a concise and logical philosophy about teaching at MSU.

Stanford University
Center for Teaching and Learning
David Halliburton, Director

The Stanford center is supported by Danforth Foundation funds and is one of several centers for the improvement of teaching throughout the United States created by Danforth. The Center for Teaching and Learning has been especially successful in designing workshops and "mini-conferences" on a wide range of topics from institutional policies about teaching to basic skills in instruction. The activities of the center attract an audience from colleges and universities in the western region of the United States. The center has developed a structured relationship with selected institutions which will help make the resources at Stanford available to assist other institutions design their own programs.

Northwestern University
The Center for the Teaching Professions
B. Claude Mathus, Director

The activities of the center represent a commitment to no one orthodoxy or solution for the examination and improvement of teaching and learning in higher education. The staff of the center are involved in a number of programs which reflect opportunities to work with faculty and graduate students, and professional associations, in a wide variety of contexts representing a broad range of needs. Examples of these program areas are as follows:

a.   The center helps departments at Northwestern plan, and itself offers, sections of a "Seminar on College Teaching" for graduate students whose career goals include a teaching obligation of some kind. The students who take the seminar obtain credit, which becomes part of their doctoral programs.

b.   The center maintains a Faculty Fellowship Program for Northwestern faculty which assists those persons who are committed to excellence in teaching to have the help they need to achieve their goals. These teacher-scholars also act as an informal faculty for the center.

c. A Learning Resource Facility is part of the efforts of the center directed at providing media support for teaching at Northwestern. Through the Learning Resource Facility, Project NU-CAT (Northwestern University-Computers and Teaching) is made available to students and faculty interested in applications of computer-assisted instruction.

d. A Visiting Scholars Program is offered to faculty from other colleges and universities who wish to spend some time at the center interacting with staff, and with the university generally, concerning some problem of faculty development which interests them.

e. The center administers The Writing Place, a no-risk resource for helping students at Northwestern improve their writing skills.

f. The center has a Program for Faculty Development which is supported by the Danforth Foundation for the thirteen private liberal arts institutions in the Associated Colleges of the Midwest.

g. The center provides opportunities for professional associations to have meetings and develop plans for elevating the role of teaching to the position of importance it should have in the activities of all professionals.

h. Edited videotapes of classroom discussions are being prepared with support of the Danforth Foundation. These "College Classroom Vignettes" are used to stimulate discussion about teaching among college and university faculty.

i. The center maintains a publications program which makes available a series of occasional papers prepared by staff and faculty involved in seminars which faculty offer for each other.

The efforts of the center in the future will involve a continuing commitment to general faculty development in higher education. Our successes suggest that the strategies and programs which will be maintained are those which will be more useful with faculty in the private sector of higher education, such as are found in institutions like those in the Associated Colleges of the Midwest and the Great Lakes College Association. We feel that the most effective criteria for assessing what we try to do at the center are those which indicate movement in individual faculty from dependence to independence, or self-direction, in the analysis, understanding and control of those factors which are crucial in influencing a positive and satisfying feeling about what one does as a teacher-scholar and about what one is able to do within an institutional culture which provides a context for professional development.

Appendix C

Selected Teaching Improvement Programs

The Community College

Staff Development at Three California Community Colleges

Introduction

Presented here are three brief reports on staff development efforts at three Northern California community colleges, De Anza College, Sacramento City College, and the College of Alameda. No claim is made that these three programs are exemplary nor that they are representative of staff development in California, much less the nation. The three colleges were selected because of the variations among them, as well as because of the concerns and processes they have in common.

A few words about each college will indicate the differences among them. De Anza is a large suburban college serving an increasingly diversified clientele. Among California colleges, it has from its inception been a pacesetter and innovator. Sacramento City College, located in California's capitol, is one of the older colleges of the state. Its history has been marked by the progression from the status of adjunct to the city secondary schools to its present status as one of three colleges in one of California's largest multi-campus districts. It is smaller than De Anza in numbers of students and personnel, but larger than College of Alameda. One of the five colleges in the Peralta Community College District, the College of Alameda is located in the City of Alameda in the heart of the eastern portion of the San Francisco Bay Area. Of the three, College of Alameda is the youngest.

To visit these campuses is to be impressed with the differences in student populations, the physical surroundings, the faculty, the governance systems and the organizational structures, the institutional histories — and the role and function accorded staff development. In view of the differences, it is not surprising that each college has moved at its own pace toward programmatic staff development.

Though there are differences, there are also similarities. These similarities are tantalizing, as they seem to suggest generalizations about regularities of process and outcome that transcend individual campuses. Take care, however! These reports were not made to provide a basis for sweeping generalizations. It is interesting to note, however, the emergence of the full-time staff development person at two of the colleges, and the difficulty with the committee system at another.

Written in Spring, 1977, the reports follow a common format. In a sense, they are already dated: in each case, the program was in the midst of growth at the time of writing. The reader can assume that the flow of events has brought changes to each college. An example of this is Sacramento City College, which recently launched a full-scale management development effort using the Higher Education Management Institute program, with the assistance of a grant from the Exxon Foundation.

Again, these reports are offered for whatever value they may have for the reader in supplying some concreteness in the midst of much abstraction, and in illustrating points made in the chapter.

College of Alameda
Alameda, California

Origins
Staff development activities at the College of Alameda (COA) were conceived and initiated by a small volunteer exploratory committee consisting of administrators, faculty, and classified employees during the Fall Quarter of 1975, following an acknowledgement by the college president that staff development was a positive avenue for the institution to grow and prosper. The persistent interest of one staff member provided some direction and organizational structure. Under his leadership the committee began functioning.

To begin establishing a staff development program at COA, an extensive review was undertaken of the literature, practices and activities related to staff development on community college campuses. The volunteer exploratory committee began to hold regular meetings, attend staff development conferences and meet with consultants in the area to gather as much information as possible on staff development.

After a year and a half of operation the committee has made progress in gaining support and recognition from many staff members. The majority of proposed projects has been initiated by faculty members. In addition, the committee has moved from being a volunteer exploratory committee to that of a regular standing committee of the college's organizational structure.

Project Development
At the outset the staff development project at COA was based primarily on the extensive review of literature, practices visible at other institutions

and the goals and philosophy of COA. To guide project activities the committee defined staff development at COA as being "a comprehensive program of activities conducive to the professional and personal growth of the personnel of the college, toward the ultimate end of improving learning opportunities for students."

Several philosophical statements were also developed so that staff development could be conceptualized on the campus, as well as becoming an integral part of the college's mission of enhancing student learning:

1. The continued growth of all individuals, whether staff or students, is an investment of inestimable, but appreciable, value which should be nurtured and promoted at all times.
2. The process of staff development involves *all* staff. . . . This process promotes the development of human potential and recognizes the unique abilities and capabilities for each individual.
3. Staff development should be a continuing process which involves not only a long-term commitment but also a renewal of values, a redefinition of purposes, and a change of attitudes on the part of all staff.
4. We are committed to a program which will seek to create opportunities for becoming.

These statements were identified as being relevant for *all* COA personnel: administrators, faculty, classified, instructional (student) aides, and other student workers.

In addition to the development of goal and philosophical statements the committee developed a questionnaire and conducted a needs assessment of COA personnel to determine possibilities for future activities. The questionnaire was a modification of several questionnaires assembled by experts in the field of staff development.

Current Status

Presently the staff development activities are generated from two sources. Initially, an assessment was conducted to identify staff needs as well as to identify the types of activities that staff members would be interested in. In the Fall of 1976 the first of a series of workshops, seminars and forums were introduced on the campus. In addition, the campus had originally funded a program known as Faculty Generated Projects that fell under the general heading of innovative grants. Both of these sources offer opportunity for staff involvement in professional development activities. All members of COA are encouraged to participate and the committee constantly requests input from staff members.

As of the date of this writing, the committee has not specified goals and objectives aside from definition of staff development and its philosophical statements. The committee, however, is in the process of reviewing other staff development programs and literature with the intention of defining and describing some basic components of a staff development program for COA.

Project Staff

The staff development committee at COA consists of eleven COA personnel: one administrator, four faculty, and six classified employees. A faculty member holds the position of chairperson of the committee. There are also two co-chairpersons. These two positions are held by one certificated and one classified employee. The committee, as a whole, has developed guidelines to approve staff development activities. Individuals or groups proposing projects or activities must follow the committee's guidelines and submit appropriate applications to the chairperson of the staff development committee. The chairperson has overall administrative responsibility of the project.

Approximately one-third of the chairperson's regular full-time teaching load is released to coordinate and facilitate the work of the committee and staff development activities. The committee is responsible for coordinating all staff development activities on campus including the Faculty Generated Projects program which is funded with district funds. It convenes once a month. There are no facilities per se from which staff development operates. However, campus facilities are made available to the committee when needed.

The committee structure seems to be functioning but not as effectively as the chairperson would like. After considerable analysis and review of literature, discussion with consultants, and visits to other campuses with staff development, the chairperson feels that a committee structure doesn't work as effectively as a staff development officer. Often times, *all* committee members cannot convene at the same time which causes several problems, from canceling the meeting to holding up proposed projects because of lack of quorum. The chairperson also felt that more time should be devoted to staff development aside from the one-third release time that is presently designated. This would allow more opportunity for staff development to circulate and provide more personalized attention to all staff members. However, the chairperson, as well as other committee members, does not believe that staff development should become a part of the evaluation of staff members.

Activities

This past Fall Quarter (1976) several activities under the heading of staff development were offered on COA's campus for the first time. Although few in numbers, the activities were well publicized and generated a fairly good response. Workshops and staff forums were sponsored by the staff development committees and facilitated or instructed by several COA staff members. This committee tries, as much as possible, to utilize COA staff in areas of expertise first. This year staff development activities include: 1) TV workshop on instruction in use and operation of the new video equipment at COA, 2) a staff forum sharing highlights of sabbaticals, faculty generated projects, educational conferences and other innovative projects, 3) a scholarship fund raising event for COA students, 4) communication workshop for college personnel (Fall, 1977), and 5), an orientation program (Fall, 1977). Other activities are in the hopper, pending publicity to generate enough support to sponsor the activities.

Relationship to College Structure

The staff development committee at COA has been officially recognized as a standing committee as of the Fall Quarter, 1976. The committee will be in continuous operation until the need for such a committee no longer exists. Aside from the fact that it is a standing committee, staff development relates to the spirit of COA's mission of enhancing student learning. Evaluation of personnel does not have a direct relation to staff development.

Evaluation

Some evaluation as to the value of various staff development activities has been conducted. The committee developed a ten-item evaluation form for COA personnel to complete after participating in staff development activities. Information from the evaluation is used to modify and improve future activities. Although returns have been small in numbers, there seems to be a general consensus that the activities have been of some value and use to the participants. No evaluation has been conducted on the committee structure and function of staff development.

Future

Future plans for staff development at COA include a better assessment of the total staff for continuous awareness of the diversity of needs to be satisfied. The committee would also like to sponsor more activities on campus and have a clearer understanding of allocation and disbursement of funds for staff development. The chairperson would also like to evaluate the effectiveness of the committee.

The chairperson feels that because the concept is new on campus, staff development will take time in gaining recognition, but activities are off to a good start.

Sacramento City College
Sacramento, California

Origins

The need to implement the staff development program at Sacramento City College (SCC) was evident when the program started. SCC is the oldest of three campuses within the Los Rios Community College District. For the past decade SCC, like many other community colleges, has been experiencing rapid and diversified changes in its student population. In addition, SCC is experiencing a "steady state" in its hiring that is evident in a low staff turnover. At the same time, public concern for accountability continues. These factors are quite evident on most community college campuses today. On SCC's campus these factors became the impetus in the establishment of some form of staff development.

Enough concern was generated by administrators, faculty and classified employees during the 1975-1976 academic school year to organize a staff development committee. The committee members played a key role in getting the program underway. The president seemed supportive of staff development at SCC and was fully aware of the needs and changing environment.

The need for staff development activities was apparent. Little was available to certificated and classified employees in the way of continually improving instruction and services at the campus. Several committee members sought resource persons in the area of staff development and several on-site visits were made to campuses with staff development programs in operation. Staff development conferences were attended and literature was reviewed. Subsequently, staff development activities at SCC became more and more visible on campus.

This report focuses on faculty, however, since it was written SCC has initiated a wide-ranging Higher Education Management Institute (HEMI) program for management development.

Program Development
During the 1975-76 academic school year, staff development was in its first phase of growth. A committee of administrators, faculty and classified employees met and were responsible for the operational functions of staff development on the SCC campus. One of the first tasks required was defining staff development at SCC in order to develop a program purpose and goals. Meetings were organized to accomplish this. However, no well-defined purpose, goals or even committee operational procedures were developed at this time because of committee members' conflicting schedules to meet regularly as a total group.

Eventually, some of the committee members were able to organize themselves to develop a purpose and goals for staff development. More and more committee members and the president became cognizant of the need for not only a staff development program, but also for a person to facilitate the committee and program activities. A position for a staff development officer was made and filled for the 1976-77 school year, thus opening the doors for better facilitation of committee procedures.

The staff development committee, in representation of its total staff, perceived staff development "as an effective and viable means of meeting changing needs in a constantly changing environment. . . . As the mission and goals change in adapting to the needs of the changing community, the staff needs the opportunity to adapt and change also." In addition, they perceived staff development as "an honest effort to provide the structure, experience and incentive for *all of the staff* (faculty, classified, and administrators) to develop." The staff development program was therefore institutionalized to "coordinate and organize opportunities for the professional and personal growth of all campus personnel."

Goals
1. Develop grater understanding of the special purposes and functions of Sacramento City College and its role in the community.
2. Provide an atmosphere and environment in which all Sacramento City College personnel may become aware of, and involved in, the educational process.
3. Increase the development of "community" among all campus personnel.

4. Foster a recognition that our diversity is a strength in facilitating the educational delivery system.
5. Encourage an awareness of the need for change in relation to the changing student population.
6. Encourage personal and professional growth certificated and classified personnel in the interest of improving services to Sacramento City College students.
7. Make creativity educationally beneficial, and both extrinsically and intrinsically gratifying for all personnel.
8. Develop understanding of special problems of learning and behavior of a diverse student population, in each area of instruction.
9. Improve the ability of certificated and classified staff to improve relevant and effective instruction and services for students' diverse racial, ethnic and economic backgrounds, and those who possess physical, language, or other disabilities.
10. Increase knowledge of available resources and instructional strategies.
11. Increase student learning.

Current Status

The staff development program at SCC is becoming more and more acceptable to its entire personnel. The committee continues to function with its staff development officer and continuous direction is sought for improvement of the committee's procedures. Staff development has been achieving an "umbrella" effect, catching and disbursing basically any and all funds for innovation, in-service training activities, and program development. Because of this, the committee has restructured itself to accommodate its diversity of responsibilities.

The committee currently has a budget of $41,150 for utilization in the funding of grants and projects for college personnel. $2,500 was allocated for an operating budget for the Staff Development Office, and $5,000 was allocated for in-service training activities. A monthly newsletter called FOCUS is published which reports staff development activities locally and throughout the state for college personnel information.

Program Staff

The program's staff consists of a full-time staff development officer (a full-time day, reassigned time faculty member), two co-chairpersons, and the staff development committee, comprised of twenty-two SCC personnel. After considerable self-assessment, a complete reorganization of the committee and its operational procedures were brought forth to the academic community. The committee is divided into three sub-committees: 1) in-service training, 2) innovation, and 3) program development. It was felt that although the large number of committee members offered diversity among the committee, operationally the large number did not seem feasible. Schedules conflicted occasionally to the point where it was impossible to conduct meetings of substance. The committee's efforts were perceived by some college personnel as being "less than sufficient, frequently redundant, and often inconsistent."

The staff development officer's primary function is to "serve as a catalyst for the improvement of instruction and other college services and as a specialist in the techniques and resources involved in the process." The officer is directly responsible to the associate dean of instruction. Basic duties of the staff development officer include the organization and development of activities for total staff participation, function as a recorder and work with co-chairpersons of the staff development committee in facilitating the process for approval/disapproval of various projects, work with the divisions, departments, and other college units in formulating, organizing, implementing and evaluating staff development projects, and encourages and assists staff members to establish individualized professional growth and development plans.

The twenty-two member committee consists of faculty, classified and administrative personnel. Each of the three sub-committees has a chairperson with the sub-committee members initially appointed by the co-chairpersons. Each sub-committee is "given the responsibility of initial consideration of proposals relevant to their broadly difined area" as well as "serve to generate in-puts and direction for the Committee as a whole."

Activities

Projects and activities have been both large in numbers as well as diverse in content. Projects have included the following: restructuring the ESL program, development of self-paced instruction in business mathematics, group subscription to CJC Journal, Faculty TV project, aerial photography, attendance at conferences, development of visual aid packages on clothing construction techniques. Activities sponsored by the Staff Development Office have included: Data Processing In-service Training Class, Reading & the Community College Instructor, Learning How to Learn:

"A Packaged Classroom," Content Vocabulary & the Classroom Teacher, Cognitive Mapping, Blacks in Nursing—A Historical Perspective, Bulk Mailing Procedures Workshop, Cardio-Pulmonary Resuscitation Certification Course, Human Potential Seminar, Secretarial Workshop, Student Volunteer Sercices Workshop, Assertiveness Training Workshop, Metric Measurement Workshop, Instructional Design Workshop, The Non-Traditional Student: Changing Services for Changing Needs, Individualized Instruction: A Packaged Approach. The majority of seminars, workshops, and faculty forums are sponsored by the staff development office. However, the academic community is encouraged to generate topics for such activities. In addition, the academic community is recognized by the staff development committee.as being of vital resource. For this reason, as much as possible the academic community is sought for its expertise in areas of campus-wide interest prior to seeking outside experts in a given area.

Relationship to College Structure

Originally being implemented as an *ad hoc* committee, the staff development committee at SCC has since gained acceptance and approval of the academic community. Consequently, it has become a standing committee within the over-all structure of SCC's governance structure.

Because of the intensity of such a program, staff development has begun to move the college in the direction of continuous reassessment of its needs. The profound effects of activities, projects, committee participants, and college personnel attitudes on individual and group needs have influenced the awareness for a comprehensive staff development program. The program has no direct bearing on the evaluation of college personnel. However, the personnel is encouraged to generate projects and, if necessary, seek out the staff development officer for assistance in developing proposals.

Evaluation

The staff development program a SCC presently has no concrete method for evaluating its program purpose and goals. However, at the end of the 1976-77 school year, an annual report was written and a self-assessment was conducted by the staff development committee on the committee's organization and direction for the coming year. It has since restructured itself into three sub-committees. The annual report for 1976-77, written by the co-chairpersons acclaimed the use of sub-committees as having a profound influence on participation of committee members. In addition, the sub-committees have "helped facilitate consistency of committee action, and enabled the Committee to give more careful consideration and greater direction to the College."

The co-chairpersons also attributed a more favorable environment for staff development at SCC to the establishment of a staff development officer position. A survey was conducted in January to assess the effectiveness of the services of staff development and over eighty per cent of the respondents considered the services to be effective and of use. The annual report has suggested that as a result of the new staff development officer's position greater coordination of committee activity has occured, coupled with the committee's ability to interact with the academic community in a more positive and proactive manner.

Future

The staff development program a SCC is moving at a fast pace toward a comprehensive staff development program. Gradually, projects, activities, seminars and workshops are being generated and sponsored to meet the needs of a college-wide personnel. The staff development committee is seeking greater understanding and awareness of staff development programs in communtiy colleges in an attempt to better define their won program. In addition, the staff development office is continuously reviewing needs assessment inventories, conducting extensive literature reviews and establishing contact for resources in the area of staff development to better equip the office and committee with updated resources and materials. Future events include: more well-defined goals and objectives, better assessment of personnel needs, establishment of more concrete criteria for approval/disapproval of proposal, clearer operational procedures for the staff development committee, and development of an evaluation plan of the total program.

De Anza College
Cupertino, California

Origins

The establishment of staff development at De Anza College was initiated primarily by student services staff when the college first opened its doors ten years ago. Their concern was to be truly effective in serving De Anza's students. Because a well-defined system was needed, staff development was established to further implement innovations and provide support in many areas for staff members.

Initial in-service activities at De Anza College included sensitivity training, team building and development of interpersonal relations. These activities focused primarily on the student services staff and administrative personnel. However, the success of such activities soon spread and encompassed a majority of De Anza's personnel, including both classified and certificated staff.

The activities grew in numbers. The time had come to implement a comprehensivedevelopment program for all segments of the college. The need for a staff development program at De Anza became increasingly apparent. The movement toward a comprehensive program has been launched. At De Anza there is agreement among the college segments that there should be a fully-funded, comprehensive staff development program. The position of a full-time staff development officer was established to institutionalize the many activities into a staff development program. Presently, two segments (administrators and faculty) of De Anza College personnel are actively involved in staff development. The classified segement is in the process of identifying specific needs in an effort to address themselves to these needs with the assistance of the staff development officer.

Program Development

The premises from which De Anza established its staff development program were the following:
   (a) be responsible to the comprehensive need of the staff;
   (b) assess needs of staff prior to creating in-service activities;
   (c) place emphasis on personalization, individualization, and more active participation of the college's total personnel;
   (d) maximum utilization of diversity of training and support activities and resources.

Current Status

Two programs presently fall underneath the broad heading of staff development of De Anza College: the Management Development Program and the Faculty Professional Renewal Program.

Management Development Program

The Management Development Program (MDP) at De Anza has established as its mission "...to provide the opportunities for the continuing development of an effective, professional management team that can lead De Anza College toward the achievement of its stated goals." The program has defined four specific objectives:

1. Assist administrators and potential administrators in career development planning.
2. Identify individual and college requirements for development training.
3. Identify, design, and evaluate various developmental training strategies for obtaining individual administrator and college goals.
4. Provide a current vita file for each administrator that records professional achievements, developmental activities, and future career planning.

The MDP serves all administrators at De Anza College. Activities for the program are planned under the general operation and direction of the staff development officer with assistance from an MDP advisory committee. This committee consists of representatives from each job speciality group and individualized activities. Assessments are conducted through joint-consultation of the staff development officer and key administrators. In the case of personalizing activities, individual admisistrators consult with the staff development officer and even immediate supervisors. Individualization of activities and consultation of immediate supervisors on both job performance needs and indivudual needs are highly encourages. "Biannual administrator evaluation interviews will emphasize not only job performance but career planning and developmental activities as well."

Faculty Professional Renewal Program

A Faculty Professional Renewal Program (FPRP) was also implemented to respond to the increasingly diversified needs of De Anza's faculty. FPRP has been defined as ". . . a planned and sustained interpersonal problem-solving process which utilizes collaborative methods to diagnose needed changes and to design a variety of interventions which result in personal and professional growth and enhance performance for staff members." At De Anza College emphasis is placed on a clearly defined process which lends support in the creation of individual and group development programs. "at the core of any such process must be a network of support which stimulates and supports the accomplishment of individual and institutional changes upon which any future progress is dependent."

The FPRP can be viewed as a process for exploration of professional and personalized growth. In this light, the goals of FPRP are as follows:

1. Support the creation of organizational conditions that support the problem solving process.
2. Provide consultant help in initiating and sustaining the process of problem solving with individuals, groups, or organizational areas.
3. Provide a number of specific offerings at the college-wide level which may be utilized by individual staff members and by groups of staff members to learn new skills, techniques, knowledge or attitudes that will enhance both personal and professional performance.
4. Provide a delivery system for problem-solving to be supported, encouraged and integrated into the college's policies.
5. Provide the president with documentation which supports the effectiveness of the FPRP, both as an independent program and as a major support system of student development.
6. Publicize and support FPRP within the college.

Individual and group initiated concerns, projects or activities are encouraged from the entire De Anza faculty. The areas for participation therefore fall into three basic divisions: individual, group and college. All plans for specified activities are brought to the attention of the staff development officer and the FPRP advisory committee (FPRPAC) who then make decisions on the nature and character of the proposed activities. This advisory committee consists of five faculty (three selected by the senate: one from the sciences, one from the humanities, and one from the behavioral/applied sciences; two selected from student services) whose functions are to plan and develop interventions for the various levels of need within the college. In addition, the committee also reviews proposals for staff development courses and activities.

Project Staff

The MDP and the FPRP are coordinated by one full-time staff development officer. There is also one half-time secretary and a student aide. The major functions of the staff development officer are to coordinate and organize those activities generated by staff interests and proposal plans. In addition, the staff development officer oversees a budget of approximately $60,000 that covers program expenses, office expenses and salaries. The program is housed in the administrative area adjacent to the library and the learning center.

Activities

As an initial step, a needs assessment is performed. Information is used to assist staff members in designing activities. Administrator and faculty needs are responded to through the activities of the staff development program in a variety of ways. Some of the more recurring activities administrators and faculty have participated in over the past few years include: workshops, seminars, and courses; independent study; conferences; professional improvement leaves; professional association activity; travel. The management of many on-campus activities for staff development has been visible with response from past years events, and activities have been widely accepted and utilized. All of the above-mentioned activities and many more are designed by individual and group staff members as the need arises. All activities are tailored to the needs of staff members and the different stages of their development.

Relationship to College Structure

Staff development at De Anza College has a direct and positive relationship with the overall structure of the college. As stated in the College's Master Plan of July 1975, "Instructional Development/Staff Development efforts must be strengthened immediately by the addition of more staff time—probably the addition of a program coordinator. The president should assume leadership responsiblilty for accomplishing this objective." This particular statement was adopted and subsequently became the impetus in developing the MDP and the FPRP at De Anza. A commitment was made to allocate resources to the college staff to implement developmental opportunities to the entire college. In addition, support from within the college itself has assisted in developing and maintaining supportive avenues for positive growth among the staff. Staff development is integrated into the entire college system. It is built directly into the administrator's evaluation. Annual renewal plans are written by faculty and given to the division/area manager for review and approval prior to submission to the staff development officer. In addition, each division or area develops management by objectives (MBS's) for the new year for the office of instruction as an indication of direction for that division. Assistance for the development of such MBO's is secured through the staff development office. Copies of the objectives are sent to the FPRP advisory committee for review.

Special Factors

The staff development officer, advisory committees and staff engage in realistic and concrete relationships to achieve the programs goals. The staff development officer and others on the De Anza campus have repeatedly stated that the development and availability of effective activities for staff members cannot begin unless a healthy and positive climate (one showing concern, commitment, knowledge and awareness of needs) is produced.

In the beginning of this program, respected personnel launched the program and have continued to secure the cooperation of other staff members and district personnel. The program has received full and continued support from the district and the president since its inception. There has been a favorable impact of the program on staff members. More and more staff are receptive to the goals set forth by their colleagues. There has been a substantial increase in the numbers of staff members participating and even presenting or supporting program-related activities.

Evaluation

The staff development officer is responsible for evaluating the program. Annual reports are presented to the advisory committees for review and recommendations. The staff development officer is responsible directly to the president of the college, to whom final evaluation reports are submitted. Evaluation of activities are done primarily by surveying participants as to the value of the activity in relation to their professional and/or personal needs.

Future

The MDP was the catalyst for staff development on the De Anza campus. Soon after the introduction of MDP, the FPRP came into existence. Future plans in staff development include assessing classified staff needs more thoroughly, defining program goals and objectives, and assisting in the development of relevant activities. In addition, the staff development office would like to collect more objective and subjective data for evaluation purposes. Future intentions are also to expand the capabilities of staff development by establishing more supportive training programs for staff members.

Appendix D

Selected Teaching Improvement Programs

Interinstitutional Setting

Associated Colleges of the Midwest
Northwestern University
Evanston, Illinois
Contact Person: Claude Mathus

The Center for the Teaching Professions

The Center for the Teaching Professions was created in 1960 at Northwestern University with funds provided by a W.K. Kellogg Foundation grant. The purposes of the center are threefold: 1) the improvement of teaching of faculty and prospective teachers (graduate students) at Northwestern University; 2) involvement with other educational institutions and organizations to help improve their teaching programs; and 3) creation of a model for developing centers at other colleges/universities to improve the quality of education at those institutions.

In January 1975 the center was notified of the award of a Danforth Foundation grant to support a program for faculty development in cooperation with the Associated Colleges of the Midwest (ACM). ACM is composed of thirteen midwestern private liberal arts colleges. The overall goals of this program are faculty development and self-renewal. More specifically, the program seeks to improve both teaching and learning and reinforce commitment to excellence in teaching as a professional goal and the primary obligation of faculty. Faculty are trained to be resources on their own campuses and to initiate faculty development efforts. It is hoped that there will also be dissemination of a wide variety of experiencs, methods and strategies.

Structure

The center currently serves a consulting and coordinating function. Initial ground work includes campus visitations to all ACM institutions by center staff to become acquainted with each college and its individual concerns and expectations for a faculty development program. An advisory committee for the faculty development program was appointed by the deans of the various institutions; one contact person per campus serves on this advisory committee. Two workshops were held at the center for selected faculty from ACM institutions for training purposes and to act as a stimulus for the format of an ACM network.

Staffing

The faculty participating in the two workshops mentioned above then formed the base for the faculty development efforts at their respective campuses. Center staff continue to serve as resources.

Financing

Approximately $1200 per campus was alotted from the Danforth grant to provide financial support for the development of two educational programs. Individualized faculty development programs based on the unique need and concerns of each campus were initiated.

Activities

The focus of the programs varies from campus to campus, but activities include workshops, seminars and other experiences dealing with course design, curriculum improvement, media use, writing skills and evaluation of the student advisory system to name a few. On one campus a teaching-learning center was established.

During implementation of these activities, two other initiatives arose for the center, separate from but related to the ACM prgram. The first was the development of a pilot program for teaching internships (Danforth Graduate Fellows) in ACM institutions. The second project involved development of a video-vignette project which has achieved major emphasis during the current funding phase of the program. This project involves video-taping of short segments of classroom behavior which are used to stimulate discussion of teaching in groups of college faculty and graduate students. Both of these initiatives have been effected and incorporated into the other faculty development efforts at the ACM institutions.

Evaluation

Evaluation of this program is carried out by center staff as part of the general evaluation of all center activities. According to the director, the most effective criteria for assessing the center's efforts are those which indicate movement in individual faculty from dependence to self-direction in the analysis, understanding, and control of those factors which reinforce a positive attitude toward one's role as teacher-scholar and one's position within the institutional culture which provides the setting for professional development.

Impacts

Four major successes or impacts have been achieved. First is the cooperation that has been established between a large university and a consortium of small liberal arts colleges jointly funded by a private foundation—quite a unique relationship.

In the area of activities the director cites the organization of traveling workshops conducted on various campuses for the benefit of other colleges nearby. These workshops are conducted by faculty in the consortium with the center serving as coordinator, that is, determining which topics are most useful, where and who the best resource people might be. These workshops have the effect of strengthening the network and hopefully will ease the center's eventual withdrawal from the program.

Thirdly, the video-vignette program has been well received and has continued success in the area of teaching improvement.

Finally, the opportunities offered to ACM faculty through the Visiting Faculty program is seen as an important plus. This activity makes available to faculty those university resources not accessible at the liberal arts college, thus providing the best of both worlds.

California State University and Colleges
Long Beach, California.

The Center for Professional Development

The Center for Professional Development was established in 1974 to assist in the development of individualized, autonomous professional development programs at the nineteen universities and colleges in the California State system. Member institutions range in size from large metropolitan universities to small semi-rural colleges.

The center acts as a mechanism to foster the campus-based operations and also serves as a clearinghouse for faculty development materials and information. Center objectives are broader than instructional development. Models of professional development being implemented include: 1) development of materials for use in improvement of instruction; 2) efforts to affect organizational structure through programs designed for deans and department chairpersons; 3) comprehensive faculty programs aimed at personal, instructional and leadership development; and 4) a plan for institutional renewal using faculty development as a prime means for change.

Structure

Currently, the center reports to the dean for the division of New Program Development and Evaluation and will soon be absorbed into this office. A policy board generates policy and determines operating procedures for the professional development efforts. The board is composed of twenty-six presidentially appointed representatives, one from each of the member campuses, three from the chancellor's office, three students, and one representative from the statewide academic service. A six-member steering committee of this board handles most of the business. The center has formal ties to six institutions which receive funds to support full-time project directors. One goal of the center is to eventually have all nineteen campuses experimenting with professional development activities.

Staffing

The center has a full-time director, but as individual campus programs take over program responsibility this position will become half-time, probably beginning next year. There is also a center secretary and consultants are used when needed.

Financing

The center is currently funded by a $175,000 grant from the Fund for the Improvement of Postsecondary Education. Hopefully, enough internal support may be garnered for the program so that member institutions will assume the cost of the respective campus programs when he grant expires.

Activities

There is a great range of programs since all are tailored to meet the individual needs of each campus. The center provides consulting and support services, acts as a linkage agent for resource people and materials and stands as a symbol of the importance and commitment to professional development activities.

Specific activities of the various programs include sabbatical leaves for faculty and staff, fee waivers for courses that aid in development (both personal and professional), pre-retirement seminars, faculty exchanges and a system of various sized award grants for innovative programs.

Evaluation

An outside evaluation team and specially trained internal faculty have performed an "illuminative evaluation," defined as "attempts to discern and discuss a program's most significant features, recurring concomitant and critical processes." This process included interviews and document review. It is designed to be formative, increase the capacity of the system to conduct its own evaluations, generate useful and valid information, assess the effectiveness of individuals and programs, and assess the interaction of programs. General findings were that at the more traditional institutions faculty spent more time on campus and became more involved with students as a result of the professional development programs. At the more innovative campuses, faculty seemed more willing to deal with personal problems relevant to their role as teachers. Suggestions for changes and improvements were provided as well as descriptive comments.

Impacts

In discussing impacts of the program, the director cites the Northridge model as having great success at establishing feelings of collegiality and a sense of community among faculty. This approach of getting faculty to "commune" together and feel loyalty to the institution has functioned to make faculty development a vehicle for institutional renewal.

Secondly, the flexibility and opportunities to test out many different models of professional development due to the large number of campuses is seen as a plus. Much information is generated as to what programs work well in which situations. Next year, additional new campuses will be involved and this knowledge will be quite valuable.

The Cleveland Commission on Higher Education
Cleveland Ohio
Contact Person: Lance C. Buhl

Educational Consulting Study

The Educational Consulting Study (ECS) is a three year project (September 1, 1974-August 31,1977) created to stimulate efforts among faculty and administrators to increase teaching/learning effectiveness in the twenty-three postsecondary institutions of northeast Ohio. Effectiveness is taken to mean the number of students achieving learning objectives at high levels of competence. Two goals inform ECS work. First if it is successful, most students will be learning effectively because most faculty will be setting up appropriate conditions for learning. Second, most faculty will be working to enhance learning because their colleagues and administrators encourage, support and reward such work. The staff of ECS are realistic enough to know that neither goal is likely to be achieved, particularly over three years. But linking the idea of appropriate conditions for learning and appropriate conditions for teaching created a strong frame of reference for determining annual operating objectives.

Structure

ECS is an autonomous entity within the legal framework of the Cleveland Commission on Higher Education. Formally, its director reports to the commission—composed of the eight presidents of Greater Cleveland colleges and universities and several law members—through an executive officer. In practice, ECS functions almost independently, its staff negotiating with funding agencies and with fifteen institutions outside the commission as well as with the eight member schools.

An advisory board was created of representatives from all twenty-three institutions, each appointed by the school's president. The board meets periodically to discuss various project goals and activities, to share ideas, and to provide channels of communication between ECS and client institutions. In several cases, members of the board are also instructional development officers who either seek ECS assistance or serve as trainer/consultants on ECS projects.

Staffing

ECS maintains a very small permanent staff—a full-time director, a part-time principal consultant, and a full-time administrative assistant/secretary. Consultants and trainers with special and known expertness were hired for particular projects and for evaluation of the project. In the opinion of the permanent staff, despite a positive experience in using consults for a lot of ECS work, the project needs more full-time staff.

Activities

ECS services include administering an institutional needs assessment survey with respect to the state of professional development in teaching; planning and conducting brief campus-based and regional conferences and workshops for building faculty (and administrator) skills in all aspects of the systematic design and conduct of courses; planning and conducting a week-long summer Institute on College Teaching; planning and conducting professional development workshops for administrators on the support of teaching; and providing short- and long-term consultative assistance to faculty and administrators on planning, implementing and evaluating professional development programs. As a central strategy of its third year, ECS organized and conducted a training program for "instructional development leaders" in which twenty persons from eleven institutions participated and from which emerged a regional association to carry on the networking that ECS initiated.

Financing

The annual ECS budget averaged approximately $70,000 in operating funds (exclusive of indirect charges for Cleveland Commission management costs, space and furniture). Save for the third year of operation, during which some ECS services were bought by institutios, funds were derived solely from grants from the Cleveland Foundation, the Fund for the Improvement of Postsecondary Education, and the W.K. Kellogg Foundation. Staff were not successful in devising other funding plans—a service subscription, for example—which would have allowed it to maintain its viability.

Evaluation

The first year's evaluation was largely a matter of internal staff assessment, focusing primarily on input (total professional days of service, number and types of service) and output (user satisfaction, developed materials). External evaluation the first year took the form of FIPSE and Kellogg review of a funding proposal. Staff of the two funding sources interviewed ECS clients about nature, extent and value of the project. Second and third year evaluations have followed a similar internal assessment procedure, but were strengthened by employing two external consultant/evaluators who visited ECS periodically, organized more systematic measurement procedures and conducted independent studies of ECS products and clients.

Impacts

During each of the three years of its existence, ECS has achieved roughly sixty to eighty percent of its objectives as defined. Other objectives either became irrelevant or impossible to achieve satisfactorily. ECS has been directly involved through training and/or consulting in the measurable growth of professional development in teaching at the four two-year colleges, at three of the four state universities, at the medical and dental schools of the large private university and at five of the small independent colleges in the region. ECS staff have provided fewer services to all but three of the remaining ten institutions. While the extent of growth (in terms of hard dollar support, numbers of faculty involved and policy adjustments) and of ECS contribution vary considerably among the institutions served, the evidence of growth and the recognition of ECS as a facilitative element for change are clear in over half of the institutions in the region. Overall, it can be said that consciousness about and programs for professional development are greatly advanced in 1977 in this region over what they were in 1974.

College Center of the Finger Lakes
Corning, New York
Contact Person: Bonnie Buenger-Larson

The College Center of the Finger Lakes (CCFL) is composed of three institutions, two colleges and one university, and is one of the oldest consortia in the country. For the last three years the main focus of the center activities has been faculty development. The purpose of the faculty development program is to "test, refine and evaluate" a comprehensive model for faculty development. In order to do this effectively, the model deals with the professional, organizational and personal roles of the faculty. The program assumes active involvement on the part of administrators and students as well as faculty since the support of all three sectors is needed to improve teaching quality. Specific objectives in professional, organizational and personal development have been outlined for faculty, administrators and students.

Structure

The consortium acts as an initial change agent, introducing ideas and concepts through workshops on professional development for faculty, administrators and students. Representatives of these three populations are also trained in professional development theories, strategies and techniques so that they may serve as internal consultants on their own campuses. These internal consultants set up an on-campus Educational Consulting Service which becomes the focal point of the campus program.

Staffing

The consortium has a small center staff which works with the Educational Consulting Service staff in the implementation of program activities. Five initial faculty members per campus were trained to organize the service at their respective campuses.

Financing

Program efforts have been funded by a three-year, $100,000 Lilly Endowment Grant and matching funds from member institutions. At the termination of the grant funding, the member institutions will assume the costs of the program.

Activities

The consortium has sponsored four seven-day residential workshops on basic instructional development. These are staffed by experienced CCFL faculty as well as professional staff. As a follow-up to these workshops, a variety of three-day experiences are offered called advanced professional development workshops, focusing on course design, alternative teaching styles and other topics.

Professional development workshops for administrators have been designed to complement the faculty workshops and provide a support system on campus for improved teaching. These cover such topics as identification of leadership and decision making styles, communication skills and basic management and institutional renewal processes.

Student workshops are provided which focus on the student role in increasing teaching effectiveness.

Through workshops and consultation, faculty members have been trained to staff the Educational Consulting Service on each campus.

Educational Consulting Service activities and services include a diagnostic and training sequence on teaching, various luncheon colloquia, practicums on classroom techniques and advising skills, workshops on using simulation techniques, and student and secretary workshops respectively, as well as individual and departmental consultation.

Evaluation

An evaluation of the faculty development program has been designed to provide information about changes in personal, professional, and organizational development and how these changes affect teaching effectiveness.

An attitude survey has been extremely useful in determining the direction of change.

Impacts

Two major goals or impacts have thus far been realized. First, the flexibility and comprehensiveness of the model have enabled program staff to be effective in different areas of the institutions. For example, a pilot project at Hartwick College involved creation of an organizational development model to aid in departmental review of three academic departments. Later, when problems arose in an administrative area, this same model was used effectively to help alleviate the concerns there. This flexibility so impressed the administration that a decision was made to support further efforts with institutional funds.

Secondly, an important task was to move the program from the consortium to the individual campuses; that is to establish program ownership by those individuals involved in the development efforts. To accomplish this, the director spent all of her time during the first year of the program in training campus people to serve as consultants for their respective campuses. These efforts were quite successful since the director now functions primarily as a consultant to the campus consultants after facilitating the change of program ownership.

Great Lakes College Association
Wesleyan University
Delaware, Ohio
Contact Person: Steve Scholl

The Faculty Development Program of the Great Lakes College Association (GLCA) was designed by a "group of teachers who were convinced that working with faculty from different institutions would foster creative thinking and provide greater support for teaching." The purposes of the program are to improve teaching skills and promote greater interest in teaching. GLCA is composed of twelve private liberal arts colleges in the Great Lakes states.

Structure

The Faculty Development Program has an advisory board composed of faculty and administrative representatives from the member campuses. A strong network has developed from which advisory committees have been formed for special topic areas of faculty development (e.g. women's studies).

Activities

Program activities of the first three years include teaching fellowships, interinstitutional workshops, a consultant service, resource development, a women's studies committee and a dissemination of papers and other materials relevant to faculty development. In addition, a GLCA Newsletter which discusses current and upcoming member projects is published regularly.

New program activities that have been approved by the advisory board include a one-week summer workshop on instructional development, weekend and one-day workshops on various topics, and a personal development weekend workshop focused on participants at the same general stage of their career.

In addition, a GLCA faculty development committee composed of two members from each campus will be formed to: 1) facilitate exchange of information, 2) advise and assist in the faculty development program, and 3) provide opportunities for new and continued training of individuals with an interest in and responsibility for faculty development on their campuses.

Evaluations

Individual evaluations of all activities are performed as well as a full scale evaluation done on a campus by campus basis. After the first year of the program an evaluation was done by an external review team. Since then internal teams have performed this function.

Impacts

Significant impact of the faculty development program has been achieved in three areas. Most controversial, but viewed as most important by the director, has been the successful integration of a personal development experience into a retreat for faculty and their families. This is perhaps the most unique aspect of the program and arouses resistance from those who believe that faculty development should remain in academic areas and not enter into the personal sphere.

On the basis of the evaluation the wide variety of weekend workshops with limited focus provided more contact and affected more people, and thus might be viewed as having greatest impact.

The third area of success is seen in the large number of activities that have been launched in the area of women's studies and issues. Workshops, seminars and general support services are only a few of the programs initiated and implemented by the network founded by the consortium.

Spelman College
Atlanta, Georgia
Contact Person: Pauline Drake

Institute for Teaching and Learning

The Institute for Teaching and Learning at Spelman College works in collaboration with twelve other predominantly black southern colleges and universities to improve instruction through curriculum and faculty development. Institute objectives are: 1) working with faculty from participating colleges in the improvement of teaching basic skills; 2) development of cross-disciplinary teaching and learning; 3) development of an information exchange network with similar institutes or centers; 4) preparation of instructional materials in selected areas for dissemination to faculty in the participating institutions; and 5) development and utilization of a data base compiled from resources available at the individual institutions.

Structure

A program policy board, composed of one representative from each campus and chaired by the president of Spelman College, monitors the program and budget of the institute. Communication between the institute and member institutions is maintained through a network of contact persons, one per campus.

Staffing

The institute is staffed by a director and secretary. Consultants, both from member institutions and outside agencies and institutions, are utilized for conferences and workshops.

Financing

The institute is funded by a Danforth Foundation grant for $210,000. The grant is for three years. During the first year of the program, member institutions provided some small contributory monies.

Activities

Consortial activities include periodic weekend workshops at various member campuses, organized by discipline, generally limited to twenty-five participants and often covering topics related to course design and implementation of audiovisual equipment. Faculty selected for summer curriculum development workshops receive a stipend plus reimbursement for lodging, meals and travel expenses.

An annual faculty development conference is held for all member institutions with primary focus on improvement of teaching skills. Consultants from member campuses are utilized as part of the program to enhance a sharing of diverse faculty development ideas.

The institute also sponsors a faculty development internship program in the Fall and Spring. Release time of up to five days is granted to faculty who are selected to observe and participate in an instructional program which has been shown to be effective at another member campus. As follow-up to this program interns are required to submit a report to the institute of how they have applied their internship experience in their own college setting. Interns are reimbursed for travel, meals and lodging costs.

In addition, the institute publishes a quarterly newsletter describing various faculty development activities and featuring articles written by individual faculty.

Evaluation

Each activity is evaluated by the participants. In addition, a comprehensive evaluation is planned during the next academic year to determine the program effects on those faculty who have been directly involved and the impacts on others who have not participated. Either an interview or questionnaire technique will be used.

Impacts

In terms of dollars spent and number of people involved, the weekend workshops would rank highest. Whether or not these have been most beneficial, or have had most impact, remains to be seen after the evaluation is completed.

The program director sees a more far reaching and measurable effect achieved through a new course that has been developed called "Moral

Values and Contemporary Issues." The course, funded by a supplementary Danforth grant, deals with values clarification and was piloted on two campuses this past year. Effects of this course have spread beyond the classroom to other faculty not originally involved. Due to this success, next year's plans include implementation of the course on three additional campuses.

Kansas City Regional Council for Higher Education
Kansas City, Missouri
Contact Person: Russell Wilson

Center for Professional Development

The Kansas City Regional Council for Higher Education (KCRCHE) is composed of seventeen member campuses, including one private and three public community colleges, one state university, ten private liberal arts colleges and one private college of art. The Center for Professional Development, a project of KCRCHE, offers services to administrators as well as faculty (a total population of approximately 2500) at the seventeen campuses.

The main focus of the center is personal development. As such, primary consulting is offered to individuals on a one-to-one basis. The center operates on the belief that by helping individuals with concerns which they identify — career planning and renewal, professional effectiveness, classroom activities, departmental and/or institutional responsibilities, personal growth issues — it assists that individual's colleagues, students and institution. In addition, the center encourages the organization of new faculty development programs and offers support to presently existing ones.

Structure

Though the center receives substantial financial support from the member institutions, it is independent of member control. There is, however, an advisory board composed of one representative from each member institution.

A variety of techniques are employed for establishing contact with faculty and administrators on the member campuses. Brochures and newsletters are sent out on a regular, frequent basis. In addition, center staff members attend on-campus faculty and administrative meetings for the purpose of outlining the services offered. Referrals to the center are also made by presidents, deans, and department chairpersons. Liaison persons are used on campus to publicize visits by center staff and arrange for appointments. A small grants program serves as an attraction to some faculty and administrators.

Staffing

The center staff includes two full-time professionals and two secretaries. Consultants in various areas are drawn from consortium members. Though this staff size has been adequate, it is the opinion of its director that a larger professional staff would allow for more project activities.

Financing

Funding for the center has been provided by the W.K. Kellogg Foundation since July 1, 1974, and will continue through June 30, 1977 with matching funds from the KCRCHE member institutions. Efforts are presently being made to obtain continued funding. Additional monies do not appear to be forthcoming from member institutions.

Activities

While the primary emphasis is on one-to-one assistance, workshops are also conducted with groups of people who have identified common concerns. The center serves as an informational clearinghouse, searching out information to assist individuals in professional development. In addition, once individual plans for professional development are made, the center will identify and arrange for a resource person to assist in the implementation of these plans. Finally, small stipends are offered to enable faculty and administrators to pursue professional development strategies and plans.

Evaluation

An evaluation of center efforts will be conducted by Dr. Laurence Barrett of Kalamazoo College. He plans to use an interview technique and will meet with center staff, individuals assisted by the center and key administrators at member institutions.

Impacts

In general, a one-to-one approach has been most effective according to the director. Both administrators and faculty have been receptive to the development efforts. Using the consortium-based professional development strategy has proven cost-effective, provides a large pool of resource people, and is a less threatening approach due to the off-campus setting and staff of the center. On the other hand, gaining visibility on member campuses and making institution-wide impact have been difficult.

The greatest impact has been achieved in personal development, particularly in the area of career planning. Two day seminars followed by one-to-one interactions with faculty and staff have been used in dealing with such issues as late job changes, retirement, and planning a lifetime career. Another part of this has been job search counseling which includes assistance in resume building, strategizing, and advice as to where jobs are listed. These activities have all been facilitated by the one-to-one approach.

New Hampshire College and University Council
Manchester, New Hampshire
Contact Person: Doug Lyon

Instructional Development Program

A four year instructional development (ID) program was started in 1973 as a project of the New Hampshire College and University Council (NHCUC). The council is composed of thirteen public and private four-year institutions. The consortium works together to share resources and enhance learning opportunities for students. The three main goals of the ID program are: 1) the redesigning of faculty selected courses to increase course effectiveness, 2) faculty skills development in teaching, and 3) establishment of an information dissemination and exchange system. Since emphasis is on action rather than holding workshops or conferences, the program focuses on actual instructional development experiments.

Structure

Council headquarters are located at Notre Dame College (Manchester, N.H.) and perform an advising and consulting function. The instructional development coordinator is based at this office.

Staffing

The program is staffed by one professional coordinator and a secretary. Outside consultants are used primarily in the area of faculty skill development to conduct small one to three day seminars on fairly specialized topics, e.g. a faculty evaluation seminar conducted for NHCUC academic deans. The program coordinator functions mainly as a circuit rider, travelling from campus to campus, consulting and assisting in the process and implementation of course redesign.

Financing

Financing is provided by a W.K. Kellogg Foundation grant of $350,000 for four years. Hopefully, the seeds of innovation and improvement in teaching that are sown during the duration of the funding will continue to reap benefits and provide encouragement for continued development after the funding terminates. Early results speak favorably to this end.

Activities

Of the three program goals, perhaps course design and redesign has been stressed the most. Much of the program coordinator's time has been spent in this area. Cost efficiency has not been stressed. The intent of redesign has been to improve the quality of courses and instruction for the same amount of dollars spent previously. This has proven to be the most effective strategy.

In addition, the program has sponsored attendance of key faculty and administrators at regional and national workshops and seminars on instructional development and evaluation so that new and different strategies and ideas might be incorporated.

Another activity has been local information sharing and dissemination meetings concerning the various campus ID projects. Since each campus determines its own focus based on its individual needs, programs are varied and these meetings often arouse interest in new course areas for exploration.

Evaluation

Consultants have been used to perform an evaluation of the program. The focus has been on gaining information about student attitudes and achievements in those courses which have either been newly developed or redesigned.

Impacts

The general focus of the ID program has been to make changes in the classroom. The program coordinator feels satisfied that changes have occurred to the benefit of students. Additionally, the program continues to have an effect as many faculty take the initiative of their own accord and include innovation and development as part of their own goals for teaching improvement. In many cases, the outside incentive and motivation is no longer needed.

Ohio Board of Regents
Columbus, Ohio
Contact Persons: Lance Buhl
                    Sandra Cheldelin Inglis

The Chancellor's Advisory Committee on Instructional Development

The Chancellor's Advisory Committee on Instructional Development (CACID) was created by the chancellor of the Ohio board of regents in September, 1973. Charged initially with the task of organizing a state-wide conference on instructional development for Ohio postsecondary institutions, the committee has evolved into a more permanent structure mandated to stimulate and support campus-based programs for professional development in teaching and to represent the needs of instructional development to the chancellor and board.

The ultimate goal (fully elaborated in the Ohio board of regents five-year MASTER PLAN, 1976) framing the committee's work is that all of Ohio's postsecondary institutions will be graced with instructional development programs which are both stable and comprehensive in scope. Nearly two-thirds of Ohio's one hundred-plus institutions have evolved some type of program for the enhancement of teaching and learning since 1972. CACID has been involved as a supporting body to most of these efforts.

Structure

CACID reports to the chancellor of the Ohio board of regents, who annually develops a charge to the committee based largely on the result of the committee's work over the preceding year and the recommendations for action included in CACIC's annual report. The advisory committee is composed of sixteen persons, including an *ex officio* but active representative of the chancellor's staff. The committee is unique in that its membership, as well as its mandate, encompasses all of Ohio's non-profit educational community. Members are appointed for indeterminate terms by the chancellor as vacancies occur. The committee and chancellor work to ensure that each segment of the postsecondary community is adequately represented.

Staffing

CACID is a working group. Typically, programs are envisioned, planned and in large part carried out by members of the committee, working in subgroups. The extent to which CACID can depend on a real "staff" is a function of its success in raising grant funds. During the 1976-77 year, a grant from the Battelle Memorial Institute Foundation has allowed CACID to purchase one-half the time of the chancellor's representative, an Education Policy Fellow.

Financing

CACID is largely dependent on external grant funding if it wishes to offer a full range of services to instructional development officers as well as represent institutional needs to the chancellor and board. The extent of the regents' support has ranged from $15,000 to $45,000 per year, some of which represents estimated value of staff time devoted to CACID activities. During the 1976-77 year, CACID was supported by a $50,000 one-year grant from the Battelle Memorial Institute Foundation.

Activities

On the consciousness-raising level, CACIC has helped sponsor regional "teaching-tips" conferences for faculty and administrators. It conducted a pilot project on a state-wide consulting network in 1975 and, more recently, has fostered the organization of regional networks of persons responsible for or committed to professional development in teaching. It published a comprehensive two-volume set of readings in college teaching in limited edition (1975) and is currently editing an up-to-date one-volume set for general publication. At the continuous planning level, CACID has conducted an annual residential conference to assist institutional teams of faculty and administrators design or redesign campus programs for professional development in teaching. So far, twenty nine teams have attended these conferences. Most significant is CACID's contribution to the structure and content of the 1976 Master Plan, HIGHER EDUCATION IN OHIO. The board of regents adopted the list of recommendations and published the set of coordinated goals drawn up by the committee. Those recommendations call on institutions to develop programs which not only provide faculty with opportunities to increase their teaching skills but which support and reward faculty who work to enhance learning.

Evaluation

The chancellor and the committee have relied largely on participant satisfaction indices as evidence of the desirability and, to a certain extent, the utility of committee activities. More substantively, the committee has examined the content of team plans and annual reports in conjunction with the residential planning conferences. This year, the committee appointed an evaluation subcommittee which is in the process of conducting interviews around the state relative to instructional development and CACID's role in fostering it and of developing stratified case study data. If further funding is to be secured, CACID will conduct a major evaluative project around the theme of the role of 1202 commissions in promoting instructional development.

Impacts

Instructional development programming has grown significantly in Ohio since 1972. Because so many persons involved in planning or running these programs at the campus level have been involved in one or more CACID programs, often to a substantial degree (particularly with respect to the team planning conferences), CACID assumes at least a correlative tie between its work and ID expansion. Certainly, the climate for instructional development programming has become increasingly favorable as a result of the committee's work on its behalf.

Small College Consortium
Faculty and Staff Development and Evaluation
Washington, D.C.
Contact Person: Joan North

Institutional Development Project

The Institutional Development Project is a four-year program started in the summer of 1976. The project involves fifty-six four-year liberal arts colleges across the country which make up the Small College Consortium (SCC). The general purpose of the project is institutional development; more specifically, the project deals in five Technical Assistance (TA) areas:

1) Planning and Management Information Systems; 2) Admissions, Recruitment and Retention; 3) Curriculum and Student Development; 4) Faculty and Staff Development and Evaluation; and 5) Fiscal Management and Fund Raising. The Council for the Advancement of Small Colleges (CASC) acts as the assisting agency and provides directors for each of these TA areas. Each college selects the areas in which they will focus and the length of that focus depending upon their own specific needs and concerns. Many choose a combination of areas. Of particular interest for the purposes of this Sourcebook are the activities in Area Four, Faculty and Staff Development and Evaluation.

Structure

Each college develops a "growth contract" with the project staff. This document integrates overall institutional concerns with specific goals and activities. The contract states the area and activities in which the college will engage and includes an evaluation plan for assessing progress and outcomes.

An advisor from the project staff assists an on-campus coordinator and ensures that project activities are incorporated into the institutional structure so as to have continued impact.

In addition, the project staff provides and/or coordinates technical assistance in each of the five areas. One project staff person serves as director for each technical assistance area.

Staffing

Each college has an on-campus coordinator who heads the development team. The teams vary in size according to the needs and goals of the individual campuses.

Financing

The project is financed by a $1,500,000 grant from the Office of Education under Title III, Basic Institutional Development. Most of the funding goes directly to the colleges; each college has a $22,200 budget which includes a two-thirds time on-campus coordinator.

The remaining funds plus a small contribution from each college are used to support the project office in Washington, D.C. and the coordinating institution which is Averett College in Danville, VA.

Activities

Approximately twenty colleges are currently working in the area of faculty and staff development and evaluation. Most of their activities thus far have been campus-based at the individual colleges. Workshops are presently being planned that will draw together groups from several colleges.

The Director of TA Area Four works with individual college teams in planning and renewing their faculty development programs. A four stage process model is used in this task. The stages include information gathering which involves needs assessment using both institutional and faculty data, goal setting and strategizing and program implementation and assessment.

Teams are notified periodically of useful resources (e.g. books, workshops). The model and resource notification comprise what is called a TA kit in Faculty Development. Similar kits are being devised on evaluation and administrative development.

The project advisor also has worked with colleges in personal development areas and has conducted short workshops on limited topics.

More activity is foreseen in the area of administrative development in the upcoming year.

Evaluation

Since each college outlines its own evaluation plan in its growth contract, a variety of methods are used. In addition to these individualized assessments, an overall evaluation of the project, including each TA area, is being done by an independent research organization. This evaluation involves use of questionnaires, case studies from each college, and document analysis.

Impacts

The greatest concentration of energy has been expanded on the pre-planning for the programs, that is, bringing planning principles to the concept of faculty development. Emphasis is constantly placed on ensuring that all strategies and activities are related to the goals of the program and are incorporable into the structure and activities of the institution. This focus helps to guarantee that programs will have impact and be continued after outside funding is terminated.

Society for Values in Higher Education
Washington, D.C.
Contact Person: Jerry Gaff

Project on Institutional Renewal through the Improvement of Teaching

The Project on Institutional Renewal through the Improvement of Teaching (PIRIT) is a three year program sponsored by the Society for Values in Higher Education. The project involves sixteen colleges and universities, eight from the southeast and eight from the midwest, selected from thirty applicant institutions.

Structure

A twenty member advisory committee performs various functions including establishment of project policy, serving as a resource for staffing project activities and providing consultation to participating institutions. One advisory committee member is assigned to each institution to serve as institutional advisor.

The advisory committee also is responsible for offering suggestions and providing criticism of the program plans prepared by institutional team members. These plans are based on careful, detailed analysis of institutional needs and goals.

The central office of the project is headed by a director; this office seeks to clarify project goals and provide coordination of institutional teams, advisory committee members, resource people and Society for Values in Higher Education members. Related to this, central office staff continue to work on refining of relationships with the participating institutions so that the project may best meet their needs and support their efforts. Additionally, information about the project as disseminated to other society members who might benefit by learning ways to improve teaching quality at their own institutions, thus furthering project impact beyond the sixteen participating institutions.

Staffing

After selection for the project each institution assembled a project team. Staff size varies from campus to campus, but all include faculty, administrators and students.

Financing

Funding for the project is provided by a grant from the Fund for the

Improvement of Postsecondary Education. First year grant support totaled approximately $130,000 with an additional $60,000 from Society and the participating institutions. Second year funding from FIPSE was increased to approximately $153,000 which is still relatively cost efficient since this represents less than $10,000 per institution. Third year FIPSE funding was $188,000.

An activity fund of up to $1000 is available to each institution on a matching fund basis to finance new or additional program activities.

Activities

Early project activities included initial visits by the project director or advisory committee members to the individual campuses (this only included the southeastern institutions) to ensure the project team had been assembled and to provide information about the national project to each institution.

Two weekend conferences staffed by the director and advisory committee — one for each geographic grouping of institutions — were held to consider issues and strategies in regard to institutional renewal and teaching improvement.

A resource notebook has been compiled including relevant materials and discussion of various topics and strategies. A dissemination service also offers articles, books and other materials on faculty and institutional development and institutional renewal. A regular newsletter and occasional papers are published.

Periodic meetings of liaison persons (one from each institution) and the project director serve as a vehicle for establishing a strong network and facilitate discussion and exchange of new information, program problems and consultant resources. In addition, these meetings help to energize team workers and promote a feeling of ownership of their programs.

Each institution receives three full days per year of institutional consulting and a visit from the project director. This consulting time is generally used for program planning, advising of program administrators and participation in program workshops and seminars.

A training workshop also has been held to help individuals at each institution learn the skills needed to assist faculty in improvement of teaching.

Team members themselves have been active in conducting interviews and distributing questionnaires to better determine and assess the needs of their colleagues. A student questionnaire also has been devised to obtain student opinion about the teaching-learning climate of the institutions.

Finally, a week-long summer conference including all sixteen participating institutions was held. Besides exploring many interesting topics, this conference also served to pull the project together since it was the first time all institutions had met together.

This large number of activities was deemed necessary to facilitate fulfillment of the diverse needs and strategies of sixteen different institutions.

Evaluation

An evaluation is planned to: 1) document and describe changes in participants resulting from the different programs; 2) determine principles and barriers relevant to the growth and development of individual faculty members; 3) determine institutional changes that occur and observe which strategies are successful and which are not; 4) explore the interaction between faculty members and institutional policy, structure and culture.

Multiple methods will be utilized; interviews will be conducted by team members with colleagues to learn in depth about their experiences, values and perspectives as teachers and members of the institution. Questionnaires will be administered to faculty and students to gather baseline data. Case studies will be prepared for each institution to monitor progress. Three advisory committee members and two independent evaluators will oversee the process.

Impacts

The hope is that the strategies and activities employed will facilitate establishment of teaching improvement programs after the initial project is terminated. Groundwork for this appears to be laid since the programs are quite satisfactory to the faculty and are already gaining administrative support. By focusing on the institution as a whole and involving faculty, administrators, and students in the commitment to teaching improvement the likelihood for continuation is greatly increased.

Bibliography
Project List

1. Lawrence Alexander and Stephen Yelon, *Instructional Development Agencies in Higher Education* (East Lansing, Michigan: Continuing Education Service, 1972).
2. Charles H. Anderson and John D. Murray, eds.; *The Professors: Work and Life Styles Among Academicians* (Cambridge, Massachusetts: Schenkman, 1971).
3. John Atkinson and Norman Leather, eds., *A Theory of Achievement Motivation* (New York, New York: Wiley, 1966).
4. Joseph Alexrod, *The University Teacher as Artist* (San Francisco, California: Jossey-Bass, 1973).
5. Don Bass, Director of Educational Development Services, (Texas City, Texas: College of the Mainland, study in progress.)
6. Howard S. Becker, Blanche Geer and Everett C. Hughes, *Making the Grade: The Academic Side of College Life* (New York,New York: Wiley, 1968).
7. William H. Bergquist and Steven R. Phillips, *A Handbook for Faculty Development – Volume I* (Washington, D.C.: Council for the Avancement of Small Colleges, 1975), and *A Handbook for Faculty Development – Volume II* (Berkeley, Calif.: Pacific Soundings Press, 1970).
8. William H. Bergquist and William A. Shoemaker, "Facilitating Comprehensive Institutional Development," in Bergquist and Shoemaker, eds., *A Comprehensive Approach to Institutional Development: New Directions for Higher Education* (San Francisco, Calif.: Jossey-Bass, 1976), pp. 1-49.
9. Paul Berman and Milbrey McLaughlin, "The Findings in Review," in *Rand Studies: Federal Programs Supporting Educational Change, Volume 4* (Washington, D.C.: HEW, R-1589/1-5, April 1975).
10. Benjamin Bloom, ed., *Taxonomy of Educational Objectives: Handbook I, Cognitive Domain* (New York, New York: Longmans, Grien, 1956).
10a Board of Governors, California Community Colleges, *California Community Colleges Five Year Plan, 1977-1982: Background Information* (Sacramento, Calif.: Chancellor's Office, 1977).
11. Charles K. Bolton and Ronald K. Boyer, "Organizational Development for Academic Departments," *Journal of Higher Education*, 44, May (1973), 352-369.
12. David S. Bushnell, *Organizing for Change: New Priorities for Community Colleges* (New York, New York: McGraw-Hill, 1973).
13. Donald T. Campbell, "Reforms as Experiments," *American Psychologist*, 24 (1969), 409-429.
14. Chester H. Case, *Professional Staff Development: A Community College Model* (Pittsburg, Calif.: Los Medanos Community College Press, 1976).
15. Chester H. Case, "Providing Staff Development Opportunities in California's Community Colleges." Prepared for the Board of Governors of California Community Colleges Five-Year Plan, 1977-82, September 1976.
15a Chester H. Case, ed., *Staff Development for the Five Clienteles: Readings on*

Community College Staff Development Programs for New Faculty, Experienced Faculty, Adjunct (Part-Time, Faculty, Classified Staff and Management (Pittsburgh, Calif.: Los Medanos Community College Press, 1976).

16. John A. Centra, *Faculty Development Practices in U.S. Colleges and Universities* (Princeton, New Jersey: Educational Testing Service, 1976).

17. John A. Centra, *The Student Instructional Report: Its Development and Uses,* SIR Report Number I (Princeton, New Jersey: Educational Testing Service, 1972).

18. Arthur Chickering, *A Conceptual Framework for Educational Alternatives at Empire State College* (Saratoga Springs, New York: Empire State College, 1976).

19. Arthur Chickering, "Developmental Change as a Major Outcome," in ed., Morris Keaton, *Experiential Learning* (San Francisco, Calif.: Jossey-Bass, 1977), pp. 62-108.

20. Arthur Chickering, *Education and Identity* (San Francisco, Calif.: Jossey-Bass, 1969).

21. Arthur Chickering, "Undergraduate Academic Experience," *Journal of Educational Psychology,* 63 (1972), 134-143.

21a Arthur Chickering and John McCormick, "Personality Development and the College Experience," *Research in Higher Education,* 1 (1973), 43-70.

22. Arthur Chickering, David Halliburton, William H. Bergquist and Jack Lindquist, *Developing the College Curriculum: A Handbook for Faculty and Administrators,* eds., Gary H. Quehl and Marguerite Gee (Washington, D.C.: Council for the Advancement of Small Colleges, 1977).

23. Arthur M. Cohen and Florence B. Brawer, *Confronting Identity: The Community College Instructor* (Englewood Cliffs, New Jersey: Prentice-Hall, 1972).

24. "College Student Questionnaire." Contact: Educational Testing Service, Princeton, New Jersey 08540.

25. Committee on Institutional Cooperation, Panel on Research and Development of Instructional Resources, *Development and Experiment in College Teaching,* Number 7 (Ann Arbor, Michigan: Center for Research on Learning and Teaching, The University of Michigan, 1971).

26. Council for the Advancement of Small Colleges, "Final Report on the Advanced In-Service Faculty Development Program," (Battlecreek, Michigan: W.K. Kellogg Foundation, 1 July 1977).

27. K. Patricia Cross, *Accent on Learning: Improving Instruction and Reshaping the Curriculum* (San Francisco, Calif.: Jossey-Bass, 1976).

28. K. Patricia Cross, *Beyond the Open Door: New Students to Higher Education* (San Francisco, Calif.: Jossey-Bass, 1971).

29. K. Patricia Cross, "Not Can, But Will College Teaching Be Improved?" in ed., John A. Centra, *Renewing and Evaluating Teaching: New Directions for Higher Education* (San Francisco, Calif.: Jossey-Bass, 1977), pp. 1-16.

30. Robert H. Davis, Allan J. Abedore and Paul W.F. Witt, *Commitment to Excellence: A Case Study of Educational Innovation* (East Lansing, Michigan: Michigan State University, 1976).

31. Robert A. DeHart, "Management Development at De Anza College," in ed., Chester H. Case, *Staff Development for the Five Clienteles: Readings on Community College Staff Development Programs for New Faculty, Experienced Faculty, Adjunct (Part-time) Faculty, Classified Staff and Management* (Pittsburgh, Calif.: Los Medanos Community College Press, 1976).

32. J.O. Derry, W.F. Seibert, A.R. Starry, J.W. Van Horn and G.L. Wright, *The Cafeteria System: A New Approach to Course and Instructor Evaluation* (West Lafayette, Indiana: Measurement and Research Center, Purdue University, 1974), pp. 1-27.

33. Robert Diamond, Paul E. Eickmann, Edward F. Kelly; Robert E. Holloway, Tom Rusk Vickery and Ernest T. Pascarella, *Instructional Development for Individualized Learning in Higher Education* (Englewood Cliffs, New Jersey: Educational Technology Publications, 1975).

34. Kenneth E. Eble, *Professors as Teachers* (San Francisco, Calif.: Jossey-Bass, 1972).

35. Bette L. Erickson, "A Survey of the Inservice Training Needs and Interests of Instructional Improvement Centers in Higher Education," Ed.D. dissertation (University of Massachusetts-Amherst, 1975).

36. Glenn Erickson and Bette L. Erickson, "Improving College and University Teaching: An Evaluation of a Teaching Consultation Procedure." Unpublished manuscript (Instructional Development Program, The University of Rhode Island).

37. Stanford Erickson, ed., *Memo to the Faculty* (Ann Arbor, Michigan: Center for Research on Learning and Teaching, The University of Michigan).

38. Stanford Erickson, *Motivation for Learning* (Ann Arbor, Michigan: University of Michigan Press, 1975).

39. Richard I. Evans, *Resistance to Innovation in Higher Education* (San Francisco, Calif.: Jossey-Bass, 1968).

40. "Experience of College Questionnaire." Contact: Arthur Chickering, Center for the Study of Higher Education, Memphis State University, Memphis, Tennessee 38152.

41. Kenneth A. Feldman and Theodore M. Newcomb, *The Impact of College on Students* (San Francisco, Calif.: Jossey-Bass, 1969).

42. John C. Flanagan, "The Critical Incident Technique," *Psychological Bulletin,* 51 (1954), 327-358.

43. J. Bruce Francis, "How Do We Get There From Here? Program Design for Faculty Development," *Journal of Higher Education,* 46 (1975), 719-732.

44. Jerome Franklin, *Organization Development: An Annotated Bibliogrpahy* (Ann Arbor, Michigan: Institute for Social Research, 1973).

45. Mervin Freedman, ed., *Facilitating Faculty Development: New Directions for Higher Education* (San Francisco, Calif.: Jossey-Bass, 1973).

46. Mervin Freedman and Nevitt Sanford, "The Faculty Member Yesterday and Today," in Freedman, ed., *Facilitating Faculty Development: New Directions for Higher Education* (San Francisco, Calif.: Jossey-Bass, 1973), pp. 1-16.

47. Wendell French and Cecil Bell, *Organizational Development* (Englewood Cliffs, New Jersey: Prentice-Hall, 1973).

48. Jerry G. Gaff, *Toward Faculty Renewal* (San Francisco, Calif.: Jossey-Bass, 1975).

49. Gordon College, *Faculty Development Manual*, First Draft (Wenham, Massachusetts: Gordon College, 1976).

50. Roger Gould, "The Phases of Adult Life: A Study in Developmental Psychology," *American Journal of Psychiatry,* 129, November (1972), 521-531.

51. Neale Gross, Joseph Giacquinta and Marilyn Bernstein, *Implementing Organizational Innovations* (New York, New York: Harper and Row, 1973).

52. The Group for Human Development in Higher Education, *Faculty Development in a Time of Retrenchment* (New Rochelle, New York: *Change* magazine, 1974).

53. Ronald Havelock, *Planning for Innovation Through Dissemination and Utilization of Knowledge* (Ann Arbor, Michigan: Institute for Social Research, 1971).

54. Paul Heist, *The Creative College Student: An Unmet Challenge* (San Francisco, Calif.: Jossey-Bass, 1968).

55. Frederick Herzberg and others, *The Motivation to Work,* 2nd edition (New York, New York: Wiley and Sons, 1959).

56. Harold Hodgkinson, "Adult Development: Implications for Faculty and Administrators," *Educational Record,* 55, Fall (1974), 263-274.

57. Ernest House, *The Politics of Educational Innovation* (Berkeley, Calif.: McCutchan, 1974).

58. "IDEA Survey Form." Contact: Center for Faculty Evaluation and Development, Kansas State University, 1627 Anderson Avenue, Manhattan, Kansas 66502.

59. *IDEA: System Handbook* (Manhattan, Kansas: Center for Faculty Evaluation and Development in Higher Education, Kansas State University, 1976).

60. "Institutional Functioning Inventory." Contact: Educational Testing Service, Princeton, New Jersey 08540.

61. "Institutional Goals Inventory." Contact: Educational Testing Service, Princeton, New Jersey 08540.

62. Christopher Jencks and David Riesman, *The Academic Revolution* (Garden City, New Jersey: Doubleday & Company, 1968).

63. Joseph Katz and Associates, *No Time for Youth* (San Francisco, Calif.: Jossey-

Bass, 1968).

64. Lawrence Kohlberg, "The Concepts of Developmental Psychology as a Central Guide to Education: Examples from Cognitive, Moral and Psychological Education," in M.C. Reynolds, ed., *Proceedings of the Conference on Psychology and the Process of Schooling in the Next Decade: Alternative Conceptions* (Washington, D.C.: Bureau for Educational Personnel Development, U.S. Office of Education, 1972), pp. 1-55.

65. David Krathwohl, Benjamin Bloom and B. Masia, eds., *Taxonomy of Educational Objectives: Handbook II, Affective Domain* (New York, New York: David McKay, 1964).

66. Daniel J. Levinson and others, "The Psychosocial Development of Men in Early Adulthood and the Mid-Life Transition," in David Ricks, A. Thomas and M. Roolf, eds., *Life History Research in Psychopathology,* Volume 3 (Minneapolis, Minn.: University of Minnesota Press, 1974), pp. 243-258.

67. Jack Lindquist, "Institutional Services for Teaching Improvement," in Clifford Steward and Thomas Harvey, eds., *Strategies for Significant Survival: New Directions for Higher Education* (San Francisco, Calif.: Jossey-Bass, 1974), pp. 33-48.

68. Jack Lindquist, *Strategies for Change: Academic Innovation as Adaptive Development* (Berkeley, Calif.: Pacific Soundings Press, 1978).

69. Jack Lindquist, "Social Learning and Problem Solving Strategies for Increasing Academic Productivity," in Leonard Romney, ed., *Faculty Enhancement of Productivity* (WCHMS, 1978).

70. Jane Loevinger, *Ego Development: Conceptions and Theories* (San Francisco, Calif.: Jossey-Bass, 1976).

71. Wilbert McKeachie, "Psychology in America's Bicentennial Year," *American Psychologist,* 46, December (1976), 819-833.

72. Wilbert McKeachie, *Teaching Tips: A Guidebook for the Beginning College Teacher* (New York, New York: D.C. Heath, 1969).

73. James H. McMillan, "The Unfinished Business of Evaluation in Faculty Development," Unpublished manuscript (Evanston, Illinois: Center for the Teaching Professions, 1976).

74. James H. McMillan, "The Impact of Instructional Improvement Agencies in Higher Education," *Journal of Higher Education,* 46, (1975), 17-23.

75. Roberg Mager, *Preparing Objectives for Programmed Instruction* (San Francisco, Calif.: Fearon, 1962).

76. Management Development and Training Program for Colleges and Universities: "Needs Assessment Questionnaire" (Forms 1-10). Contact: Higher Education Management Institute, Dr. Richard S. Webster, Research Director, 2699 South Bayshore, Coconut Grove, Florida 33133.

77. Richard Mann, *The College Classroom* (New York, New York: John Wiley, 1970).

78. W. Many, J. Ellis and P. Abrams, "In-Service Education in American Senior College and Universities: A Status Report," *Illinois School Research,* Spring (1969), 46-51.

79. Claude B. Mathis, *"Persuading the Institution to Experiment:* Strategies for Seduction," Occasional Paper Number 9 (Evanston, Illinois: Center for the Teaching Professions, 1974).

81. Samuel Messick and Associates, *Individuality in Learning* (San Francisco, Calif.: Jossey-Bass, 1976).

82. Matthew Miles, *Learning to Work in Groups: A Guide for Educational Leaders* (New York, New York: Teachers College, 1959).

83. W. Starr Miller and Kenneth Wilson, *Faculty Development Procedures in Small Colleges: A Southern Survey* (Atlanta, Georgia: Southern Regional Education Board, 1963).

84. Robert W. Moats, "Undergraduate Teaching: Instructional Improvement Progress at Ten Major Universities." Ph.D. dissertation (Northwestern University, 1975).

85. Paul J. Munson and Elizabeth Wells, *Integrating Professional and Personal Growth* (Richmond, Virginia: Virginia Commonwealth University, 1976).

86. "Myer-Briggs Type Indicator." Contact: Mary McCaulley, Center Applications of Psychological Type, 1441 Northwest 6th Street, Suite B-400, Gainesville, Florida 32601.

87. John Cardinal Newman, *The Idea of the University* (Garden City, New Jersey: Doubleday & Company, 1959).

88. John F. Noonan, "Faculty Development Through Experimentation and Institutional Cooperation," in Mervin Freedman, ed., *Facilitating Faculty Development: New Directions for Higher Education* (San Francisco, California: Jossey-Bass, 1973).

89. Terry O'Banion, *Programs that Work* (Tucson, Arizona: University of Arizona Press, forthcoming).

90. Ernest Palola, Richard Debus, Timothy Lehmann, and A. Paul Bradley, *Program Effectiveness and Related Costs Handbook* (Saratoga Springs, New York: Empire State College, 1976).

91. Malcolm Parlett and Gary Dearden, eds., *An Introduction to Illuminative Evaluation* (Berkeley, Calif.: Pacific Soundings Press, 1977).

92. Talcott Parsons and Gerald M. Platt, *The American University* (Cambridge, Massachusetts: Harvard University Press, 1973).

93. Gerald Perkus and Diana K. Christopulos, "Change of Life at Hartwick College," in William H. Bergquist and William A. Shoemaker, eds., *A Comprehensive Approach to Institutional Development: New Directions for Higher Education* (San Francisco, Calif.: Jossey-Bass, 1976), pp. 69-81.

94. William G. Perry, *Forms of Intellectual and Ethical Development in the College Years* (New York, New York: Holt, Rinehart and Winston, 1970).

95. Jean Piaget, "Intellectual Development from Adolescence to Adulthood," *Human Development,* 15 (1972), 1-12.

96. Robert M. Pirsig, *Zen and the Art of Motorcycle Maintenance* (New York, New York: Morrow, 1974).

97. Everett Rogers and F. Floyd Shoemaker, *Communication of Innovations* (New York, New York: Free Press, 1971).

97a Robert Rosenthal and Lenore Jacobson, *Pygmalion in the Classroom* (New York, New York: Holt, Rinehart and Winston, 1968).

98. B.A. Ryan, *PSI – Keller's Personalized System of Instruction: An Appraisal* (Washington, D.C.: American Psychological Association, 1974).

99. Nevitt Sanford, *Where Colleges Fail* (San Francisco, Calif.: Jossey-Bass, 1967).

100. John Shtogren, ed., *Administrative Development Programs* (Berkeley, Calif.: Pacific Soundings Press, forthcoming).

101. Walter Sikes and Laurence Barrett, *Case Studies on Faculty Development* (Washington, D.C.: Council for the Advancement of Small Colleges, 1976).

102. Walter Sikes, Laurence E. Schlesinger and Charles N. Seashore, *Renewing Higher Education from Within: A Guide for Campus Change Teams* (San Francisco, Calif.: Jossey-Bass, 1974).

103. Elizabeth Steltenpohl and Jane Shipton, *Guide to Resources for Life/Career/ Educational Planning for Adults* (Saratoga Springs, New York: The Center for Individualized Education, Empire State College, 1976).

104. "Student Biographical Inventory." Contact: Office of Research and Evaluation, Empire State College, 2 Union Avenue, Saratoga Springs, New York 12866.

105. "Student Information Form" (SIF). Contact: Alexander Astin, University of California at Los Angeles or American Council on Education, One Dupont Circle, Washington, D.C. 20036.

106. "Student Orientation Survey." Contact: Barry Moirtain, Education School, University of Delaware, Newark, Delaware 19711.

106a Daniel L. Stufflebeam and others, "Educational Decision Making," in *Educational Evaluation and Decision Making* (Ithaca, Illinois, 1971), pp. 49-105.

107. "Teaching Analysis by Students" (TABS), in William Bergquist and Steven R. Phillips, *A Handbook for Faculty Development – Volume 2* (Berkeley, Calif.: Pacific Soundings Press, 1977), pp. 90-102.

108. Jonathon R. Warren, "Student Behavior Underlying Faculty Judgments of Academic Performance" (Princeton, New Jersey: Educational Testing Service, 1973). ERIC: ED 081 326.

109. Alfred North Whitehead, "Harvard: The Future," *Atlantic Monthly* 138, September (1936), 267.

110. Robert Wilson, Jerry Gaff, Evelyn Dienst, Lynn Wood and James Bavry, *College Professors and Their Impact on Students* (New York, New York: John Wiley, 1975).

PROJECT LIST

111. Academic Leadership Development Program, Edward I. Stevens, Project Director, Association for Innovation, P.O. Box 12560, St. Petersburg, Florida 33733 (813) 867-1166.

112. Administrative Development Project, Council for the Advancement of Small Colleges, Gary H. Quehl, President, One Dupont Circle, Washington, D.C. 20036 (202) 659-3795.

113. Center for Faculty Evaluation and Development, Steven Brock, Director, Kansas State University, 1627 Anderson Avenue, Manhattan, Kansas 66502 (913) 532-5970.

114. Center for Individualized Education, Thomas Clark, Director, Empire State College, 28 Union Avenue, Saratoga Springs, New York, 12866 (518) 587-2100.

115. Center for Instructional Development, Robert M. Diamond, Director, Syracuse University, Syracuse, New York 13210 (315) 423-4258.

116. Center for Instructional Resources and Improvement, Sheryl Riechmann, Director, University of Massachusetts, Amherst, Massachusetts 01002 (413) 545-3480.

117. Center for Professional Development, Russell Wilson, Project Director, Kansas City Regional Council for Higher Education, 912 East 63rd Street, Kansas City, Missouri 64110 (816) 361-4143.

118. Center for Teaching and Learning, David Halliburton, Director, Stanford University, Stanford, California 94305 (415) 497-1326.

119. "College 1," William H. Bergquist, 1217 Campus Drive, Berkeley, California 94708 (415) 848-3412.

119a. Council for the Advancement of Experiential Learning, Morris Keeton, Director, American City Building, Columbia, Maryland 21044 (301) 997-3535.

120. Educational Development Program, Robert H. Davis, Director, Michigan State University, East Lansing, Michigan 48823 (517) 355-1855.

121. "Facilitating Faculty Development Through Department Chairpersons," John F. Noonan, Director, Center for Improving Teaching Effectiveness, Virginia Commonwealth University, Richmond, Virginia 23284 (804) 770-8253.

122. "Faculty Development in a Competency Based Curriculum," David Knisley, Director, Mars Hill College, Mars Hill, North Carolina 28754 (704) 689-1111.

123. Faculty Development Program, Will Gartman, Director, Davis and Elkins College, Elkins, West Virginia 26241 (304) 636-1900.

124. Faculty Development Program, Eugene Rice, Director, University of the Pacific, Stockton, California 95204 (202) 946-2011.

125. Faculty Resource Center, Anthony F. Grasha, Director, University of Cincinnati, Cincinnati, Ohio 45221 (513) 475-2228.
126. Individualized Program for Faculty Development, R. Judson Carlberg, Director, Gordon College, 255 Grapevine Road, Wenham, Massachusetts 01984 (617) 297-2300.
127. "Instructional Development Project," Doug Lyon, Director, New Hampshire College and University Council, 2321 Elm Street, Manchester, New Hampshire 03104 (603) 669-3432.
128. Kellogg Faculty Development Program, Carol Gene Brownlee, Sterling College, Sterling, Kansas 67579 (316) 278-2173.
129. Kellogg Faculty Fellowship Program, Reynold Feldman, Director, Northeastern Illinois University, Bryn Mawr and St. Louis Avenues, Chicago, Illinois 60625 (312) 583-4050.
130. Management Development and Training Program, Higher Education Management Institute, Jack B. Levine, Director, 2699 South Bayshore, Coconut Grove, Florida 33133 (305) 854-2318.
131. Office of Leadership Development in Higher Education, Charles F. Fisher, Director, American Council on Education, One Dupont Circle, Washington, D.C. 20036 (202) 833-4780.
132. The Professional Development Center, Elmer Van Egmond, Director, Illinois State University, Normal, Illinois 61761 (309) 438-2531 and the Teaching-Learning Center, John Sharpham, Director, Illinois State University, Normal, Illinois 61761 (309) 438-2431.
133. Program of Faculty Development, Bonnie Buenger-Larson, Director, Houghton House, College Center of the Finger Lakes, Corning, New York 14830.
134. "Project on Institutional Renewal Through the Improvement of Teaching," Society for Values in Higher Education, Jerry Gaff, Director, 1818 R Street, N.W. Washington, D.C. 20009 (202) 462-4846.
135. Resource Center for Planned Change, Kent G. Alm, Director, American Association of State Colleges and Universities, 2010 Massachusetts Avenue, Washington, D.C 20036 (202) 492-3621.
136. "Video Vignettes Project," Robert Menges, Director, Center for the Teaching Professions, Northwestern University, 2003 Sheridan Road, Evanston, Illinois 60201 (312) 492-3621.